Advance praise for *Wrongful Conviction in Sexual Assault*

"This book provides an important contribution to existing wrongful conviction literature by providing an insightful and comprehensive analysis of cases of sexual assault, rape, and child sexual abuse where innocent suspects have been convicted of crimes they did not commit. The risks of wrongful conviction which are unique to sexual offenses are specifically addressed. It is a must read."

—**Robert J. Ramsey**, PhD, Associate Professor of
Criminal Justice, Indiana University

"*Wrongful Conviction in Sexual Assault* is an important read. As the global world attempts to address racial justice, such an in-depth book that discusses the multi-dimensions of wrongful criminal convictions contributes to this progress. Johnson provides a thorough and rigorous analysis, which lends to building new models of addressing the inherent flaws that lead to disparate treatment within the criminal justice system."

—**William T. Hoston,** PhD, Associate Dean and Professor of
Political Science, Prairie View A&M University

"*Wrongful Conviction in Sexual Assault* unravels the unique legal and social context, the biases, challenges, and misconceptions that surround sexual crimes, both in the public eye and in investigative and legal practices, and that make it particularly prone to wrongful arrests and convictions. A thorough analysis of the current issues, research, and justice reform needs. A must read for social scientists and criminal justice professionals alike."

—**Marina Sorochinski**, PhD, Investigative Psychologist,
Professor of Criminal Justice, St. John's University, NY

"As a leading advocate and exoneree, I know firsthand the stigma and obstacles faced by those wrongfully convicted of sexual assaults. In *Wrongful Conviction in Sexual Assault*, Dr. Johnson presents the different wrongful conviction risks associated with various types of sexual assault cases, while exploring the role of the media, race, and other causes of wrongful conviction. Readers are exposed to the basic issues in the field of wrongful conviction and then introduced to Dr. Johnson's new contributions. The case illustrations are clear, comprehensive, and compelling. If you did not have a good grasp of wrongful criminal conviction before reading this book, you will afterwards. Read it!!"

—**Jeffrey Deskovic**, MA, JD; Founder—The Jeffrey Deskovic
Foundation for Justice; Advisory Board Member—
It Could Happen To You; Global Advisory
Council—Restorative Justice International

"This timely book is a must for anyone interested in bias, racism, wrongful conviction and the (mis)use of science. It is a wake-up call to bring science, transparency and justice to the criminal justice system"

—**Itiel Dror**, PhD, Cognitive Neuroscientist,
University College London

Wrongful Conviction in Sexual Assault

Stranger Rape, Acquaintance Rape, and Intra-Familial Child Sexual Assaults

MATTHEW BARRY JOHNSON

OXFORD
UNIVERSITY PRESS

OXFORD
UNIVERSITY PRESS

Oxford University Press is a department of the University of Oxford. It furthers
the University's objective of excellence in research, scholarship, and education
by publishing worldwide. Oxford is a registered trade mark of Oxford University
Press in the UK and certain other countries.

Published in the United States of America by Oxford University Press
198 Madison Avenue, New York, NY 10016, United States of America.

Library of Congress Cataloging-in-Publication Data
Names: Johnson, Matthew Barry, author.
Title: Wrongful conviction in sexual assault : stranger rape, acquaintance
rape, and intra-familial child sexual assaults / Matthew Barry Johnson.
Description: New York, NY : Oxford University Press, 2021. |
Includes bibliographical references and index.
Identifiers: LCCN 2020026322 (print) | LCCN 2020026323 (ebook) |
ISBN 9780190653057 (hardback) | ISBN 9780190653071 (epub) |
ISBN 9780190653088
Subjects: LCSH: Judicial error—United States—History. | Rape—Law and
legislation—United States—History. | Child sexual abuse—Law and
legislation—United States—History. | Sex crimes—Law and
legislation—United States—History.
Classification: LCC KF9329 .J64 2021 (print) | LCC KF9329 (ebook) |
DDC 345.73/0253—dc23
LC record available at https://lccn.loc.gov/2020026322
LC ebook record available at https://lccn.loc.gov/2020026323

9 8 7 6 5 4 3 2 1

Printed by Integrated Books International, United States of America

This book is dedicated to my parents, Jay Robert Johnson (1922–1999) and Ann Stevenson Johnson (1927–).

CONTENTS

LIST OF FIGURES AND TABLES

FIGURES

TABLES

AUTHOR'S NOTE AND ACKNOWLEDGMENTS

My interest in wrongful conviction is the result of the convergence of my work in the areas of disputed confession evidence and death penalty abolition over the past 20 years. Beginning in the 1990s, I consulted on numerous cases involving disputed confession evidence and authored a number of papers and law reviews in this area. In 2002, I was appointed to the Executive Board of New Jerseyans for Death Penalty Moratorium (later renamed New Jerseyans for Alternatives to the Death Penalty, NJADP). Through my service with NJADP, which included research, public education, lobbying, and testimony before legislative and administrative committees, I met and developed personal acquaintances with exonerees David Shephard, Nate Walker, Ray Krone, Kurt Bloodsworth, Byron Halsey, Larry Petersen, and James Landano. Each of these exonerees (except Landano) was wrongly convicted of sexual assault and spent multiple years in prison prior to exoneration. I learned much about the "legal" process of wrongful conviction from their cases. I also learned about the personal ordeal of wrongful conviction these men endured. The public education and lobbying efforts these men provided were instrumental in the eventual success of the campaign to abolish the death penalty in New Jersey in 2007.

I remain tremendously appreciative of the opportunity to be part of the campaign and accomplishments of NJADP. I cannot name everyone I met and worked with, but I want to acknowledge June Post, and the late Lorry Post, whose advocacy initiated the death penalty abolition campaign in New Jersey. I also want to acknowledge Celeste Fitzgerald, Kevin Walsh, and Sandra Manning who played key leadership roles. The abolition of the death penalty in New Jersey was particularly significant because it was accomplished through the legislature and demonstrated that voting against the death penalty was not a political liability. Thus, following abolition in New Jersey, five other US states (New Mexico, 2009; Illinois, 2011; Connecticut, 2012; Maryland, 2013; and Delaware 2016) followed suit and abolished the death penalty via legislative action.

In addition, my interest and concern about wrongful conviction in sexual assault were enhanced further by my association and subsequent friendship with Jeffrey Deskovic, who was one of my students at John Jay College of Criminal

Justice, CUNY. Jeffrey also endured multiple years of imprisonment for a rape (and murder) he did not commit. After being exonerated, Jeffrey established the Jeffrey Deskovic Foundation for Justice (http://www.thejeffreydeskovicfoundatio nforjustice.org) to advocate for others who have been wrongly convicted. In 2009, I authored a paper on false confessions focused on the exonerations of Jeffrey Deskovic and Byron Halsey. This article was primarily a critique of the "Reid" technique, interrogation methods. After publication, I realized I had overlooked the shared sexual assault element in the two prosecutions.

A major background consideration, a subtext for this study, is the enormous and seemingly perpetual crime of sexual assault. Though not exclusively, rape/ sexual assault is overwhelmingly a crime where men attack women. In this examination of wrongful conviction in sexual assault, I have regarded it as a challenge to focus on wrongful conviction while simultaneously recognizing the parallel problem of failure to convict actual offenders. It is my impression that wrongful conviction can be reduced without risking actual offenders escaping apprehension. In fact, reducing wrongful conviction will result in fewer sexual assaults, as suggested by the findings reported in Chapter 4 and other sources.

A pivotable development in the realization of this book-length treatment of wrongful conviction in sexual assault was the manuscript, "African-Americans Wrongly Convicted of Sexual Assaults Against Whites: Eyewitness Error and Other Case Features," which I authored with Shakina Griffith and Carlene Barnaby in 2013. From this modest study emerged the essential ideas and framework that led to the current book, *Wrongful Conviction in Sexual Assault: Stranger Rape, Acquaintance Rape, and Intra-Familial Child Sexual Assaults*.

After examining Black defendants wrongfully convicted of sexual assaults against whites, I wanted to examine the broader question of wrongful conviction in rape considering all race/ethnic configurations. The question in my mind was whether the risks of wrongful conviction, apparent in the Black defendant/white victim cases, were apparent among other wrongful convictions in sexual assault. The initial formulation of the book was a catalogue focused on the prevalence of sexual assault among confirmed wrongful convictions, which would also examine race and the history of racial discrimination in the prosecution of sexual assault in the United States.

In the process of examining rape and wrongful conviction, other highly relevant findings emerged. The lack of transparency in the production of prosecution of evidence (which I refer to as "black box" investigation methods) was identified through recognizing the functional similarity between false confessions and misidentifications. This led to other observations and formulations, such as the continuum of intentionality, describing how the manufacture of evidence ranged from inadvertent to more deliberate. These formulations gave rise to other important distinctions, such as secondary evidence (forensic analyst, "scientific," and incentivized informant testimony) that commonly supports unreliable confession and witness identification testimony, distinct victim status paths, the influence of moral correction pressures, and a stranger rape thesis that draws from these observations and findings.

No doubt, the introduction of DNA science to crime investigation in the 1990s and the subsequent revelation of hundreds of confirmed wrongful convictions in the United States provided a new context that allowed the realization of the work reflected in this volume. However, in addition to the catalogue of injustice in the wrongful conviction literature, my vision for this book was also heavily influenced by my exposure to the earlier work of Ida B. Wells, as revealed in her autobiography *Crusade for Justice* edited by Alfreda M. Duster (1970), which I read in the early 2000s. Wells' investigative journalism documented the terroristic lynching violence perpetrated against African Americans, often related to rape allegations. Also, William Patterson's (1951) *We Charge Genocide* was another influential source in framing the current volume.

There are several researchers whose vital work influenced my approach and analysis as presented in this volume. I mention them here in the order in which I became acquainted with their contributions: Gisli Gudjonsson, Thomas Grisso, Saul Kassin, Richard Leo, and Samuel Gross. I have benefitted from their innovative research and scholarship, as well as their supportive correspondence. I extend a special acknowledgment to Saul Kassin, my colleague at John Jay College of Criminal Justice, CUNY.

I also extend acknowledgments to key people who support and inspire my work. First and foremost is Christine Baker, my devoted wife, life partner, and primary collaborator in all things of value. My brothers, Mark S. Johnson and Bradford S. Johnson, both support and inspire. My dear friends Larry "Adimhu" Hamm, Akili Buchanan, "Cheo Halili" Jones, the late Gregory "Mfalme" King, Larry Adams, Zayid Muhammad, Angenetta Robinson, Ingrid Hill, Jean Ross, Donald and Karen Rucker, Carlene Barnaby, and Delores Jones-Brown—I am grateful for our friendship. I am also deeply appreciative of all my friends and colleagues with the Peoples' Organization for Progress as well as those with the Association of Black Psychologists.

I also recognize the invaluable legal expertise, support, and consultation provided by Verna Leath, Ronald Hunt, Bernado Henry, Robyn Veasey, Theresa Owens, Susan Van Amburgh, Alonda Sullivan, Andrew Manns, and Laura Bryant over the years.

My two sons, Kali Baker-Johnson and Jay Baker-Johnson, are a primary source of joy in my life, and I think of them in all my endeavors, large and small.

I am also thankful to Donna Boles, my sons' godmother, who allowed me to use her Oak Bluffs home during my sabbatical leave when I began writing this book.

I also acknowledge influential and admirable professors and mentors such as James Harris, Duncan Walton, the late Clement Alexander Price, H. Bruce Franklin, Daniel E. Williams, Maulana Karenga, Peter Oliphant, Fred Halper, the late Joel Kovel, Gerald Markowitz, and the late Steve Friedman.

I am especially thankful to a small group of forensic psychologists in New Jersey who contributed to my early career professional development, notably Louis B. Schlesinger, James Wulach, Frank Dyer, and Susan Esquilin.

I earned my PhD in clinical psychology at the Derner Institute (formerly the Institute for Advanced Psychological Studies) at Adelphi University in 1984. I am grateful that I had the opportunity to be a student of Gordon Derner, George Stricker, and the other faculty. Gordon Derner created and sustained a unique doctoral training program that supported my intellectual and personal development. I continue to benefit from the support and encouragement I receive from the current Derner Institute dean, Jacques Barber, and the faculty.

I am also quite grateful to Tom Litwack, who, very generously, read and commented on the chapters of the book. He also provided recommendations to additional sources that improved the content and presentation of the material. Likewise, Kate Brown provided very helpful copy editing.

Also, two special people warrant mention. Sarah Harrington, my editor at Oxford University Press, expressed an informed interest in making this book a reality on her initial review of the proposal. She continued to be supportive and patient with me as I labored to complete it. It has been a pleasure to work with her, and I am very grateful. Sydney Melendez was one of many research assistants who contributed to the completion of this volume. However, in addition to her research assistance, Sydney had a vision of the potential significance of the research on wrongful conviction in sexual assault, and our discussions and exchange helped to shape this volume.

Many John Jay College of Criminal Justice students provided essential research assistance throughout the process of completing this project. I relied substantially on Stephanie Cunningham, Ana Paredes, and Candice Coll during the initial work on this project. Zamorah Kennedy, Jason Lee, Amy Rampuran, Daun Jung, Brittany Finn, Brittany McCollough, Nadia Baichoo, Renee Joseph, Kasandra Martinez, Riki Martinez, Rukiya King, Damascus Rice, Janquel Acevedo, and Shereen Bell are other students who provided substantial contributions.

Angela Crossman served as chair of my academic department (Psychology) during the period when I was completing this project and provided essential support and assistance. Also, Anila Duro served as the administrative director of our department, and she always was supportive and responsive to my many requests.

I also acknowledge the support and assistance provided by the John Jay College of Criminal Justice librarians, particularly Ellen Sexton, Karen Okamoto, and Nancy Egan.

Introduction and Overview

There can be no doubt that for every proven case of wrongful conviction there are many more that remain unproven.

—GISLI GUDJONSSON (2003, p. 163)

In 2010, Edward Carter was exonerated and released from prison after 35 years of confinement for a crime he did not commit. At age 19, he was convicted of the knifepoint rape of a white university student in Detroit, Michigan (Gross & Shaffer, 2012). The only evidence against Carter was the victim's identification, though he had a verifiable alibi. After exhausting all appeals, Carter sought DNA testing through a Michigan Innocence Project. The crime scene DNA had been destroyed, but fortunately a police officer did further investigation, locating fingerprints from the crime scene. The prints were submitted to the FBI Automated Fingerprint Identification System and matched to a convicted sex offender then imprisoned for similar rapes at the university during the same time period. Carter reported that his trial public defender urged him to plead guilty and failed to effectively defend him when he refused. According to Carter, he was actually in police custody on an unrelated charge at the time of the offense; nevertheless, the victim picked him out of a photo spread that included multiple photos of him. The victim then identified Carter in a live lineup where the others did not fit the description of the perpetrator. Carter's parents and girlfriend died while he was imprisoned. His major regret on release at age 55 was that he never had children. In 2017, he was awarded a 1.7-million-dollar settlement through recently enacted legislation (E. Anderson, 2017). It is worth noting that Carter was a suspect with prior criminal justice exposure and the offense he was convicted of was actually committed by a serial sex offender. Carter's exoneration received virtually no media attention (Gross & Shaffer, 2012), but in many ways, his case is emblematic of wrongful conviction of sexual assault in the

United States—an innocent Black defendant misidentified by a white victim of a "stranger rape."

WRONGFUL CONVICTION AND RAPE

This book is focused on two sets of egregious violations, rape/sexual assault and wrongful criminal conviction. Both are tragic and traumatic occurrences with multiple adverse, chronic consequences. By far, the large majority of confirmed wrongful convictions in the United States have occurred in cases of rape and sexual assault where prosecutors were able to convict innocent suspects of major crimes, resulting in grave injustice for the defendants, the crime victims, and society at large. This book highlights characteristics of rape/sexual assault that increase the risk of wrongful conviction.

Rape

Rape and sexual assault produce severe acute and chronic injuries to victims. In some cases, victims are murdered (rape/murder) in the course of the crime.[1] Estimating the extent of the damage from rape is difficult for a variety of reasons. *Incidence rates* assess the emergence of cases within a certain time frame, typically a year. *Prevalence* addresses the number of existing cases at a given time. Garland (2009), citing information from the Bureau of Justice Statistics for the mid-1990s, reported 335,000 US rape and sexual assaults a year, with only a third of victims filing reports with law enforcement. Garland also cited varying sources suggesting the lifetime prevalence of sexual victimization (a broader term) among women to be 12% to 50%. The use of multiple terms for these crimes ("rape," "forcible rape," "sexual violence," "deviant sexual battery," and so on) also contributes to a lack of reliable incidence and prevalence rates.

What is clear is that rape is a notoriously underreported crime. Typically, victims are unwilling to make official reports, and according to Garland, some (mistakenly) regard their assault as something other than rape. Ambiguity stemming from state variation in defining rape and prevailing cultural biases leads some victims to believe "real" rape is when she has "been brutally beaten by a minority stranger" (Garland, 2009, p. 8; also see Estrich, 1987). Rape victims are often confused, ashamed, fearful of the assailant, and also afraid that they will not be believed by friends, family, and law enforcement.

More recent Bureau of Justice Statistics data on rape and sexual victimization were provided by Planty, Langton, Krebs, Bersofsky, and Smiley-McDonald (2013). The encouraging news is that the rate of sexual violence decreased substantially (by 64%) from 1995 to 2005. The decrease was apparent across race/ethnic groups, though lower socioeconomic status continued to be associated with increased victimization. The large majority of victims (78%) knew their offender; stranger assaults occurred in only 22% of cases. Victims reported use of a weapon by the perpetrator in 11% of the cases. The percentage of victims who reported assaults to police increased from 29% in 1995 to 35% in 2010, with fear of reprisal as the most commonly cited reason for failure to report. The percentage of reports that produced arrests decreased from 47% to 31%.

During the decade of the 2000s, the US Centers for Disease Control and Prevention (CDC) promoted multifaceted initiatives to define rape and sexual violence as a public health issue and to support (primary) prevention research and intervention approaches (Degue et al., 2012). The indices cited previously of reduced sexual victimization suggest that the CDC's initiatives, in conjunction with other efforts, contributed to a reduction in sexual violence and related harm; however, sexual violence remains a major source of adversity with traumatic and, at times, fatal outcomes.

Wrongful Conviction

While there is a lengthy history of research on wrongful conviction and miscar-riage of justice (Bedau & Radelet, 1987; Borchard, 1932; Gould & Leo, 2010; Leo, 2005), the past 30 years have witnessed a growing academic, professional, and public interest associated with DNA science confirming wrongful convictions. Borchard's 1932 book, *Convicting the Innocent: Sixty-five Actual Errors of Criminal Justice*, is regarded as the first academic study of wrongful conviction in the United States. The work documents and examines 65 wrongful criminal convictions and served as a rebuttal to influential circuit court Judge Learned Hand's 1923 re-mark that, "The ghost of the innocent man convicted . . . [was] an unreal dream" (Krajicek, 2015).

As noted by Leo (2005), subsequent decades produced more wrongful con-viction scholarship and journalist contributions. Typically, these works identified additional cases and echoed a familiar narrative that began with an innocent defendant tried and convicted despite the axiom that it is better to allow some number of criminals go unpunished than to convict one innocent. The narra-tive was completed by heroic efforts marshaled to exonerate and free the wrongly convicted. In 1987, Bedau and Radelet (1987) published a major law review that presented 350 wrongful convictions in capital cases dating back to the beginning of the 20th Century. While this work was very well regarded among scholars in-terested in wrongful conviction, the broader influence of the research was limited because it relied, in large part, on the authors' judgments about innocence.

A good deal of informed literature has addressed the topic of how to identify and define wrongful conviction and exoneration (Bedau & Radelet, 1987; Gross, Jacoby, Matheson, Montgomery, & Patil, 2005; Gudjonsson, 2003). Identification of a wrongful conviction requires some type of process for evaluating and thus confirming the defendant was indeed innocent. Proving innocence in an abso-lute way may be difficult or impossible. *Exoneration* is an official process; one leader in the field, Gross (Gross, O'Brien, Hu, & Kennedy, 2014; Gross & Shaffer, 2012) used the term to refer to cases in which, following conviction, some kind of official statement is made that the defendant was not guilty. Examples are ex-ecutive pardons based on evidence of innocence, charges dismissed based on evidence of innocence, and defendants acquitted at retrial where evidence of in-nocence was previously unavailable. Consistent with Gross, for the purpose of the current presentation, here the term *wrongful conviction* is used to refer to cases that have received an official declaration the defendant was not guilty. It is important to note there are several cases in which there is substantial evidence of innocence, but an official exoneration has not occurred for any number of reasons unrelated to criminal evidence.[2]

DNA EXONERATIONS

The first DNA exoneration in the United States occurred in 1989. Gary Dotson was convicted in 1979 for the rape of Cathleen Crowell-Webb (Garrett, 2011; "Gary Dotson—Northwestern School of Law," n.d.). The case was investigated as a stranger rape when actually there was no crime at all. Prior to the presentation of exculpatory DNA, the purported victim testified under oath in postconviction hearings that she lied about the accusation against Dotson; she fabricated the rape story to conceal her sexual activity with her boyfriend because she feared she was pregnant (she was 16 years old at the time). However, her testimony was not sufficient for the exoneration. Mr. Dotson's release, after 10 years, occurred when DNA evidence was presented at subsequent hearings. In addition to the intention-ally false rape charge, the case involved faulty scientific testimony about serology (blood typing) and hair analysis, as well as apparent prosecutorial misconduct.[3] It should be noted that "false rape charges" as in the Dotson case are not typical of wrongful convictions in sexual assault.

The application of DNA science to criminal investigation has altered the meaning and perception of criminal evidence in many ways. First, DNA science has made it much more difficult to ignore or dismiss the reality of wrongful crim-inal convictions in the US legal system. As DNA analysis has become increasingly more efficient (Scheck, Neufeld, & Dwyer, 2001), it has provided conclusive evi-dence of guilt in many cases, as well as innocence in others. But DNA analysis can only be applied to the small proportion of criminal cases (5%–10%; see Innocence Project, 2009) in which human bodily residues (blood, sweat, tears, semen, sa-liva, hair, etc.) are taken into evidence. Nevertheless, the yield from DNA analysis extends beyond the particular cases in which it is applied. Postconviction excul-patory DNA evidence has demonstrated that major forms of criminal evidence typically relied on to prove guilt (e.g., eyewitness testimony, informant testimony, confessions, hair, fiber, footprint, and dental bite mark impression analyses) are often unreliable (Garrett & Neufeld, 2009). This has profound relevance to virtu-ally all criminal prosecutions regardless of the existence of DNA evidence in any given case.

Manufactured evidence is a term that has been a staple of wrongful conviction scholars and researchers as far back as Borchard (1932). While the prevailing perception of criminal investigation is that evidence is discovered and collected, the reality is that evidence presented to prove guilt is often created or "manufactured" by the police or prosecution. The manufacturing of evidence occurs via concealed interrogation and witness identification procedures, secret (or otherwise unacknowledged) incentives provided to informants for testimony, undisclosed informal relationships among prosecutors and forensic experts, and other means. The failure to objectively preserve the evidence from these procedures amounts to a suppression of evidence. The term *black box* is used in this book to characterize the secret domains where evidence is manufactured. As noted, the primary two black boxes are unrecorded custodial interrogations and unrecorded witness identification procedures, though there are others.

A major milestone in wrongful conviction research and awareness occurred with the 1996 publication *Convicted by Juries, Exonerated by Science: Case Studies in the Use of DNA Evidence to Establish Innocence After Trial* (Connors, Lundregan, Miller, & McEwen, 1996). This report, commissioned by the National Institute of Justice, presented findings from early cases in which postconviction DNA evidence was used to exonerate defendants convicted of major offenses. Attorney General Janet Reno noted in the Preface, "The criminal justice system is not infallible, and this report documents cases where the search for truth took a tortuous path" (p. iii). The authors' comment, "All 28 cases profiled in the report involved some form of sexual assault" (p.12) is remarkable for what is stated, as well as what was unstated. All the cases did include "some form of sexual assault" allegation; however, in at least one case (Gary Dotson's) there was no rape at all. In two others (Mark Bravo and Gerald Davis) it was not clear whether a rape occurred. Bravo was convicted in 1990 of raping a patient in a psychiatric hospital where he worked. Postconviction DNA testing matched none of the crime scene semen to Bravo; furthermore, the complainant recanted her testimony, so it was not apparent whether this was a misidentification or a no-crime case (Connors et al., 1996). Davis was convicted of raping a woman who reported that she was a family friend. Trial testimony from discredited forensic chemist Fred Zain[4] indicated Davis could not be eliminated as a source of semen recovered from the complainant, but postconviction DNA results excluded Davis as a contributor of the crime scene semen. Thus, again, it was not apparent if this was a no-crime case or misidentification. A more substantial finding in the report, though not articulated by the authors, was that 25 of the 28 cases were stranger rapes as opposed to the more common "acquaintance" or "date" rape (or they were mistakenly prosecuted as stranger rapes, as in the Dotson case).

As noted, available data strongly suggest that the less frequently occurring type of rape, stranger rape, is disproportionately associated with wrongful conviction when compared to the more common "acquaintance rape."[5] By and large, informed commentators, such as Neufeld and Scheck (as cited in Connors et al., 1996), viewed the matter of wrongful convictions being concentrated among "some form of sexual assault" to be an artifact of the availability of DNA evidence in sexual assaults. This left unexamined and underappreciated the unique features of stranger rapes (with regard to the offenses themselves, investigation into the

Figure I.1 Percentage of Offenses Among the First 250 DNA Exonerations (from Garrett, 2011).

crimes, and prosecution) that increase the risk of wrongful conviction. These features include, but are not limited to, pressure on law enforcement officials and the enhanced risk of misidentification. Multiple sources indicated common misidentification error to be in the range of 30% (Gaulkin, 2010), and this is likely increased where there is traumatic victimization (Bookbinder & Brainerd, 2016; Deffenbacher, Bornstein, Penrod, & McGorty, 2004). Further, additional obstacles to reliable identification exist when the witness and subject are from different race/ethnic groups—cross-racial identification (Connelly, 2015)—as elaborated in Chapter 3.

Several researchers (Free & Ruesink, 2012; Gross et al., 2005; Gross & Shaffer, 2012) have noted that the most common offense associated with wrongful conviction is murder/homicide, and the second most common offense is rape/sexual assault. But, this is an artifact of classifying cases by the most serious charge, the classification approach employed for purposes of criminal prosecution. The focus of this book is on classification that informs processes involved in wrongful conviction.

As presented in Figure I.1, when rape/sexual assault cases are combined with murder/homicide cases that included sexual assault charges, it becomes evident that the majority of confirmed wrongful convictions in the United States have involved rape/sexual assault charges (89% of the DNA exonerations; Garrett, 2011). This is especially significant given that sexual offenses account for only about 10% of the prison population (Gross et al., 2005).

The Frequency of Wrongful Conviction

How common is wrongful conviction? Virtually all researchers (Garrett, 2011; Gross et al., 2014; Gross & Shaffer, 2012; Kassin et al., 2010; Leo, 2008; Neufield &

Scheck as cited in Connors et al., 1996) agreed that known or confirmed wrongful convictions represent only a fraction of innocent defendants found guilty at trial or by guilty plea. Several investigators have sought to estimate the frequency of wrongful convictions. Krajicek (2015) referred to calculation of the aggregate number of wrongful convictions as "the Holy Grail" question in the field. Huff, Rattner, and Sagarin (1996) offered an estimate of 0.05%–1.0%, drawing on a survey of judges, attorneys, and law enforcement officials in Ohio. While this suggests a high degree of accuracy, it also would mean at least 10,000 wrongful convictions among the 2 million defendants convicted a year at the time of their study. Risinger (2007), critiquing Supreme Court Justice Scalia's suggestion of a 0.027% rate of wrongful criminal convictions in the United States, calculated "a minimum factually wrongful conviction rate" (p. 762) for rape-murders as 3.3% and suggested the rate across all crime could be as high as 5%.

Gross and O'Brien (2008) found a 2.3% exoneration rate among defendants sentenced to death from 1973 to 2003 but noted the rate could not be generalized beyond their particular sample. Gross and O'Brien described enormous methodological obstacles in determining the prevalence of false convictions and stated, "It will be difficult to learn more" (p. 958).[6] Leo and Gould (2009), critical of the pessimism conveyed in the Gross and O'Brien formulation, pointed out that the unknown aggregate wrongful conviction figure need not deter ongoing empirical research to discover, understand, and prevent wrongful conviction, noting other criminological research advances in the context of unknowns. In addition, Leo and Gould recommended the adoption of social science methods to capture the multifactorial and contingent interaction of variables that contribute to wrongful convictions. In a subsequent publication, Gross et al. (2014) reported a new analysis of US death sentences from 1973 to 2004 and found that 117 (1.6%) of the defendants had been exonerated. Gross and his colleagues estimated that another 200 prisoners from this sample may have been innocent but were without access to the legal resources to demonstrate their innocence. According to these researchers, this was suggestive of a 4.1% wrongful conviction rate, though Gross and his colleagues referred to the aggregate wrongful conviction rate as "unknowable" (Gross et al., 2014, p. 7230).

This limited review indicates estimated rates of wrongful conviction from leading investigators ranging from 0.05% to 5%. As Leo and Gould (2009) suggested, arguably the aggregate wrongful conviction rate is not necessary to further advance meaningful research. However, it is an important metric if only because critics (e.g., US Supreme Court Justice Scalia, as noted previously) attempt to dismiss or marginalize the investigation of wrongful criminal conviction in the United States, characterizing it as a rare aberration, and promote an image of the US legal system as fair, impartial, and efficient. Stated differently, these critics aim to advance the ideal of the US legal system as "imperfect but the best in the world" and thus to curtail what are characterized as frivolous postconviction appeals, providing closure and finality to legal rulings. Thus, in many ways, wrongful conviction is an area of investigation that runs contrary to deeply held beliefs about US government institutions (police and law enforcement, "first responders," and the court system) and the narrative of a legal system based on democratic ideas of liberty, justice, and equal protection of law.

Disaggregating Wrongful Conviction

The current project is guided by the Leo and Gould (2009) formulation that despite obstacles, much has been learned and much more can be discovered about wrongful conviction. The current examination asserts the increasingly visible wrongful convictions in sexual assault (a major portion of all wrongful convictions) can be reduced substantially through recognition of the unique wrongful conviction risks in different types of rape/sexual assault cases, that is, "stranger rape" versus "date/acquaintance rape" versus "child sexual abuse" cases. While stranger rapes garner the most press and public attention (and fears), they are much less common than date and acquaintance rapes (Maston & Klaus, 2003; Planty et al., 2013). The confirmed wrongful convictions in sexual assault are highly concentrated among stranger rapes and associated with faulty identifications and police-induced false confessions (as well as other factors). Wrongful conviction in date and acquaintance rape is associated with false rape charges, is less common,[7] and is associated with complainant characteristics (which converge with other factors). Child sexual abuse cases can also be divided in stranger versus acquaintance assaults, but in addition there are special risks associated with the manner in which the victim/complainants are assessed and interviewed, interpersonal discord associated with divorce and separation, plea bargaining in the context of severe penalties, and social hysteria associated with many prosecutions. These features are presented in greater detail in subsequent chapters.

An overview of the general disaggregation approach used in this study is illustrated in Figure I.2. There are confirmed/exonerated wrongful convictions and an unknown amount of unconfirmed wrongful convictions. Among the confirmed wrongful convictions, there are sexual assaults (including sexual assaults that include murder), murders, and other offenses. Among the sexual assaults, there are "stranger rapes," "acquaintance rapes," "intrafamilial child sexual assaults,"[8] and cases where the offense type was undetermined. Among the stranger rapes, there are differential risks associated with cases with capable victims versus cases with incapacitated victims.

So, through disaggregating the wrongful conviction database by offense, and grouping the sexual assaults together (rather than categorizing the rape/murders as murders), it is apparent a distinctively large proportion of cases involve rape/sexual assault. Further disaggregation indicates the wrongful convictions are not distributed randomly among rape and sexual assaults but occur disproportionately among the less common type of rapes, stranger rape. In disaggregating by offense, we are not so much concerned with the total aggregate number but rather with the distribution among a population. Disaggregation enlists a public health or epidemiological perspective. For instance, in examining suicide, we want to know not only the aggregate suicide rate but also the rate is higher among

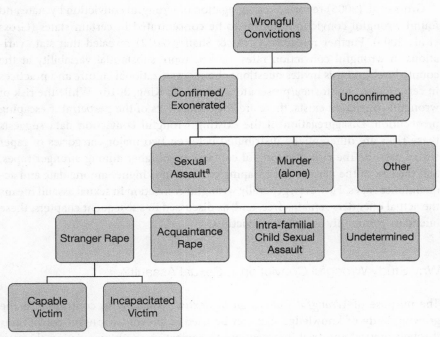

Figure I.2 Disaggregating Wrongful Conviction Diagram.
Diagram prepared by Riki Martinez

adolescent males, and maybe higher still among Latina adolescents, or among the elderly with certain chronic conditions. In the examination of automobile or airline accidents, it is valuable to know the general rate of occurrence and even more valuable to know the general rate is increased in the presence of certain risk factors (weather, driver/pilot fatigue and distraction, substance abuse, the design of roadways or airports, and so on).

Disaggregating the wrongful conviction database by race/ethnicity reveals other important findings. For instance, a disproportionate concentration of Black and Latino defendants are wrongfully convicted. Garrett (2011) reported that 75% of rape exonerees are Black or Latino, while these ethnic groups make up only 30%–40% of rape convicts. Further disaggregation based on race/ethnicity of both victim and defendant indicates a concentration of wrongful convictions in sexual assaults associated with white victims of stranger assaults by Black and Latino assailants, a decidedly rare offense. Alternatively, if we disaggregate by the circumstances of conviction, we see that a number of innocent defendants pled guilty to rape (M. B. Johnson & Cunningham, 2015), which raises questions about the operation of the judicial system. Examining wrongful conviction in stranger rape, we find that a considerable portion of the offenses are actually committed by serial rapists, which warrants a focus on characteristics of the offense and investigation that contribute to the prosecution of innocent suspects.

Gross et al. (2005) reported disaggregation of wrongful conviction by state and found wrongful convictions appear to be concentrated in certain states (Gross et al., 2005). Further research (Gross & Shaffer, 2012) revealed that state variations in wrongful conviction rates masked more substantial variability at the county level, and this invites questions about organizational culture and practices in certain district attorney/prosecutor's offices (R. King, 2016). While the risk of wrongful conviction exists, there are coexisting risks of the perpetrator escaping prosecution. Disaggregation of the existing wrongful conviction data suggests these risks are differentially distributed between two major categories of rape/ sexual assault. The risk of wrongful conviction is higher among stranger rapes, and the risk of the perpetrator escaping conviction is higher among date and acquaintance rapes. However, generally wrongful conviction in sexual assault means the actual offenders remains free, and, as discussed in subsequent chapters, these offenders commonly assault other victims.

Why Study Wrongful Conviction in Sexual Assault?

The purpose of *Wrongful Conviction in Sexual Assault* is to contribute to the growing body of knowledge that can be used to prevent wrongful convictions through pretrial and trial intervention; to correct wrongful conviction through postconviction relief appeals; and to generate policy recommendations that will reduce the occurrence of wrongful convictions. In addition, the findings presented here will be useful in clarifying potential flaws in the US criminal justice system and suggesting alternative approaches and models of adjudication and intervention.

OUTLINE OF THE CHAPTERS

This book proceeds by examining wrongful conviction in sexual assault from several perspectives. Chapter 1 provides an overview of the rape law reform movement that began in the 1970s and continued at least through the 1990s. The movement sought a series of reforms designed to encourage victims to make official reports that would facilitate the successful prosecution of rapists and sex offenders. The movement was quite effective in achieving legislative reform, but there was no discernible increase in sexual assault convictions. The rape law reform movement solidified an alliance of concern that strengthened vigorous prosecution of stranger rapes but had little impact on the more common type of rape, acquaintance rape.

Chapter 2 focuses on the concentration of rape cases among confirmed wrongful convictions, examining how stranger rape differs from date and acquaintance rape with regard to risk of wrongful conviction. Chapter 2 also examines the pressures on law enforcement authorities and the roles of primary evidence (misidentifications and false confessions); and secondary evidence, "black box" investigation methods and "victim status" in stranger rape. In addition, Chapter 2 presents a "stranger rape thesis" to distinguish the unique challenges faced in the investigation of stranger rape. The moral outrage that tends to result from stranger rape results in great pressure on police for arrests and convictions, yet reliable identification of the perpetrator is often compromised in stranger rape.

Chapter 3 examines the current disproportion of Black defendants wrongly convicted of sexual assault through a historical lens, noting the history in the United States of statutorily separate sexual assault penalties based on race. Chapter 3 presents how race, rape law, and prosecution have been manifest in different historical eras in the United States and how racial bias against Black defendants continues in the post–civil rights era.

Chapter 4 describes a common pattern in which innocent defendants are tried and convicted of crimes committed by serial rapists. This chapter highlights the difficulty encountered by law enforcement in the investigation of stranger rapes despite the expanding literature on crime scene investigation and offender profiling.

Chapter 5 reviews the series of day care–based child sexual abuse prosecutions that occurred in the United Sates from the mid-1980s to the mid-1990s. Charges in these cases often relied on highly implausible accusations. Suggestive questioning of children, prosecutorial overcharging, and a prevailing social hysteria contributed to a substantial number of innocent defendants being convicted.

Chapter 6 discusses concepts and models used to describe and explain processes in wrongful criminal conviction, such as "tunnel vision," "confirmation biases," "misinformation effects," and "escalation of commitment." This chapter considers the research focus on "causes" or contributors to wrongful conviction with an emphasis on trial evidence and variables; it also draws on several theoretical sources to introduce the notion of wrongful conviction as a form of "moral correction" that results in emotional and cognitive factors that adversely affect the evaluation of evidence and contribute to the risk of wrongful conviction.

Chapter 7 summarizes the findings from the previous chapters and examines recommendations for reform from across the field. Chapter 7 not only makes note of the obstacles to reducing wrongful conviction but also highlights the guidance that has emerged from the expanding academic research and legal engagement in the past two decades.

The wrongful conviction data reported and relied on in this book are provided online (www.oxfordclinicalpsych.com/WCSA). This includes the following appendices:

A Wrongful convictions in sexual assault as reported on the Innocence Project website
B Wrongful convictions in sexual assault as reported on the National Registry of Exonerations
C Exonerees wrongly convicted of sexual assaults committed by serial sex offenders
D Wrongful convictions related to the child sexual abuse hysteria as reported on the National Registry of Exonerations

NOTES

1. Michelle Bosko (Chapter 4), Lori Roscetti (Chapter 3), Nancy DePriest (Chapter 2), Angela Corea (Chapter 2), Deborah Sykes (Chapter 3), Tyrone and Tina Urquhart (Chapter 3) were all rape/murder victims, and innocent defendants were convicted of the crimes.
2. See the discussion by Gross et al. (2005) of "foot dragging" by government officials, guilty pleas with release provisions offered to avoid risk of retrial, and other situations amounting to negligence. Also see where exonerations are bargained for terms acceptable to the original prosecuting authorities, as in the Kerry Max Cook case (M. Hall, 2017).
3. In closing arguments, the prosecutor stated the forensic analyst "matched" Dotson's hairs to the victim when the analyst only said they were similar (Garrett, 2011).
4. As noted in Connors et al., 1996, Fred Zain provided unsubstantiated incriminating testimony for the prosecution in several cases. Also see the work of Garrett and Neufeld (2009).
5. Another observation made by Connors et al. (1996) was that a substantial proportion of the defendants (15 of the 28) were known to police prior to arrest, suggesting prior police contact may be associated with vulnerability to wrongful conviction.
6. However, Gross and O'Brien reported a "strong demographic pattern" where "black men accused of raping white women face a greater risk of false conviction than other rape defendants" (Gross & O'Brien, 2008, p. 958).
7. False rape charges are rare though highly publicized when identified, as in the Gary Dotson case as well as the Brian Banks case presented in Chapter 2.
8. In addition, there are intrafamilial adult sexual assaults that are no doubt underreported and are not addressed in this work.

1

The Modern Politics of Sexual
Assault Prosecution

There have been 214 exonerations based on DNA evidence, almost all of
them in rape cases...

—LIPTAK (2008)

In 2017 came a watershed moment in US history. Substantial press coverage of
several sexual assault and harassment allegations against award-winning film producer Harvey Weinstein (*BBC News*, 2017) led to a flood of accusations against
others (James Rosen, media journalist; Morgan Spurlock, documentary filmmaker;
Alex Kozinski, federal appeals judge; Trent Frank, Congressman; Matt Lauer, TV
host; Charlie Rose, TV host; John Conyers, congressman; Russell Simmons, en-
tertainment executive; Al Franken, US senator; among many others) (Almukhtar,
Gold, & Buchanan, 2018). The 2016 presidential campaign was a precursor in that
multiple women made sexual assault complaints against candidate Donald Trump
(Ford, 2017), who nevertheless ascended to the presidency. Trump's chief rival,
Hillary Clinton, was not completely immune; she was forced to answer questions
about her defense of her husband (former President Bill Clinton), who previously
faced charges of sexual assault and harassment (Wilkinson, 2016).

Major press accounts involved sexual assault allegations against entertainer Bill
Cosby (Kim, Littlefield, & Etehad, 2017) and former US House of Representatives
Speaker Dennis Hastert (Stack, 2017), and the Catholic priests' sex abuse scandal
dominated press attention in the 1990s (Terry, 2008). Common to all of these
cases is that they involved "acquaintance sexual assault" allegations, as opposed to
"stranger rape" allegations. Despite rape law reforms that were adopted beginning
in the 1970s, victims of sexual assault by acquaintances (bosses, coworkers, dates,
friends, former and current lovers) found it difficult to pursue criminal cases
against offenders. Advocacy for these assault and harassment victims became
known as the "Me Too" movement and the associated "Time's Up" campaign.

The law develops and evolves, typically slowly, though there are isolated instances of rapid and even dramatic change. While there is a tendency to view law and illegality as settled, there is an appreciation that legal judgments are influenced, if not determined, by changing social values and historical processes. Rape law is not unique in this way. The law and social attitudes toward sexual assault and rape share these features with other aspects of law. The investigation of wrongful conviction in sexual assault recognizes these processes, which are also presented in some detail in the Chapter 3 discussion of race and rape prosecution in the United States.

The current chapter examines the rape law reform movement that emerged in the United States in the latter part of the 20th Century. As suggested in the Introduction, distinctions between stranger rape and acquaintance rape inform the analysis. The varied reforms that comprised the rape law reform movement, by and large, were designed to remedy obstacles to the reporting and prosecution of acquaintance rapes rather than stranger rapes (Klein, 2008; Gruber, 2009). This could be seen as reflecting that acquaintance rapes were (and remain) more common than stranger rapes. Alternately and importantly, it suggests the reporting and prosecution of stranger rapes were not burdened with such obstacles. This chapter provides an overview of the agenda and accomplishments of the rape law reform movement, as well as notes the unfinished work.

While the rape reform movement had various allies, it was initiated and sustained principally by feminist activists and scholars. The rape law reform not only targeted legal rules and practices that interfered with the prosecution of defendants charged with acquaintance rapes but also, in that process, solidified a coalition of interests that further strengthened the prosecution of stranger rape defendants. While certain feminist critiques and analyses were central to initiating and sustaining the rape reform movement, alternative feminist perspectives clarify the challenges that emerged.

RAPE LAW REFORM

According to Klein (2008), a convergence of "feminist" advocacy, with the "law and order" backlash against perceived liberal "excesses" of the 1960s, led to a period of more aggressive sexual assault prosecution that emerged in the 1970s. The intention of advocates was to counter prejudicial and patriarchal perspectives in the Western legal tradition (Reddington, 2009; Garland, 2009; Klein, 2008). Advocates for sexually assaulted women sought a series of "rape law reforms," such as "rape shield" laws; eliminating corroboration, resistance, and prompt reporting requirements in rape statutes; and eliminating the marital exception. These reforms were designed to encourage victims to report assaults and facilitate the successful prosecution of rapists and sex offenders. Reformers also hoped legal reform would result in change in normative behavior, that is, reduced sexual offending. Pursuit of this agenda continued and escalated further through the 1980s and into the 1990s.

Klein (2008) differentiated two waves of rape law reforms. The first wave focused on reporting and prosecution of sexual assault. Here, the concerns were primarily facilitating the prosecution of date and acquaintance rapes, that is, cases where defendants did not challenge there was a sexual encounter but denied force was used, denied there was criminal intent, or asserted the complainant consented to the sexual encounter. A second wave focused on sex offender registration, Megan's laws, and the civil commitment of "sexually violent predators."

Gruber (2009) suggested that prior to the rape reform movement, rape criminalization in the United States discounted female interests. Rape law reinforced male dominance through chastity expectations and notions of male ownership and functioned to reinforce "white racial supremacy" (p. 587). The prevailing legal paradigm for rape was the assault by a stranger, characteristically a Black man, hiding in wait of the innocent white victim. Thus, African Americans were the principal targets of official prosecutions (legal lynching) as well as mob actions (extrajudicial lynching, discussed in greater detail in Chapter 3). According to Gruber (2009), the rape reform agenda strengthened "society's condemnation of paradigmatic rape" (p. 594) but was limited in advancing the cause for nonparadigmatic victims, victims acquainted with their attackers, victims without physical injuries, and victims in the sex trades.

In the 1990s, with the application of DNA science to criminal investigation, the number of unambiguous wrongful convictions began to mount. Emerging data indicated a large majority of the DNA exonerations were in sexual assault cases (Klein, 2008). The first DNA exoneration in the United States involved Gary Dotson, who was wrongly convicted of rape in 1979 and exonerated in 1989. As presented in the Introduction and Overview, in Dotson's wrongful conviction and incarceration, the young victim reported a stranger rape that was later established to be a "false rape charge." The evidence (cited in material that follows) suggests the increasingly aggressive prosecution of rape and sexual assault initiated in the 1970s and through the 1980s had a negligible impact on the prosecution of date and acquaintance rape but contributed to the continued aggressive prosecution of stranger rapes, where wrongful convictions are concentrated.

OVERVIEW OF THE RAPE LAW REFORM AGENDA

Rape laws prior to the 1970s made it difficult to convict (certain) perpetrators (Klein, 2008; Estrich, 1987). This was the result of statutes and juror skepticism about the motives of complainants. Kalven and Zeisel (1966) found jurors more likely to acquit in rape than other crimes. In the 1970s, the National Organization for Women (NOW) joined with police, prosecutors, and "tough-on-crime" politicians to reform rape criminal codes across the country. One researcher (Brownmiller, 1975) noted only 5% of rapes were even reported to police, though other data suggested reporting rates were higher (McDermott, 1979). Some commentators remarked women's lives were described as being "controlled by fear of rape" (Klein, 2008).

Several aspects of rape law were targeted for reform. It was noted that rape was unique among crimes because statutes required the complainant's charge to be corroborated, a feature not required for other criminal convictions. The corroboration requirement had a long history, stemming from English common law (Klein, 2008), and was reiterated in the 1962 Model Penal Code, recommending no conviction "upon the uncorroborated testimony of the alleged victim" (as cited in Klein, 2008, p. 986). By 1974, the corroboration requirement had been abandoned by 35 states and was virtually nonexistent by 2001.

Skepticism about rape accusations was also reflected in legal requirements where rape victims must present evidence they exhibited "utmost resistance" to the assault. This was a burden faced by victims of acquaintance rape, that is, proving the sexual encounter was not consensual. Victims of stranger rape, without a prior relationship with the perpetrator, typically were not burdened with proving it was an unwanted attack. Through advocacy, "utmost resistance" requirements were reduced to "reasonable" resistance in many states and eventually eliminated in others (Klein, 2008). It became widely recognized resistance could result in more severe injuries to victims.

Probably the most well-known rape law reform was establishing "rape shield" protections. These were reforms that limited the in-court questioning of rape complainants about their sexual history. Advocates for rape law reform recognized this type of questioning was an obstacle to women filing formal charges against perpetrators. The State of Michigan was a leader in this area, with a 1975 statute indicating the complainant's past sexual behavior was inadmissible (Klein, 2008). Congress passed a similar federal rape shield law in 1978. It was expected these reforms would not only encourage victims to report but also prevent juror bias stemming from stereotypical, gendered notions about appropriate behavior.

However, rape shield provisions were controversial in that they collided with defendants' rights to confront and cross-examine witnesses. In practice, rape shield protections had limited effect because behavior proximal to the alleged offense was clearly open to question and might reveal the complainant and the defendant met at a singles bar or that she visited his apartment at night. These facts could be enough to influence a biased juror. Also, typically judges retained the discretion to determine in-court questioning, and the rape shield was a presumption rather than a rigid prohibition. The rape shield was designed to protect a rape victim from a defendant's claim she invited or consented to sexual relations, which would be characteristic of an acquaintance attack rather than an attack by a stranger.

According to Klein (2008), judicial expansion of the rape shield was apparent in several rulings and most evident in the 1992 Ninth Circuit ruling in *Wood v. Alaska*. The defendant acknowledged the sexual intercourse and sought to present evidence the complainant had shown him her nude pictures in a men's magazine and also told him she had acted in pornographic films. According to the defendant, this was relevant to assessing whether she consented to the intercourse. The trial judge ruled this evidence was inadmissible consistent with the state rape shield law. The Ninth Circuit affirmed the trial court, ruling such evidence would be more prejudicial than probative. Klein (2008) suggested the fact the complainant had posed nude or acted in pornographic films would properly be excluded by the rape shield statute, but the complainant's volunteering of this information to the defendant was relevant to the jury's deliberation. As was the case with other rape law reforms, the rape shield law targeted disputes in acquaintance rape prosecutions.

Marital rape is the quintessential acquaintance rape, where victims were deprived, by law, of remedy. Like the corroboration requirement, the marital exemption was rooted in English common law (Klein, 2008) and supported by patriarchal doctrine. As late as 1980, the exemption was articulated in the Model Penal Code commentary; however, by 2008 it had been virtually eliminated in all states.

The rape reform agenda continued through the latter part of the 20th Century and converged with the growing emphasis on crime and strategies of criminal incapacitation that characterized the period. This took the form of sex offender registration policies and, in some states, the civil commitment of those deemed "sexually violent predators."

Assessment of rape law reform suggests mixed results. No doubt the ambitious legislative agenda was broadly achieved. However, available data suggest the impact of rape law reform on the reporting and prosecution of rape was rather limited. Several studies, including comprehensive reviews of empirical research (Reddington, 2009; Bryden & Lengnick, 1997; Spohn & Horney, 1992, 1996), found the reforms failed to produce increased reporting, increased prosecutions, or decreased rape offending. Bachman and Paternoster (1993) found no significant difference in reporting rates or system response, though convicted defendants were more likely to receive a prison sentence. As suggested by Gruber (2009), prior to the rape law reform movement, rape prosecution was focused on the paradigmatic rape, a stranger rape typically by a minority assailant. While rape law reform sought to secure redress for victims of acquaintance assaults ("nonparadigmatic rape") and achieved many of its legal reforms, its impact on rape reporting and prosecution was limited. However, the convergence of forces and interests that enacted rape law reform also enhanced prosecution of stranger rape.

ALTERNATE FEMINIST PERSPECTIVES

Gruber (2009), from a feminist perspective, outlined several limits and complications for feminist advocates in pursuing and relying on criminal prosecution remedies for sexual assault victims. According to Gruber, rape is a product of gender inequality and gender norms that are broadly pervasive in society. That is, males are encouraged to be sexually aggressive and adventuresome, while females are socialized to be passive and dependent. In this view, rape is encouraged (if not abetted) by the common gender socialization of males, as well as females, and related messages that prevail throughout the culture. While the feminist advocacy for rape law reform was valuable, and even heroic, as a result of its alliance with police, prosecutors, and so-called tough-on-crime politicians, it allowed rape to be defined and perceived, principally, as criminal pathology. In this way, the outcome of rape law reform was the perpetuation of focus on the paradigmatic rape while the more common acquaintance and date rape remained extremely difficult to prosecute.

Essentially, rape law reform was effective in reforming certain laws, was largely ineffective in altering practice, and by accepting the criminal pathological notion of rape offending, could not influence normative behavior. Paradigmatic (stranger) rapists would face prosecution and severe penalties, but the more common acquaintance offender remained beyond the reach of criminal law. The rape law reform agenda also neglected to address the abuse of rape prosecution against African Americans. Gruber (2009) pointed out that the 1962 Model Penal Code language advising against rape convictions based on uncorroborated reports was in response to tainted prosecutions of African Americans charged with rape, principally in southern states (as elaborated in Chapter 3). Also troublesome, rape law reform adopted presumptions contrary to progressive feminism, such as fostering female dependency on the state, undermining female agency, and supporting civil liberty infringements. Ultimately, rape law reform efforts became allied with the late 20th Century overcriminalization regime in the United States.

Gruber (2009) was not the lone, or the first among feminists, to express these concerns. J. D. Hall (1983; as well as Davis, 1983; Wriggins, 1983; McGuire, 2010) pointed out that rape fears were stoked in prior generations, primarily in the south, to justify terroristic violence against African Americans for the purpose of maintaining white male privilege. Hall described the antilynching advocacy of Jessie Daniel Ames, as well as the earlier work of journalist Ida B. Wells, as examples of critical feminist perspectives that challenged the promotion of (stranger) rape fears in order to justify racial intimidation and violence (also see Gray, 2015).

The nature of the revisions made to the law in response to the rape law reform movement now warrant renewed attention given that the "vast majority" (Klein, 2008, p. 1057) of DNA exonerations are for defendants wrongly convicted of rape (also see Liptak, 2008). Rape law reform advocacy produced dramatic and rapid legislative change, change that was clearly warranted not only for victims of sexual assault, but also for its contribution to the integrity of the US legal process. However, altering the written law, a daunting endeavor in itself, may be insufficient in achieving desired goals in practice and in behavior. The numerous, persistent, and credible acquaintance assault allegations that characterize the current Me Too movement, 40 years after the initiation of the rape law reform agenda, illustrate the complexity of the modern politics of sexual assault prosecution. This dilemma has been observed in the legal campaigns to eliminate racial segregation, to secure abortion rights, and in other areas of US law. In addition, such legal campaigns may contribute to unintended byproducts, such as the predominance of sexual assaults among the wrongfully convicted as observed by Klein (2008) and elaborated further in this work.

2

Rape and Wrongful Conviction

> We suspect that systematic research would certainly uncover more cases of
> wrongful conviction ... especially for crimes of rape.
> —BEDAU & RADELET (1987, p. 35)

The relationship between rape and wrongful conviction has been recognized in
the wrongful conviction literature. As noted in the Introduction, Connors et al.
(1996, p. 12) described the first 28 US DNA exonerations as all involving "some
form of sexual assault." Gross, Jacoby, Matheson, Montgomery, and Patil (2005)
sought to explain the connection, indicating the observation was the product of
two related features. The combination of erroneous identifications by victims
coupled with DNA-testable biological residues meant that wrongful convictions
in sexual assault had an increased chance of being confirmed (also see Gross,
2008). Klein (2008), in reviewing rape law reform advocacy, also inquired about
the apparent prevalence of rape cases among exonerated defendants.

In this chapter, the relationship between rape and wrongful conviction is
considered through disaggregation of sexual assault data. These data indicate that
wrongful conviction in sexual assault is strongly associated with a particular type
of sexual assault, stranger rape. Wrongful conviction does occur in acquaintance
rape and intra-familial child sexual assaults as well but less frequently.

There are special challenges presented in the investigation of stranger rape,
as noted in the criminal investigation literature and illustrated in cases. Huff
et al. (1996) suggested Packer's (1968) "crime control" versus "due process" dichotomy provides a valuable model for understanding wrongful conviction (also
see Leo, 2005). According to Huff et al., an emphasis on crime control will result
in more wrongful convictions, while an emphasis on due process will produce
fewer. A reasonable alternate perspective is wrongful conviction can be reduced
by improving investigation methods and efficiency, resulting in improved assessment of innocence and guilt (Findley, 2009). The existing wrongful conviction
literature is largely due process in orientation. As presented in the material that

follows, the crime control–focused, sexual assault investigation literature helps to inform the relationship between rape and wrongful conviction. Toward that goal, this chapter also elaborates on several concepts introduced in the Introduction, such as "manufactured evidence," "black box" investigation methods, defining stranger rape, and designating "victim status" in stranger rape.

The occurrence of wrongful conviction warrants consideration in the context of the related finding that "Most crimes are never solved." (Gross, 1996, p. 476). As stated by Gross, homicides (as compared to other violent crimes) have greater clearance rates. In the typical homicide, the perpetrator is a friend, family member, or acquaintance. The investigation and prosecution are rather straightforward. Gross explained police are tasked with more difficult homicide investigations as well, and when a body has been recovered, tremendous effort and resources are typically devoted. The taking of human life provokes strong reactions, the impulse to protect the vulnerable and to punish the offender. Gross pointed out other horrendous crimes (i.e., kidnapping and serial rape) produce similar reactions. Pressures from the community, coupled with law enforcement officers' own internally generated pressures, result in the greater clearance rates in homicides.

The circumstances that produce increased, sometimes heroic, efforts can also lead to circumventing procedures and short cutting rules. Gross (1996, p. 478) stated, "And if [police] believe they have the killer-perhaps [they will] . . . manufacture evidence to clinch the case." Here, Gross used the term *manufacture evidence* to refer to intentional deliberate efforts. The unintentional manufacture of evidence is also addressed below. According to Gross, this risk is increased where police are under public scrutiny and pressure.

Gross illustrated this process through presenting the rape/murder of 12-year-old Jeanine Nicarico and the resulting wrongful conviction of Rolando Cruz and Alejandro Hernandez. More than a decade after the conviction, a police officer admitted he gave false incriminating trial testimony regarding admissions by Cruz. This revelation, along with a corroborated confession from the actual perpetrator, led to the exoneration of Cruz and Hernandez. Gross commented the police were convinced they had the perpetrators, and they manufactured evidence to secure the conviction. Similarly, Leo (2008) reported, 20 years after Earl Washington was convicted of murder and rape in Virginia, it was established, via civil litigation, that Officer Wilmore had fabricated Earl Washington's confession.

Findley and Scott (2006, p. 323) pointed out, "Highly publicized unsolved crimes foster public fear of crime, which in turn undermines public confidence in and support for police." The capacity of the police to solve crimes is limited, and sizable proportions of violent crime are never solved. Unrealistic public expectations often result in pressure on police investigators to solve crimes or face the loss of confidence. Certain crimes, or characteristics of crime, present unique and formidable obstacles to police investigators. In some circumstances, these are the very offenses where there is greatest pressure on police for arrests and convictions. Stranger rapes have many of these features.

Consideration of unique risks associated with stranger rape has been conspicuously absent from research and theorizing about wrongful conviction, even though a dramatically large proportion of the confirmed wrongful convictions were stranger rapes. The landmark early National Institute of Justice exoneration study (Connors et al., 1996) noted the large proportion of sexual assault cases without noting the overwhelming majority were stranger rapes. The term *stranger rape* is rarely used in the wrongful conviction literature. An exception is Gould's (2008), *The Innocence Commission: Preventing Wrongful Convictions and Restoring the Criminal Justice System*. In this volume, focused on confirmed wrongful convictions in the State of Virginia, Gould remarked stranger rape, "was the most common crime found in the Virginia exonerations" (p. 129). Yet, he did not offer any discussion or analysis of the finding as though it were incidental. Gould presented a "Table of Factors Found in Virginia's Erroneous Convictions" and omitted mention that 8 of the 11 cases were stranger assaults (and 6 involved cross-racial misidentification).

Similarly, Garrett (2010), in his rigorous legal research study, "The Substance of False Confessions," described how interrogators provide crime details to innocent suspects, who then incorporate the crime details in incriminating "confession" narratives. The prosecution's case is constructed around these confessions, which purportedly include knowledge only the perpetrator would know ("specialized knowledge"). These confessions become the heart of the prosecutor's appeal to the jury for conviction and are cited in appellate rulings that affirm the convictions. Garrett (2010, p. 1061) stated, "The study set [40 cases] includes mostly cases involving a rape by a stranger", but did not address the prevalence of stranger rape among the series of cases or any potential relationship between the nature of the offense and the police interrogation tactics he described.[1] Another example of the conspicuous absence of discussion of stranger rape, in the context of wrongful conviction, is the widely cited elaboration of "tunnel vision" by Findley and Scott (2006). The Findley and Scott law review used four wrongful convictions (Marvin Anderson, Steve Avery, the Central Park Five defendants, and Christopher Ochoa) to illustrate various aspects of tunnel vision without mentioning the shared fundamental characteristic of the four cases: as stranger rape (also see G. L. Wells et al., 1998).

Attention to the challenges presented by stranger rape is apparent in the sexual assault investigation literature. Harbers, Deslauriers-Varin, Beauregard, and Van Der Kemp (2012, pp. 259–260) stated, "The idea that anyone can become a victim of a sexual crime committed by a stranger (i.e., an offender with no personal relationship with the victim prior to the day the offence was committed) is terrifying and has an immense impact on the quality of life." Slater, Woodhams, and Hamilton-Giachritsis (2015, p. 261) referred to "'hard to solve' crimes such as those committed by a stranger who had no previous connection to the victim." Likewise, Santtila, Junkkila, and Sandnabba (2005, p. 88) pointed out, "Serial rapists are overwhelmingly strangers to their victims (LeBeau, 1987), apparently attempting to maximize anonymity in order to avoid apprehension." As developed further in this chapter, stranger rapes challenge law enforcement authorities with increased pressures for prosecution coupled with unique obstacles related to motive, reliable identification, and victim status.

STRANGER RAPE, REAL RAPE, AND LEGITIMATE RAPE

In addition to the special challenges presented in investigation, the perception and response to stranger rape differ from those for other rapes. Estrich (1987), in *Real Rape: How the Legal System Victimizes Women Who Say No*, noted the law distinguishes between aggravated and "simple rape." Aggravated rape involves assaults with physical violence, multiple perpetrators, and assaults by strangers. Simple rapes are cases where these aggravators do not exist. This common distinction in the law is consistent with the perception of police, prosecutors, and jurors. Estrich cited research (Kalven & Zeisel, 1966) indicating jury conviction in aggravated rape approached four times the rate in simple rape cases. Further, Estrich pointed out stranger rape, as opposed to simple rape, is prosecuted more frequently and successfully than many violent crimes (citing Galvin & Polk, 1983). Consistently, across studies from different US cities, stranger rapes are more likely to lead to indictments and serious prosecution than are rapes by assailants known to victims. As noted in the Introduction, generally rape victims with a prior relationship with the accused must overcome the presumption "victim contributory behavior" (appearance, manner of dress, or presence at certain locations) played a role in the attack. When the victim is attacked by a stranger, this burden is reduced. The result is stranger rape, the less frequent type of rape, is the most likely to be prosecuted fully (also see Shaw, Campbell, & Cain, 2016).

Arguably, stranger rape warrants a more rigorous response than other rapes. The notion of "victim contributory behavior" can lead potential rape victims to believe their conduct and good judgment can protect them from rape. However, when attacks are being committed by strangers this perceived protection does not exist (Harbers et al., 2012). In addition, there is reason to believe there is a gendered consideration in the evaluation of stranger rape as distinct from simple rape. Males are likely to share the outrage at stranger rape. In the male mind, the stranger rapist will attack "his" wife, sister, mother, or daughter. Yet the male will remain skeptical about simple rape claims because most men have aggressively pursued sexual acts with reluctant partners. Estrich noted the fear in the male mind about rape is an accusation, the day after, a night of consensual sex. So, as Estrich pointed out, women assaulted in the more common type of rape (assaults by dates, former lovers, coworkers, or "friends") face legal and social obstacles in prosecuting the assailants that do not exist for victims of stranger rape. Stated differently, there is an alliance of moral outrage in response to stranger rape that does not exist in the response to simple or acquaintance rapes.

This distinction drawn by Estrich, 30 years ago, is no relic of the past. In 2012, Missouri Congressman Todd Akin drew a similar distinction, stating in "legitimate rape" a woman would not become pregnant (Moore, 2012; Davidson, 2012). Akin was asserting if pregnancy was the result, the sexual encounter must have been consensual and was not a legitimate rape. According to Heggie (2012), this particular medical fallacy originated in the 13th Century and has endured in some circles. More recently, responding to reports of increased rapes in a Brooklyn neighborhood, Captain Peter Rose of the New York City Police Department (NYPD) was quoted as stating, "It's not a trend that we're too worried about because out of 13 [rapes and attempted rapes], only two were true stranger rapes. . . . If there's a true stranger rape, a random guy picks up a stranger off the street, those are the troubling ones. That person has, like, no moral standards" (Wang, 2017). A subsequent prepared statement by a NYPD spokesperson, to allay spiraling concerns, clarified the department's position that all rape reports, regardless of the relationship between the assailant and victim, were taken seriously and investigated thoroughly. The prepared statement also included a recognition of the special challenges inherent in stranger rape investigation, that is, "Due to the anonymous and random nature of rapes committed by strangers, detectives often face greater challenges in these types of crimes" (Wang, 2017). Thus, stranger rapes present more difficulties in investigation and yet are prosecuted more aggressively. As a result, there is an increased risk of wrongful conviction in stranger rape as compared to other types of rape and possibly other crimes in general. This "stranger rape thesis" is elaborated in material that follows.

DEFINING STRANGER RAPE

For the purposes of this discussion, stranger rape is operationalized as follows: *Stranger rape* indicates the sexual assault victim is attacked by someone she did not know prior to the assault. In this context, *rape* refers to an unwanted physical sexual attack, including but not limited to an attack resulting in penetration. Unwanted verbal or visual exposure to sexual material maybe damaging as well, but does not fall within the category of rape as used here.[2]

LeBeau (1987) described 6 categories of victim–offender relationships in rape.

1) Stranger with no previous contact.
2) Casual acquaintance where the offender becomes known to the victim just before the attack (an offender who uses brief casual conversation or hitchhiking as a prelude to the attack).
3) Acquaintance when the victim knew of the offender through employment or residence but they had no relationship.
4) Family friend where the offender is a friend of a victim's family member, often at the victim's home and trusted.
5) Close friend or boyfriend where the offender is often in the victim's home and had close, direct, or frequent contact with the victim.
6) Family/relative where the offender is the father, stepfather, brother, cousin, uncle, or other.

VICTIM STATUS: CAPABLE OR INCAPACITATED

Assaults characterized by LeBeau's categories 1 and 2 (stranger and casual acquaintance attacks) are being considered as stranger rape here and referred to as a "stranger rape in fact." Recognition of a stranger rape implies certain attendant circumstances with regard to how the offense is regarded by the public, as well as the law enforcement response and investigation.[3] During the initial investigation of an offense, it may not be known whether it was a stranger rape as opposed to some other type of rape. This is likely connected to the circumstances that prompt the police investigation. That is, a report of a rape (typically by a "capable victim") versus the discovery of a body (in rape/murder) or an otherwise "incapacitated victim" unable to describe the attack or the perpetrator(s), such as the brain-injured victim in the Central Park jogger assault (Burns, 2011). In some cases, stranger rape status cannot be definitively determined without certain identification of the offender.

Three well-known wrongful convictions that involved stranger rape in fact are the New York Central Park Five defendants (Burns, 2011; M. B. Johnson, 2005), the Kurt Bloodsworth wrongful conviction from Maryland (G. L. Wells & Hasel, 2007), and the Ronald Cotton/Jennifer Thompson case from North Carolina (Thompson-Cannino, Cotton, & Torneo, 2009). While there are major differences, these cases share that the victims were sexually attacked by strangers. In each of the three cases, the stranger rape character of the offense was correctly formulated by the investigators. This contributed to aggressive investigations. However, the police and prosecutors were mistaken regarding the identity of the offenders. The victim in the Bloodsworth case was a 9-year-old child, and the victim in the Central Park Jogger case was a high-status adult (white investment banker). In these two cases, the victims were unable to make identifications, due to the murder of the child victim in the Bloodsworth case and the traumatic brain injury suffered by Trisha Meili in the Central Park Jogger case (Meili, 2003). Thus, an obstacle in these two investigations was that the victims were incapacitated; they could not name the perpetrator(s), describe the attack or attacker(s), or rule out suspects. The Cotton/Thompson case, however, had a "capable" victim, Jennifer Thompson, who did describe the attack and the perpetrator.

The field of wrongful conviction research has highlighted the recurring problem of unreliable evidence of various types (Scheck et al., 2001; Garrett, 2011; Cutler, 2012; Gross & Shaffer, 2012; Garrett & Neufeld, 2009) that forms the basis of the state's prosecution of innocent defendants. Stemming back to Borchard's (1932) pioneering work, a substantial body of scholarship and research has developed and accelerated since the DNA era. This research has identified and described the frequent lack of reliability associated with eyewitness identification, "confessions," evidence and testimony from forensic analysts, "experts," and "scientists," as well as incentivized testimony from informants. As noted in the Introduction, even though DNA evidence is only available in 10% of criminal cases, DNA analysis has demonstrated that forms of evidence previously regarded as highly reliable and valid are often neither. Also, the available research demonstrates that the conviction of innocent defendants is typically characterized by multiple erroneous evidence sources, such as a false confession accompanied by unreliable testimony from an expert analyst or a misidentification along with unreliable testimony from an informant (Gross & Shaffer, 2012; Kassin, Bogart, & Kerner, 2012; Castelle & Loftus, 2008).

To further elaborate the challenges encountered in the investigation of stranger rape (and other offenses), certain terms and concepts are useful to clarify the context and the emergence of unreliable evidence of various forms. As noted by Leo and Gould (2009), the wrongful conviction factors and features mentioned, often referred to as "causes" of wrongful conviction, are not actually causes. These features also occur in sound convictions, as well as in acquittals. If these features are regarded as causes, it only raises the question of what causes them (Leo, 2005). Wrongful conviction is complex and multidetermined, as are virtually all social phenomena (Leo & Gould, 2009). The elaboration presented in this work is informed by Leo's (2005, p. 213) proposition that wrongful conviction is about "human error in social and organizational contexts," thus suggesting a multidimensional social process. The social context of wrongful conviction is criminal investigation and adjudication.

While wrongful conviction is multidetermined, there is evidence to suggest certain contributors may be more influential, or carry more weight, than others. Differences in weight are manifest in one factor accounting for more variance in an outcome (wrongful conviction) than another factor. This potentially can be measured with multivariate social science research designs (as suggested by Leo & Gould, 2009). Differences in weight may also be operative in a sequence where factors that emerge early may influence subsequent factors (see Lowrey-Kinberg, Senn, Gould & Hail-Jares, 2017). In this regard, Leo and Gould (2009) suggested "path analysis" approaches to enhance research by describing contingent relationships among emerging evidence in wrongful conviction. Similarly, Castelle and Loftus (2008) described how "mis-information" (such as a misidentification) and "cross-contamination" can divert an investigation and result in wrongful conviction. The authors described the erroneous evidence in the wrongful rape conviction of William Harris, where the faulty victim/witness identification shaped erroneous laboratory analyst evidence, which in turn reinforced and increased confidence in the faulty identification, suggesting a sequence and also circular feedback.

Focusing on similar observations, Kassin et al. (2012) examined the effects of false confessions on other incriminating evidence in wrongful convictions. Testing a "temporal order hypothesis," Kassin et al. (2012, p. 42) found false confessions and witness misidentifications were more likely to be obtained first, while forensic science, analyst, and informant "errors" were more likely to follow. Among a sample of Innocence Project (IP) confirmed wrongful convictions, both false confession and witness misidentification evidence appeared to have influenced ("corrupted") other evidence sources (expert analyst and informant evidence), with the effect being stronger for confessions than eyewitness identifications.[4] Citing these and related findings, Kassin (2015) called for "blind" investigation by expert and lay examiners to maintain the integrity of evidence assessment and prevent "forensic confirmation bias."

"BLACK BOX" INVESTIGATION: THE MANUFACTURE OF EVIDENCE

As noted in the Introduction, in many respects unrecorded custodial interrogations function in the same way as unrecorded witness identification procedures. They are nontransparent, closed, and thus secret procedures (spaces) where evidence can be "manufactured." Manufactured evidence is created by the investigation rather than discovered in the investigation. The term *black box* investigation is used, in this work, to highlight the lack of transparency, or an objective record, of what occurred. This does not mean the evidence produced is necessarily unreliable, but the absence of an objective record is clearly an obstacle to assessing reliability. Moreover, in confirmed wrongful conviction the evidence was unreliable. This manufacture of evidence may be inadvertent and unintentional. In other cases, it may be clearly intentional, as in the case with Rolando Cruz and Alejandro Hernandez as well as in the prosecution of Earl Washington. Borchard (1932) in his early work referred to evidence being intentionally manufactured. Here, inadvertent manufacture is considered as well, through processes referred to as *misinformation, confirmation bias,* or *tunnel vision.*

A Continuum of Intentionality in Manufactured Evidence

The distinction between inadvertent and intentional has limitations because intentions are not readily discernible. Typically, more than one person is involved in the manufacture of evidence, such as the witness and the investigator(s) in eyewitness identification or the suspect and the interrogator(s) in interrogation. It is useful to conceive of the distinction as a continuum, or spectrum, rather than a dichotomy. The continuum of intentionality in black box manufacture of evidence is presented in Figure 2.1.

Drawing from the distinctions between misidentifications and other supplemental evidence described by Castelle and Loftus (2008) as "misinformation" effects, as well as confession evidence and "temporal order effects" described by Kassin et al. (2012), the term *primary evidence* is used to refer to incriminating "confession" or "identification evidence." The other typically supplemental forms of prosecution evidence, such as forensic analyst, scientific, and incentivized informant testimony, will be referred to as "secondary evidence." The continuum is mainly focused on the manufacture of primary evidence, but various forms of secondary evidence are also often manufactured.

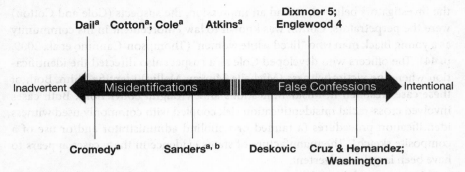

Figure 2.1 Continuum of Intentionality in Manufactured Evidence. [a] Cross-racial misidentification; [b] acquitted at trial.

The continuum presents several examples of relatively inadvertent manufacture of eyewitness misidentifications on the left and other eyewitness misidentifications that were more intentional toward the right. However, there are virtually no inadvertent police-induced false confessions because the police initiation of interrogation reflects a presumption the suspect is deceptive and thus likely guilty (Inbau, Reid, Buckley, & Jayne, 2013). Thus, on the continuum, the false confessions are near the center or toward the right.

On the far left of the continuum, there is the completely inadvertent, spontaneous, mistaken identification by an assault victim such as the 12-year-old who misidentified Dwayne Allen Dail as her rapist. The child encountered Dail on the street, weeks after the sexual assault in her home. She immediately told her mother Dail was her attacker. There were no indications of suggestive or biased questioning of the witness. She had not been exposed to Dail's photo by investigators (WRAL, 2008a). It was a cross-racial misidentification; the child was African American, and the offender was white. There was no indication the misidentification was "manufactured" by the investigation process. However, manufactured secondary evidence, in the form of incriminating testimony about hair similarity, did emerge to support the child victim's erroneous identification (WRAL, 2008b).[5]

Shifting toward the right on the continuum is the wrongful conviction of McKinley Cromedy (State v. Cromedy, 1999), also misidentified by the rape victim in a chance street encounter. In Cromedy's case, the victim's faulty identification occurred 8 months after the offense. Cromedy's photo was among a series of mug shots shown to the victim (D. S.) 5 days after the rape, and thus it is likely the postoffense exposure to Cromedy's photo contributed to a false memory (referred to as unconscious transference, that is recall of a face with incorrect recall of where the face was seen previously; Cutler & Kovera, 2010; Deffenbacher, Bornstein, & Penrod, 2006). Thus, the misidentification was manufactured inadvertently during the investigation process. Further to the right, in the Ronald Cotton wrongful conviction, as well as the Tim Cole case, the identification procedures were tainted by "nonblind" administrators. Prior to the victims' misidentifications, the investigators believed, or had an impression, the suspects (Cole and Cotton) were the perpetrators. Cotton was known to law enforcement in his community as a young Black man who "liked white women" (Thompson-Cannino et al., 2009, p. 44). The officers who developed Cole as a suspect also directed the identification where the victim/witness (Michelle Murray-Mallin) identified him. Both of these cases resulted in misidentifications and wrongful convictions. Both cases involved cross-racial misidentification risk coupled with commonly used witness identification procedures (a tainted or nonblind administrator and/or use of a composite sketch). The manufacture of state's evidence in these cases appears to have been largely inadvertent.

Shifting toward the right, suggesting investigators' more active manufacture of evidence, there is the Willie Sanders prosecution. In the Sanders case, an investigator informed the victim/witness a "painter" who fit her general description of the offender was working near the crime scene. Later, during a subsequent presentation of photos, the investigator told the victim/witness Willie Sanders' photo was the painter. The victim/witness subsequently identified Sanders as the rapist (Klibanoff, 1980a, 1980b). It is quite obvious how this evidence was manufactured. In this case, three other eyewitnesses later identified Sanders after his arrest photo was presented in the media (producing multiple eyewitness misidentification [MEM]). Sanders, however, was acquitted (see elaboration in Chapter 3).

Another illustration, further to the right on the continuum, is defendant Herman Atkins, who was selected by the victim/witness from a lineup in which he was the only African American (Weinberg, 2003; "Herman Atkins—National Registry of Exonerations," n.d.). Atkins was wrongly convicted and imprisoned for 12 years before his release and exoneration. Prior to the biased lineup, the victim/witness had seen Atkins' photo on a wanted poster stemming from an unrelated offense. Thus, the victim's misidentification of Atkins was manufactured by her exposure to the wanted poster and then supported by the sham lineup. In addition, secondary evidence was manufactured when the prosecution secured a second witness who identified Atkins from the wanted poster as someone observed in the vicinity at the time of the crime, resulting in MEM. In these cases where capable victims of rape misidentify assailants, it is not only that law enforcement directed eyewitness identification procedures failed to detect the error in identification, but also the identification procedures often make a questionable identification appear reliable. An initial tentative impression is developed into a firm (but erroneous) identification.

The black box manufacture of evidence via police-induced false confessions is further toward the right of the continuum. As noted, there is an increased degree of intentionality in the manufacture of evidence via interrogation that proceeds after a determination that the suspect is not innocent. Leo's (2008, p. 187) description of US criminal interrogation clearly conveys the black box character of the process, "Police interrogation in America for the most part remains a hidden, low-visibility practice. Detectives keep their methods and strategies hidden by questioning suspects inside closed interrogation rooms that are secluded from the potential view or intrusion of nonparticipants. They also . . . fail to create an objective or reviewable record of the interrogation."

In the wrongful conviction of 16-year-old Jeffrey Deskovic, he was subjected to an all-day interrogation, including a polygraph examination, without counsel or parental support. After hours of his repeated denials of the rape and murder of a high school classmate, he incorporated details derived from the questioning and provided an incriminating admission (M. B. Johnson & Drucker, 2009). This coerced false confession was obviously manufactured, and, on the proposed continuum, it would be toward the right, that is, more intentional than inadvertent. However, to say the confession was intentionally manufactured does not mean the officers knew Deskovic was innocent. On the one hand, it is likely they believed he was guilty and merely used court-approved (coercive and deceptive) tactics to elicit a false admission of guilt. On the other hand, it is difficult to imagine the prosecution never entertained the matter of Deskovic's innocence, particularly when the pretrial DNA results indicated Deskovic was not the contributor of the crime scene semen. It raises the question whether persistent belief in the defendant's guilt, despite exculpatory evidence, is a form of self-deception.

Garrett (2010) examined false confessions leading to wrongful convictions, drawing from a series of 40 cases where postconviction DNA evidence led to exoneration. Garrett noted the evidence included detailed confessions corresponding to available case facts that resulted in narrative accounts that appeared realistic and authentic. Since each defendants' innocence was subsequently established postconviction, and because interrogations are not routinely recorded in the United States, it is not clear if the case facts and details were inadvertently leaked during interrogation, intentionally provided under the assumption it was harmless because the suspects were guilty anyway; or whether the details were provided, and the suspects (regardless of their guilt or innocence) were pressured to adopt the details. Therefore, even where it is clear false evidence was intentionally manufactured (as in a coerced false confession), it does not mean the parties responsible for the fabrication knew the defendants were in fact innocent.[6]

Further to the right in terms of the continuum of intentionality in manufactured evidence are the instances where Cook County, Illinois, interrogators fabricated confession statements and associated narratives with seemingly realistic inner-city slang terminology and coerced Black juvenile suspects to adopt these admissions (Drizin, 2013). On the extreme right are cases where law enforcement authorities provided false testimony as well. In the prosecution of Cruz and Hernandez described previously, more than a decade after the initial conviction, an officer admitted his earlier testimony about Cruz's admissions was not true. In the case of Earl Washington, who was also wrongly convicted of rape and murder and sentenced to death in Virginia, it was 20 years later when civil litigation established a state police officer manufactured evidence by fabricating details of a confession attributed to Washington.

Now to return to the three case illustrations of stranger rape in fact, the investigators in the Bloodsworth case (without a capable victim/witness) took witnesses to the black box and emerged with mistaken identifications of Kirk

Bloodsworth. Five witnesses testified at the first trial that Bloodsworth was seen with the child on the day she went missing (Junkin, 2004). Since the witness identification procedures were not transparent, it was not apparent that five witnesses were making the same error. In retrospect (with the benefit of hindsight and vigilant discovery), informed by the misinformation process, evidence corruption, and the exculpatory DNA data, there is some clarity about what occurred during the black box investigation. The victim, Dawn Hamilton, was last seen by two preteen boys entering a wooded area with a man. The boys were interviewed and helped create a composite sketch. When the sketch was released in the media, someone reported it resembled Kirk Bloodsworth. Following the media reports of Bloodsworth's arrest, where his actual face was shown, other witnesses reported Bloodsworth was seen with the child victim. From this process, the state obtained five eyewitnesses to identify Bloodsworth at trial (see "South Carolinians Abolishing the Death Penalty," n.d.). IP data indicate 38% of the wrongful convictions connected to eyewitness misidentifications involved this phenomenon of MEM (Innocence Project, 2009; G. L. Wells & Hasel, 2007).[7]

Similarly, investigators in the Central Park jogger case, also without a capable victim/witness, took suspects to the black box and emerged with coerced false confessions. Without direct knowledge of the methods and tactics employed in the interrogations, as well as clarity regarding the source of the content of the confessions, the defendants' ability to argue against the admissibility of the statements, to present a defense at trial or to pursue appellate relief, was fatally compromised (M. B. Johnson, 2001, 2005). The racial dynamics in the Central Park Jogger prosecutions are described in Chapter 3.

The Cotton/Thompson case differed from the Bloodsworth and Central Park Jogger cases in that the investigators had a capable victim/witness. Jennifer Thompson was available to describe the attack she survived and the perpetrator. However, the stranger rape status meant the victim had no prior relationship with the perpetrator, thus making it unlikely the offender would be considered as a suspect; also, the victim's ability to reliably identify the offender was limited. According to Jennifer Thompson, during the attack she made a conscious effort to remember the rapist's face so she could identify him in the future (Thompson-Cannino et al., 2009). However, her initial visual perception was impaired by "event-related" variables, limited lighting, stress/trauma, the cross-racial identification challenge, and the presence of a weapon (Innocence Project, 2009). The resulting black box investigation, rather than aiding her visual memory, undermined it.

That is, the process of creating the composite sketch (G. L. Wells & Hasel, 2007; Innocence Project, 2009); the repeat presentation of Ronald Cotton in the mug shots; and live lineup (Innocence Project, 2009; Finkelstein, 2009; Haw, Dickinson, & Meissner, 2007; Deffenbacher et al., 2006); and the positive feedback from the investigator introduced additional variables that further distorted Thompson's initially fragile perception. The result was a confidently held, erroneous identification of an innocent suspect (Cotton). The black box nature of the identification process meant the full record of what occurred was not available or preserved. The stranger rape character of the assault meant the capable victim (Thompson) was burdened with the accurate recall of a strange face, which is difficult in general, and even more difficult in the context of trauma (Bookbinder & Brainerd, 2016; Deffenbacher et al., 2004), and further compromised by the cross-racial challenge (Connelly, 2015; Meissner & Brigham, 2001, as described in Chapter 4). So, even though the law enforcement investigators correctly identified the offense as a "stranger rape" and there was a capable victim/witness, an innocent suspect was prosecuted and (twice) convicted.[8]

These three cases with stranger rape in fact illustrate even where the stranger rape aspect, that is, the "relational aspect," is correctly formulated, there are substantial obstacles to reliable identification of the perpetrator. This highlights the identification obstacles encountered by police investigators in stranger rape, whether the victim is "capable" or "incapacitated." So, with stranger rape we have accumulating risk in the form of pressure and demands on police investigators stemming from the pronounced moral violation associated with the offense, the absence of potential suspects to connect to the victim, coupled with either a lack of information from incapacitated victims or an increased risk of unreliable identification by capable victims.

FAULTY FORMULATION OF THE RELATIONAL ASPECT

There are other cases where incorrect assessment of the "relational aspect" complicates the formulation and rape investigation. For instance, there are stranger rapes that were incorrectly formulated by investigators as acquaintance rapes, which misled the investigation and resulted in wrongful conviction. Rossmo (2006, p. 6) has characterized this type of error as an "anchoring effect," where an initial erroneous impression influences the subsequent investigation. In the Westchester County, New York, wrongful conviction of Jeffrey Deskovic, the police and prosecution proceeded under the mistaken theory the offense was an acquaintance assault (M. B. Johnson & Drucker, 2009; Synder, McQuillan, Murphy, & Joselson, 2007). Consistent with the acquaintance rape formulation, the investigators focused on the victim's high school peers and incorrectly determined Jeffrey Deskovic was the likely perpetrator. Black box investigation led to prolonged secret interrogation of Deskovic, a coerced false confession, and wrongful conviction. Had the relational aspect of the offense been correctly formulated in the investigation, Jeffrey Deskovic would not have become a suspect. Realistically, in many cases, it is not possible to know with certainty that a rape was a stranger assault during the investigation. However, when the pretrial DNA results ruled out Deskovic as the contributor of the crime scene semen, the likelihood of a stranger assault warranted serious consideration. At that point, the prosecution had already won an indictment based on the (erroneous) acquaintance rape formulation, and that error would be ratified at trial and through the multiple denied appeals associated with Deskovic's ordeal with US justice. So, clearly, the confusion about the stranger rape element of the offense was a significant contributor to Deskovic's 16-year imprisonment. Postconviction DNA matching indicated it was indeed a stranger assault (M. B. Johnson & Drucker, 2009), committed by a serial sex offender.

Another instance where the relational aspect was mistakenly formulated was the Gary Dotson case from Illinois, described in the Introduction. This case was reported to the police and investigated as a stranger rape but actually was a false rape charge—no crime case. The erroneous formulation and prosecution of the case as a stranger rape eventually resulted in the wrongful conviction of the innocent Gary Dotson. Similarly, in 1995 John Grega was wrongfully convicted of the rape and murder of his wife, Christine ("John Grega—National Registry of Exonerations," n.d.). The prosecution theorized it was an intra-familial offense where Grega killed his wife secondary to marital problems and to obtain insurance monies. Grega was convicted on circumstantial evidence and was sentenced to life without parole in the State of Vermont. In 2008, a new Vermont law entitled Grega to postconviction DNA testing. The testing completed in 2012 identified an unknown male contributor of crime scene semen and excluded Grega. His conviction was reversed; he was released and awarded compensation.

Faulty assessment of the relational aspect in rape investigation is a feature in many other wrongful convictions.[9] A notable example is the acquaintance rape prosecution of James Lee Woodard in Dallas, Texas. In 1981, Woodard was charged with the rape and murder of his girlfriend, Beverly Ann Jones. He refused to plead guilty in exchange for a 3-year sentence. He was convicted at trial and remained imprisoned for 27 years. During his imprisonment, he filed multiple appeals, which were routinely rejected. He was consistently denied parole because he refused to admit guilt for a crime he did not commit. In 2008, attorneys and investigators from the Texas Innocence Project, in cooperation with the current Dallas County District Attorney Craig Watkins, located and tested the DNA evidence from James Woodard's case. They found it did not match Woodard. They also discovered the prosecution knew that Beverly Ann Jones was in the company of another man on the night she was killed, another man with a history of sexual assault charges. This potentially exculpating information was not shared with the defense (Fager, 2008).

THE PREVALENCE OF STRANGER RAPE AMONG CONFIRMED WRONGFUL CONVICTIONS

Review of the two major data sources on US exonerations (the IP and the National Registry of Exonerations [NRE]) revealed that a distinctly large proportion of the cases fall into the category of sexual assault, though differentially between the two data sources. Cases are considered sexual assaults where rape or rape-related charges (e.g., such as "forcible rape," "sexual violence," "deviant sexual battery" "deviant sexual conduct," "sodomy," "attempted rape" or "burglary with intent to commit sexual assault") were noted to be part of the offense.

Table 2.1 TOTAL (*N* = 346) INNOCENCE PROJECT[a] EXONERATIONS BY OFFENSE TYPE

Offense Type	Number	%
Sexual assault only	213	62
Sexual assault and murder	87	25
Murder only	37	11
Other	9	2
Total	346	100

[a] Innocence Project website January 2017.

Innocence Project Data

The IP website lists cases where exoneration was supported by DNA evidence of innocence. As of January 2017, the IP listed 346 exonerations. The narrative and bullet-point accounts of these cases were reviewed and cases were classified as

> Sexual assault = where the attack involved and/or defendant was charged with "rape," "forcible rape," or related charges as noted previously, including cases where there were also higher charges such as murder.

> Stranger rape = where the victim had no prior relationship with the assailant (LeBeau, 1987) as previously defined.

> Among the (*N* = 346) IP-reported exonerations, 300 (87%) were cases with sexual assaults, and 46 (13%) were cases without sexual assault. The 300 IP sexual assault exonerees are listed in Appendix A. Further disaggregation indicated 213 (62%) were exclusively sexual assaults, 87 (25%) were sexual assaults with murders, 37 (11%) were murders only, and 9 (2%) were other types, as presented in Table 2.1.

Disaggregation among the (*n* = 300) sexual assaults finds 249 were stranger rapes (83% of the sexual assaults), 34 were acquaintance rapes (11%), two were intra-familial child sexual assaults (<1%), and 15 were undetermined (5%). It is relevant to note the 249 stranger sexual assaults accounted for 72% of the total IP cases. The IP sexual assault exonerations by case type are presented in Table 2.2.

Table 2.2 INNOCENCE PROJECT SEXUAL ASSAULT EXONERATIONS (*N* = 300) BY CASE (PROSECUTION[a]) TYPE

Case Type	Number	%
Stranger assaults	249	83
Acquaintance assaults	34	11
Intra-familial assaults	2	<1
Undetermined	15	5
Total	300	100

[a] How the case was prosecuted.

Among the N = 346 IP cases, 284 cases listed both defendant's and victim's race/ethnicity. Among these cases, 106 cases (37%) involved the Black defendant/white victim dyad. Among the (n = 300) IP sexual assaults, 257 listed both defendant and victim race/ethnicity, and 99 were Black defendant/white victim cases, 39% of all IP wrongful convictions in sexual assault where race/ethnicity was reported. This is highly disproportionate to the frequency of Black perpetrator/white victim sexual assaults. Multiple sources indicated rape and sexual assault are highly intra-ethnic crimes. For example, Gross et al. (2005) reported the Black defendant/white victim dyad accounted for 5%–6% of all rapes, but half (39 of 80) of all rape exonerations. Similarly, Garrett (2011) reported 49% (84 of 171) of rape exonerees were Black defendant/white victim cases, while 10% of sexual offenses were interracial (also see Connelly, 2015). The overrepresentation of Black defendant/white victim cases among the wrongfully convicted is considered further in the Chapter 3 presentation of race and rape prosecution in US history.

National Registry of Exonerations Data

The NRE website lists documented exonerations in the United States (total = 2,112 as of May 2017), including those reliant on DNA as well as those independent of DNA evidence. The NRE website was searched electronically for all cases where the terms *sexual assault* or *rape* were used in the narrative account or bullet-point data. O review, a number of these cases were determined not to involve sexual assault, or sexual assault allegations, such as where the narrative included reference to another defendant wrongfully convicted with evidence from a forensic expert who gave unreliable testimony in the search-identified case. Among the (N = 2,212) NRE cases, 588 (27%) were sexual assaults as defined previously. The 588 NRE sexual assault exonerees are listed in Appendix B. Among the 588 sexual assaults, 342 (58%) were stranger rapes, 133 (23%) were acquaintance assaults, 89 (15%) were intra-familial child sexual assaults, and 24 (4%) were undetermined. These data are presented in Table 2.3.

Unlike the IP, the NRE does not typically report victim race/ethnicity. However, disaggregation of the available NRE data by offense and race/ethnicity also

Table 2.3 NATIONAL REGISTRY OF EXONERATIONS[a] SEXUAL ASSAULT EXONERATIONS (N = 588) BY CASE (PROSECUTION) TYPE

Case Type	Number	%
Stranger assaults	342	58
Acquaintance assaults	133	23
Intra-familial assaults	89	15
Undetermined	24	4
Total	588	100

[a] National Registry of Exonerations website May 2017.

revealed the prominent Black defendant/white victim dyad in wrongful conviction in sexual assault. Among the (n = 588) NRE sexual assault cases, 88 included race/ethnicity data of both the defendant and the victim. Among the NRE cases with these data, 52 (59%) were Black defendant/white victim cases, further illustrating the disproportionate representation of Black defendant/white victim cases among confirmed wrongful convictions.

WRONGFUL CONVICTION IN STRANGER RAPE: "VICTIM STATUS" PATHS

There are two identifiable patterns or paths in wrongful conviction in stranger rape. Delineation of these two paths helps to clarify the sequence or contingent relationship among investigation errors, that is, how errors are connected (and potentially how they can be reduced). While a significant portion of confirmed wrongful convictions in stranger rape follow one of the two paths, there is divergence from these two paths, also described in this chapter. A distinguishing early aspect in a rape investigation is victim status: whether there is a capable or an incapacitated victim/witness. A capable victim/witness is a critical asset in the investigation of rape. There is a common lay assumption that memory with strong emotional content, such as the memory of a crime, is protected against distortion. This assumption is undermined by empirical findings (Bookbinder & Brainerd, 2016; Deffenbacher et al., 2004) that indicate false memories increase in the context of emotional content, demonstrating memories that are associated with negative emotions may be misremembered. These findings suggest witnesses being required to recall crime scene material may be at an increased risk for false memory formation, as crime scene content is often associated with highly negative emotions. Such identifications are further undermined where there was the presence of a weapon, limited time or otherwise opportunity for facial observation, limited lighting, or a cross-racial identification challenge (Innocence Project, 2009).

The wrongful conviction literature contains many examples of capable victims of stranger rapes who mistakenly identified innocents as their attackers.[10] The risks of wrongful conviction in stranger rape with capable victims differ, in various ways, from stranger rape with incapacitated victims. Where victims of rape are incapacitated by death or pronounced disability, the risk of misidentification is not as pronounced as it is with capable victims. With incapacitated victims, the risk of wrongful conviction is associated with false confession. As presented in Figure 2.2, wrongful conviction in stranger rape with capable victims is associated with misidentifications as primary evidence, supplemented by flawed expert or scientific evidence and/or some form of incentivized testimony as secondary evidence. Wrongful conviction in stranger rape with incapacitated victims is associated with false confessions as primary evidence and flawed expert or scientific evidence and/or incentivized testimony as secondary evidence.

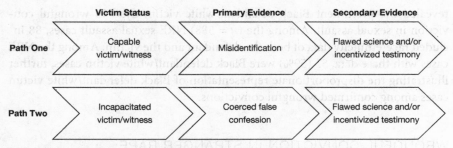

Figure 2.2 Victim Status Paths in Wrongful Conviction in Stranger Rape

STRANGER RAPE, CAPABLE VICTIM, BLACK BOX INVESTIGATION, AND MISIDENTIFICATION

Cases illustrating the common path of wrongful conviction in stranger rape with capable victims are presented next, followed by wrongful convictions with incapacitated victims. These are followed by illustrations and discussions of wrongful conviction cases that diverge from these two common paths.

Steve Titus: A Pre-DNA Exoneration

Steve Titus was wrongly convicted of a stranger rape that occurred on October 11, 1980, in Seattle, Washington. Titus was convicted by a jury in 1981. The primary evidence introduced by the state was an identification by the rape victim (Nancy Van Roper). There were defense allegations of official misconduct (planting evidence and altering records). The rape victim had been hitchhiking and was picked up by a lone male. She reported being driven to a deserted area near the Seattle–Tacoma Airport and raped in the assailant's car. She then found her way to a home in the area and called the police. Steve Titus was stopped by police because he was driving a car similar to the description provided by the rape victim (Henderson, 1981; Loftus & Ketcham, 1991). He also loosely fit the description of the offender and allowed the police to take his photo. Titus's photo, as presented in an array with five other photos, was distinguishable. It was the only Polaroid photo, smaller than the others, and with a different border. The victim's original identification was that Titus's photo was closest to her memory of the rapist. However, in court she testified Titus definitely was the rapist. Postconviction investigation by Titus's attorney, as well as journalist Paul Henderson, linked the offense to serial rapist Edward Lee King, who confessed to the crime (Olsen, 1991; R. Anderson, 2013). Psychologist Elizabeth Loftus was retained by counsel representing Titus in civil litigation against the Port of Seattle Police. Dr. Loftus prepared testimony to explain how the victim's identification of Titus was a product of the suggestive identification procedures. Titus died of a heart attack in 1985, at age 36, three weeks before his civil case was scheduled to begin. His estate was awarded a 2.8-million-dollar settlement (R. Anderson, 2013).

Steve Avery: *Making a Murderer*

One of the most widely publicized wrongful convictions in recent years was the Steve Avery case featured in the documentary film *Making a Murderer* (Ricciardi & Demos, 2015; also see Lautenschlager, 2003). The Steve Avery case involved the misidentification by a capable, stranger rape victim. The assault victim, Penny Ann Beerntsen, was attacked on July 29, 1985, while jogging along the shore of Lake Michigan in Two Rivers, Wisconsin. She was taken to a secluded wooded area, raped, and strangled until she lost consciousness. A rape kit was subsequently taken, and Beerntsen provided a description of the attacker. As reported by Ricciardi and Demos (2015), the detective believed the description was consistent with Avery. A prior mug shot of Avery was referenced to create a "composite" sketch. Beerntsen identified the composite sketch as her assailant. She thereafter chose the reference mug shot from a photo spread and subsequently identified Avery in a lineup. At trial, the victim identified Avery, and a forensic specialist testified a hair recovered from Avery's shirt was consistent with Beerntsen's hair. The black box, biased identification process was overlooked (Lautenschlager, 2003), and despite multiple alibi witnesses and relevant documentation Avery was convicted at trial on December 14, 1985.

Avery was denied appellate relief until 1995, when a petition was granted for DNA testing of the victim's fingernail residuals, which was inconclusive. In 2002, DNA testing of hairs recovered from the victim after the offense were matched to Gregory Allen, who was serving time for a sexual offense committed after the attack on Beerntsen. It was reported in the press that prior to the rape of Beerntsen, Allen had committed a sexual assault at the same location in 1983 (Chandler, 2006). According to Beerntsen (Thompson, 2016), she was never told the perpetrator might not be among the photos she was shown. Avery was released, and in 2003 the charges were dismissed.[11] Additional cases with stranger rape, capable victims and misidentification are provided in Chapters 3 and 4.

STRANGER RAPE, INCAPACITATED VICTIM, BLACK BOX INVESTIGATION, AND COERCED FALSE CONFESSION

The most widely known stranger rape, wrongful conviction with an incapacitated victim is the New York City Central Park Jogger case noted above and presented further in the Chapter 3 discussion of "Race and Rape Prosecution." There are several other cases that followed the path of incapacitated victim and coerced false confession, such as the Earl Washington case from Virginia and the Ruffin, Bivens, and Dixon wrongful convictions in Mississippi. Next, the pattern of stranger rape, incapacitated victim, and coerced false confession is illustrated with cases from Texas, Nebraska, and Long Island, New York.

Christopher Ochoa: Stranger Rape, Incapacitated Victim, Coerced Confession

Christopher Ochoa was released by Texas authorities in 2001 after his innocence in a 1988 stranger rape and murder was established by DNA exclusion
and matching. He had falsely confessed and entered a guilty plea to avoid the
risk of trial conviction and a death sentence. The victim of the attack, Nancy
DePriest, was a Pizza Hut employee. Ochoa was employed at a different Austin,
Texas, Pizza Hut. The police believed the offender had knowledge of the facility.
Ochoa became a suspect when he visited the restaurant, shortly after the offense, with another coworker (Richard Danzinger). Ochoa and Danzinger were
interrogated separately. After more than 20 hours of interrogation, where death
penalty and other threats were used, Ochoa made admissions to the rape and
murder and also implicated Danzinger (Weinstein, 2006). According to Ochoa
(2005), the interrogator selectively recorded incriminating statements but did
not record the instructions and threats. Danzinger did not give an incriminating
statement. Ochoa agreed to testify against Danzinger at trial to avoid a death
sentence. His testimony, along with less-than-scientific blood typing evidence,
led to Danzinger's trial conviction in 1990. Both defendants were sentenced to
life in prison.[12]

   In 1998, Achim Marino, a born-again Texas inmate, wrote the governor and
other officials reporting he alone had raped and murdered DePriest. In subsequent
letters, Marino revealed detailed knowledge of the crime scene and informed police where physical evidence from the crime could be found. With the assistance
of the University of Wisconsin Innocence Project, subsequent DNA tests excluded
Ochoa and Danzinger and confirmed Marino's confession (Weinstein, 2006). It
is relevant that Ochoa was neither intellectually limited nor psychologically impaired. He completed law school in 2006.

   Without a description of the perpetrator or offense, investigators relied on
black box methods, including prolonged, secret interrogation strongly supporting
Ochoa's report of physical abuse and threats. Through this process evidence was
manufactured to wrongly convict Christopher Ochoa and Richard Danzinger. The
actual offender remained at large and committed other serious sexual offenses (as
discussed further in Chapter 4).

The Beatrice Six: Stranger Rape, Incapacitated Victim, Multiple False Confessions

The prosecution of the Beatrice Six is another dramatic illustration of unreliable
manufactured evidence. The irregularities and due process violations apparent in
the black box investigation are peculiar even among other confirmed wrongful
convictions. Notable aspects of the case were the defendants' psychological
vulnerabilities, the dual roles of psychologist Dr. Wayne Price, the selective recording of interrogations, and the search for the blood type B suspect.

The crime involved the 1985 stranger rape and murder of Helen Wilson in Beatrice, Nebraska. Six defendants (Joseph White, Thomas Winslow, Ada JoAnn Taylor, Debra Shelden, James Dean, and Kathy Gonzalez) were wrongly convicted. One defendant (Joseph White) was convicted at trial, and the remaining five accepted plea arrangements (Dunker, 2017). Three of the defendants (Taylor, Dean, and Shelden) provided incriminating testimony for the prosecution at White's trial (Pilger, 2016).

During the summer of 1983, there were three attempted sexual attacks on other elderly women within blocks of Helen Wilson's residence. The suspect was described as a thin, tall, white male. An FBI report indicated these four attacks were committed by the same lone assailant ("Debra Shelden—National Registry of Exonerations," n.d.). Semen and blood residuals were collected from the crime scene. There was evidence the perpetrator's blood was type B.

Bruce Allen Smith, an early suspect, left Nebraska for Oklahoma shortly after the 1985 offense. Oklahoma officials secured biological samples from Smith and incorrectly ruled him out as a suspect. The case went cold. However, a private citizen, Burdett Searcey, told Helen Wilson's daughter he would investigate the case further. Searcey was a farmer and a former Beatrice Police officer. Two years after the rape and murder of Wilson, Searcey left farming and returned to law enforcement as a Gage County deputy sheriff (Aviv, 2017). The case was officially reopened in 1989 when Searcey prepared arrest warrants for White and Taylor based on information he developed during his private investigation. As reported in Aviv (2017), a source had informed Searcey that Taylor and White bragged about committing the offense.

In March 1989, Deputy Sheriff Searcey, Dr. Wayne Price (a licensed psychologist who was also a deputy sheriff), and another officer flew to Alabama to interrogate Joseph White. White responded to the accusatory questions by requesting an attorney. White did, however, give blood, saliva, and hair samples. The following day, the officers flew to North Carolina to arrest Taylor. Searcey did not record the interrogation until Taylor had assumed responsibility for the offense. Taylor was noted to say her involvement was secondary to her domination by White (Aviv, 2017; Huddle 2009). When Taylor denied recall of the crime details, Searcey suggested she was blocking it out. Taylor reported a history of childhood intra-familial sexual abuse. Taylor also had been treated previously by Dr. Price, who diagnosed Taylor with borderline personality disorder and recommended she surrender her child to the child protective agency. When Taylor returned to Beatrice, she requested counseling with Dr. Price, who subsequently assisted her in "recovering" memories from the 1985 offense. However, neither White nor Taylor had type B blood.

In a subsequent photo lineup, Taylor chose Thomas Winslow as someone also present during the attack on Helen Wilson. Winslow was questioned, and the video recording begins when he has already accepted blame for the offense (Aviv, 2017). His account is sketchy; he reported he was pressured by White and Taylor. Winslow had a history of depression with suicide attempt and past treatment by Dr. Price. Winslow also did not have type B blood.

Debra Shelden was the grandniece of Helen Wilson, the crime victim. She was known to be in the circle of associates with Taylor and White, though a bit older. Reportedly, she also had been sexually abused as a child, and there were records suggesting intellectual impairment (Aviv, 2017). Her limited admission was that she helped the other three gain entry to Helen Wilson's apartment. Shelden also did not have type B blood. Her court-appointed lawyer (Paul Koursland) assumed her lack of recall of the offense was due to the trauma of the murder (Aviv, 2017). Koursland had Shelden examined by Dr. Price. Dr. Price had treated Shelden in the past to improve her parenting skills, but she subsequently surrendered her parental rights. After consultation with Dr. Price, Shelden reported she dreamed her husband's friend James Dean was at the crime scene. Dean was arrested and held at the county jail. He was observed to be frantic and pacing. The jail staff called in Dr. Price to calm Dean. Through consultation, Dean revealed a history of physical abuse by his father and brother-in-law. Dean denied involvement in the assault on Helen Wilson and was told he failed the polygraph (Huddle, 2009). Six days after meeting with Dr. Price, Dean confessed to a role in the crime recovered via a dream (Aviv, 2017). But, Dean also did not have type B blood. He was urged to name another participant. About 2 weeks later, he recalled, again via a dream, Kathy Gonzalez was also there. Gonzalez had lived in the apartment above Helen Wilson. At the time of the investigation in 1989, Kathy Gonzalez was working in a restaurant in Denver, Colorado. She was taken into custody on May 25, 1989, and questioned. Gonzalez denied knowledge of the crime but agreed to return to Nebraska to clear up the reports (Huddle, 2009). On return, she continued to deny knowledge of the offense and even requested to be hypnotized. Gonzalez consulted with Dr. Price, and he convinced her there was considerable evidence she was involved. Gonzalez had type B blood.

Ultimately, White was the only defendant to go to trial. Taylor, Shelden, and Dean entered guilty pleas and testified against White. Winslow and Gonzalez entered no-contest pleas. According to reports (Aviv, 2017), at various times Taylor, Dean, Winslow, and Shelden had doubts about their innocence, that is, they internalized their false confessions to some degree.[13] However, they were also exposed to death penalty threats associated with a trial conviction, and this likely contributed to the guilty pleas as well (Duggan, 2016). Postconviction and removed from contact with the investigation, Dean recognized his innocence and sought to withdraw his guilty plea, without success (Aviv, 2017). White persisted in his efforts to establish his innocence. In 2001, White took advantage of a new state statute that allowed convicted felons to seek DNA exoneration. In 2008, White, Winslow, and Dean were excluded as the source of the crime scene semen and blood. Shortly afterward, the biological evidence was matched to Bruce Allen Smith, the early suspect. Smith had died in 1992. In early 2009, the attorney general's office confirmed White's, Taylor's, and Winslow's innocence, and they were released. Shelden, Dean, and Gonzalez had been released 5 years earlier. The six were subsequently pardoned and won a $28 million civil compensation award (Healy, 2019).

The exoneration of the Beatrice Six defendants revealed another instance of multiple false confessions manufactured by black box investigation methods in a sexual assault. The Beatrice Six case shares this feature with the New York City Central Park Five cases; the Ollins, Ollins, Saunders, and Bradford prosecution; the Dixmoor Five; and Englewood Four cases from Cook County, Illinois (discussed in Chapter 3), as well as the Norfolk Four wrongful convictions (Leo & Davis, 2010) from Virginia presented in Chapter 4.

The Beatrice Six investigation proceeded with a faulty formulation that White and Taylor had committed the offense. The precise methods used to generate the false confessions are not known because, as is characteristic of a black box investigation, an objective record was not maintained. The available record, however, indicates the interrogators' approach was not effective in securing an incriminating statement from White. Though with Taylor minimization was effective, where she confirmed the faulty formulation through indicating her involvement was forced/ dominated by White, in this way Taylor then adopted "facts" of the offense as presented by the interrogators. Similarly, Winslow's admission came through attributing his involvement to White and Taylor, and Shelden limited her involvement to providing entry for White, Taylor, and Winslow.

Kassin has noted that multiple false confessions can be likened to a "house of cards" (as cited in Drizin & Leo, 2004, p. 973), where an initial false confession is used to leverage a second one, a third one, and so on. In addition, the "Reid Technique" (Inbau et al., 2013) explicitly instructs interrogators to fabricate an initial confession as a tactic to persuade an assumed accomplice to provide an alternative incriminating admission. This is all maintained through black box selective recording of the interrogation that omits from the record what investigators say to the suspects.

Further, there are clear indications several of the Beatrice Six defendants had psychological vulnerabilities that were exploited during investigation. Four of the six defendants (Taylor, Shelden, Dean, and Gonzalez) had histories of sexual and/ or physical abuse as children, suggesting an increased vulnerability to authority figures. Three of the defendants (Taylor, Shelden, and Winslow) had been treated by Dr. Price prior to becoming suspects. Each of the defendants (the exception being White) were seen by Dr. Price in connection with the charges, and Dr. Price encouraged them to give evidence to support the state's case. Where suspects denied recall of the offense, the psychological interpretation was their inability to recall was confirmation they were present during the traumatic rape and murder. Thus, through a process that has been called "confirmation bias," "tunnel vision," "outcome bias," or "ratification of error," suspects were added until a suspect with type B blood type was found.

Kogut, Restivo, and Halstead: Stranger Rape, Incapacitated Victim, Black Box Investigation

John Kogut, John Restivo, and Dennis Halstead were charged with the rape and murder of a 16-year-old, whose naked body was discovered in Lynbrook, New York, in December 1984 (Centurion Ministries, n.d.). The youthful victim had been missing about 3 weeks. Autopsy determined the manner of death was strangulation. Semen and spermatozoa were recovered from the body; however, serological examination was not conducted. The Nassau County Police were under considerable pressure because another teen had been missing from a neighboring community since June, and within months of the discovery of the body, a third teen went missing from the area (Levy, 2015; Gootman, 2003). Without a capable victim to inform the investigation, officers sought information from various sources. In January 1985, a tip led to the questioning of John Restivo. Restivo did not make an incriminating statement but mentioned his 21-year-old employee, John Kogut. Kogut was subsequently subjected to an 18-hour interrogation, where he was falsely told he failed a polygraph examination. Kogut signed a "confession," handwritten by one of the interrogating officers, in which he implicated Halstead, Restivo, and himself in the crime with the rape occurring in Restivo's van. A search of the van resulted in the recovery of hairs that were examined forensically.

At trial, the prosecution's case relied on the confession and a forensic analyst who testified the recovered hairs matched the victim and thus corroborated the confession. In addition, the state produced testimony from incentivized informants, who tied the offense to the defendants. Despite an alibi, Kogut was convicted in April 1986. Restivo and Halstead were tried together and convicted in November of the same year.

The initial postconviction DNA testing excluded the three defendants, but the prosecution held the samples may have been limited. Further investigation by the defense led to an untested and intact vaginal swab. In 2003, advanced DNA testing of the associated spermatozoa excluded the three defendants and indicated a single unknown male profile. Also, defense attorneys secured a report from Detective Nicholas Petraco, an expert who testified for the state at the initial trial. Petraco's updated assessment indicated the hairs in evidence exhibited characteristics of "postmortem root banding," that is hairs that were attached to the corpse for at least 8 hours. This was contrary to the state's theory the victim shed the hairs while in Restivo's van prior to being killed, and suggested the victim's hairs from the autopsy had found their way (inadvertently or intentionally) to the collection of evidence from the van. The defendants' convictions were reversed, but the prosecution retried Kogut. He was acquitted in a bench trial in December 2005. The wrongful conviction of Kogut, Restivo, and Halstead illustrates the familiar sequence of stranger rape, incapacitated rape victim, pressure on investigators, black box investigation via secret interrogation, and supplemental incentivized testimony coupled with flawed forensic analyses.

PATH DIVERGENCE

While a large proportion of stranger rape wrongful convictions proceed along the "incapacitated victim, false confession path" or the "capable victim, misidentification path," there are also cases that diverge from these two paths. For instance, the Kirk Bloodsworth wrongful conviction cited previously (as well as the Darryl Hunt prosecution described in Chapter 3) involved an incapacitated victim and erroneous identifications by witnesses other than the victim. Three other wrongful rape convictions (Ray Krone, Levon Brooks, and Kennedy Brewer) with incapacitated victims relied on bite mark misidentification as the state's primary evidence. The Rodney Roberts wrongful rape conviction involved a capable victim, a false guilty plea, and confinement as a sexually violent predator. The Krone and the Roberts cases are described next.

Ray Krone: Incapacitated Victim, Bite Mark Misidentification

Ray Krone was twice convicted of the December, 29, 1991, fatal assault on waitress Kim Ancona. The victim's nude body was discovered in the male bathroom of the bar where she worked. There were multiple stab wounds and bite marks on the breast and neck. There was no semen collected, but saliva was taken from her body. Krone was a regular of the bar, and it was reported Ancona was overheard stating Krone was going to help her close up the bar. Krone agreed to make a styrofoam dental impression, which became the primary evidence used to convict him. He was arrested and charged with murder and sexual assault 2 days after Kim Ancona's body was found.

At trial, the state presented two forensic odontologists, one experienced and the other new in the field (Garrett & Neufeld, 2009). They both testified the marks on Ancona were made by Krone. Krone was convicted and sentenced to death in 1992. In 1995, Krone won a new trial when the appellate court cited the state's failure to disclose exculpatory evidence, results from another expert indicating the bites did not originate from Krone. Krone was convicted a second time in 1996 and sentenced to life. In 2002, DNA testing of saliva from the crime scene excluded Krone and was matched to Kenneth Phillips, who was serving time for a sexual assault he committed after the attack on Ancona (Davenport, 2006). Without a capable victim to make or rule out identifications, the prosecution relied on black box, manufactured evidence, in the form of unreliable bite mark identification, erroneously connecting Krone to the attack on Ancona (Garrett & Neufeld, 2009).

Rodney Roberts: False Guilty Plea and Sexually Violent Predator Confinement

The wrongful rape conviction of Rodney Roberts was not reliant on misidentification by the surviving victim. A law enforcement officer's false report that the victim had identified Roberts, coupled with inadequate defense representation, led Roberts to accept a plea arrangement, which resulted in 17 years of confinement despite his innocence ("Rodney Roberts—National Registry of Exonerations," n.d; Zambito, 2014). The record suggests Roberts was also vulnerable secondary to an earlier juvenile court judgment against him for a sexual offense.

In 1996, a 17-year-old Black woman reported she was abducted and raped by a Black male in Newark, New Jersey. She was examined at a hospital, and a rape kit was taken. While at the hospital, a suspect was presented, but she did not identify him as the assailant. Two weeks later, Roberts was arrested, in the area, on an unrelated robbery charge. According to the police, Roberts' (who had a juvenile adjudication for a sex offense) photo was shown to the victim, and she identified him as the attacker. Six weeks later, at the urging of his assigned counsel, Roberts agreed to plead guilty to kidnapping, and the prosecution dismissed the sexual assault charge. Four years later, Roberts was denied parole principally because he refused to admit guilt to the kidnap or sexual assault. Six months later, he filed pro se to withdraw his guilty plea to the kidnap charge. The motion was dismissed, by the original trial judge, before an attorney was assigned. Nevertheless, the assignment was received by an attorney who interviewed the victim, and she denied identifying Roberts as the rapist. Roberts completed his sentence in 2004 but was civilly committed as a sexually violent predator.

In the following years, Roberts filed unsuccessful motions to withdraw his plea, and the original rape kit could not be located. In 2010, the judge denied Roberts's request for a third time, but the ruling was reversed by the appellate court. By 2013, the original trial judge had retired. Following requests from Roberts' new assigned counsel, the original rape kit was located. DNA results excluded Roberts as the source of the semen from the rape kit. The new trial judge vacated the plea and conviction. The prosecutor dismissed the case, and the state withdrew the sexually violent predator designation. In 2015, Roberts filed a federal civil suit against the Newark Police, the county prosecutor, and other defendants (Gialanella, 2016).

This was a stranger rape with a capable victim, but postconviction investigation revealed the victim never identified Roberts. In addition, DNA testing excluded Roberts as the contributor of the crime scene semen. However, pretrial, Roberts feared he was facing false rape charges from a consensual sex partner. The defense counsel told him the victim identified him and knew him from the neighborhood. Roberts, already jailed on an unrelated matter and unable to make bail, faced considerable pressure to accept a plea deal. According to Roberts, since he had been wrongly convicted by jury in a prior sex offense case, he doubted he would be acquitted if he proceeded to trial ("Rodney Roberts—Innocence Project," n.d.; M. B. Johnson & Cunningham, 2015).

A STRANGER RAPE THESIS

The available literature, data, and case illustrations cited provide a framework for a stranger rape thesis that outlines an increased risk of wrongful conviction in stranger rape as compared to sexual assault in general and other offenses. While this thesis is presented as hypothetical, and warrants further assessment, it can be useful in prospective and retrospective analyses of rape and other investigations. The proposed stranger rape thesis includes four basic elements.

1. In stranger rape, the victim has no prior connection with the assailant; therefore, it is difficult to formulate a motive and thus generate potential suspects.

2. In stranger rape, there are substantial obstacles to reliable identification of suspects where the memory of a face, not previously known, is difficult for a (capable) victim of a traumatic assault (due to a host of estimator and system factors) and impossible for the deceased or otherwise incapacitated victim, which leads to reliance on black box manufacture of evidence. The obstacles to reliable identification, as well as the other three elements of the stranger rape thesis, are increased in Black defendant/white victim cases (discussed further in Chapter 3).

3. The "moral outrage" response to stranger rape leads to increased pressure on law enforcement and thus more aggressive and hasty investigation and prosecution. With stranger rape, there is a combination of the moral violation, a generalized sense of fear in the community, and special contempt for the perpetrator. Everyone, and anyone, is vulnerable to attack by a stranger, and it is difficult for elements in the public to blame the victim, such as when a prostitute or college student is raped. The sexual aspect of the offense suggests an absence of impulse control and morality, making the offender especially reprehensible. Once the allegation of stranger rape has been leveled, there is great sympathy and empathy for the victim, and the press, public, and professionals are reluctant to support the alleged sex offender.

4. "Moral correction"—the moral outrage that results from the offense—creates an emotional response, a tension experienced by the victim, family, police, prosecutors, press, and community. This tension or anxiety seeks resolution (homeostasis) through action that corrects the outrage. A swift and severe corrective response (a publicly announced arrest, a press conference assuring the criminal has been apprehended, an indictment, a conviction, and sentencing) is sought. The desire/need for a correction is so compelling that people will accept, as a corrective action, a remedy that may not actually be linked to the outrage. Operating under the influence of the tension/anxiety, or "priming" by the moral outrage, the threshold for an acceptable corrective is lowered. This leads to a moral correction bias in the evaluation of evidence, where an insufficiently supported and/or invalid solution is accepted and fulfills the desire for a moral correction. This is one of the reasons why wrongful convictions are apparently more common in high-profile cases (Dror & Fraser-MacKenzie, 2009; Drizin & Leo, 2004). Moral correction warrants consideration in the context of literature describing other biases contributing to wrongful conviction, such as tunnel vision, outcome bias, confirmation bias, and ratification of error. With time, the moral outrage

tension/anxiety will be reduced and allow for more reasoned evaluation of the evidence and legal processes. This moral correction process is elaborated further in the Chapter 6 discussion of processes, models, and concepts in wrongful conviction'.

WRONGFUL CONVICTION WHERE ACQUAINTANCE RAPE IS CHARGED

There is general recognition among criminal justice researchers that acquaintance rape is the most common type of sexual assault; that is, more common than stranger assaults or intra-familial child sexual assaults. As noted in the Introduction and Overview, 78% of sexual assault victims knew the offender (Planty et al., 2013). Acquaintance rape encompasses assaults by friends, former (and current) lovers, coworkers, and anyone with whom the victim had a prior relationship. This includes assaults often referred to as college campus "date rape" as well as the problem of sexual assault among US troops (Katz, Huffman, & Cojucar, 2017; Holland, Rabelo, & Cortina, 2016). Chapter 1 described the rape law reform movement, which was focused largely on facilitating prosecution of acquaintance rapes, which were typically more difficult to prosecute to conviction than stranger rapes.

In the lead up to the 2016 US presidential election, candidate Hilary Clinton changed some of the content on her website statement related to campus sexual assault. The message shifted from "you have the right to be believed" to "you have the right to be heard" (Wilkinson, 2016). This was in response to the reemergence of allegations candidate Clinton's husband (former President) Bill Clinton had sexually assaulted Juanita Broaddrick in 1978 and Hilary Clinton had threatened Broaddrick not to go public with the allegation. Clinton's revised message illustrates the challenge presented in assessing rape reports and allegations.

Should sexual assault "victims" be believed, or should their reports be viewed with skepticism? How can it be determined that complainants are indeed victims without ruling out other possible explanations? Is sexual assault *complainant* a preferable term compared to *victim*? Can law enforcement officers and/or specialists conduct assessments that are both supportive to the complainant and effectively rule out alternative formulations? False and fabricated charges are not unique to rape (Galvin & Polk, 1983). False criminal complaints are filed alleging theft, burglary, assault, robbery, and other offenses. Investigators are also required to evaluate and substantiate claims related to insurance matters and civil compensation. However, victims of rape and sexual assault have unique injuries, burdens, and vulnerabilities.

False rape charges undoubtedly occur, although there is dispute regarding the prevalence (Lisak, Gardinier, Nicksa, & Cote, 2010; Gruber, 2009) and, more fundamentally, how false rape charges are defined. There has been a considerable debate among researchers, including feminist scholars, about the prevalence of false rape charges. Findings have been cited to indicate false rape charges are rather common, that is, in the range of 40%–60% of all rape reports (McDowell, 1985; Kanin, 1994). However, critics of these findings make two substantial points. Studies citing high rates of false rape charges typically are counting law enforcement determinations the complaints were "unfounded" or "unsubstantiated" as false rape charges, when a variety of other reasons exist that the police or prosecution did not proceed with the case. Actual victims have been known to recant if they find the investigation and/or prosecution process to be further distressing (Belknap, 2010). While recantation is relevant and may be associated with a false accusation, it can be difficult to assess without knowledge of context and circumstances of the recantation. A second point critiquing high rates of false rape charges is that rape is a notoriously underreported crime. Therefore, according to Belknap (2010), if 5% of all rapes reported are false reports, that would be a miniscule proportion (about 0.005%) of all rapes that occur.

The concern about false rape charges is commonly a consideration where the accusation involves an acquaintance rape. It can be said that false rape charge is the common response (whether true or a false denial) of the defendant in acquaintance rape. A well-known acquaintance rape wrongful conviction was the prosecution of Brian Banks. Wanetta Gibson, a 15-year-old high school student, informed her sister she was raped by 16-year-old Banks at a "make-out" spot in the high school ("Brian Banks—National Registry of Exonerations," n.d.). An intended private false accusation grew into a major criminal case.

Banks was arrested and charged with rape and related counts. Banks pled guilty, at the advice of private counsel, to avoid a possible 40-year sentence if found guilty at trial (M. B. Johnson & Cunningham, 2015). Banks served 5 years and was then released on parole. Gibson reached out to Banks via social media, and Banks arranged a meeting where he secretly recorded her acknowledgment there was no rape. Gibson, however, was unwilling to go on record with the recantation because her family had received a 1.5 million-dollar civil settlement from the school system. The recording became the newly discovered evidence that led to Banks's exoneration.

Engle and O'Donohue (2012) discussed a range of psychological factors as well as complex motives that may contribute to false rape allegations (also see Aiken, Burgess, & Hazelwood, 1999). The presentation that follows does not focus on the motive or psychology of false rape charges, though in certain cases the available facts highlight apparent motives. The focus here is on describing instances of false complaints and determining if there are "red flags" in accusations that warrant increased scrutiny in investigation.

The matter of wrongful conviction in acquaintance rape revolves around the veracity of the charge, typically made by the victim/complainant. Review of the record of wrongful convictions in acquaintance sexual assaults reveals different types of considerations or disputes. There are cases where there is dispute regarding whether there was sexual contact, and other cases where the opposing parties agree there was sexual contact but the dispute is about whether the sexual contact was consensual. Arguably, where the dispute is about consent, complainants and the accused may provide conflicting but truthful accounts. There are also a small number of cases where the accusation came from a third party rather than the "victim/complainant." Across cases, there are three features frequently operative: the youthful complainant (as in the Dotson and the Banks cases), official misconduct in the form of withholding exculpatory evidence, and the role of inadequate defense representation.

Mark Clark: Dispute About Sexual Contact

The Brian Banks case noted involved a dispute about whether there was sexual contact, that is, intercourse as alleged by the complainant. Similarly, in the Mark Clark wrongful rape conviction in 1998, the defendant denied sexual contact with Regina Birendelli, the accuser. Birendelli reported to the police that on May 16, 1998, she was abducted and handcuffed by Clark and two other males, who raped her orally and vaginally and videotaped the assault ("Mark Clark—National Registry of Exonerations," n.d.). When evidence emerged one of the defendants was in jail on the date of the assault, Birendelli then stated the crime had occurred on May 17, 1998. The case proceeded to trial against Clark and the remaining defendant. There was no physical or forensic evidence from the alleged assault, and thus the state's case relied on Birendelli's testimony. Even though both defendants had alibis, they were convicted by the jury. After the trial and prior to sentencing, Clark's wife hired a private investigator, who learned Birendelli was a police informant and drug abuser who had a grudge against Clark because she believed he was responsible for the loss of her husband's car. The investigator also learned Birendelli was actually in jail (under a prior name) on the date of the alleged rape. The trial judge vacated the sentence, and the charges were dismissed by the prosecutor.

Christopher Burrowes: Dispute About Sexual Contact

In 2007, 21 year old, Christopher Burrowes was convicted of the sexual assault of a 12-year-old child. The child reported the sexual assault occurred in her home, and she knew Burrowes from the local basketball court ("Christopher Burrowes—National Registry of Exonerations," n.d.). There was no forensic or physical evidence connecting Burrowes to the offense. Burrowes denied the allegation and rejected a plea offer. He was convicted at trial and sentenced to a 3-year term. In 2009, during questioning by police on an unrelated matter, the "victim" at age 16 volunteered she had fabricated charges against Burrowes in response to her mother's suspicions about her sexual activity. The victim revealed she named Burrowes to conceal a sexual relationship with an uncle. The district attorney investigated further, found the recantation to be credible, and dismissed the charges against Burrowes.

Jarrett Adams: Dispute About Consent

Jarrett Adams was a 17-year-old Black defendant charged with the sexual assault of a white college student in Wisconsin. Adams' defense was the sexual contact was consensual (Esposito, 2010). He was convicted by an all-white jury.[14] Adams was tried along with a codefendant. A third Black defendant was tried separately, and after exculpatory evidence emerged during his second trial, the charges were dismissed. According to Adams, the victim and her roommate invited him and the two other males to her dormitory room. On the way, the roommate made a stop. When the roommate arrived, she found the victim engaged in sexual acts with two of the males. The roommate left the room and used disparaging language to describe the victim. Later, the victim called her boyfriend and reported she had been raped. He urged her to go to the hospital and make a police report. The following day she went to the hospital, and the next day the police took a report that led to the charges. The victim denied the men were invited to her room and indicated they appeared behind her as she entered the room. However, at trial, she acknowledged she left the room to seek her roommate at one point and then returned to the room and had "nonconsensual" sex with the males. During Adams' postconviction habeas appeal with a new attorney, exculpatory evidence that had led to the acquittal of the third defendant was identified—the record of a witness who observed the victim socializing in the smoking lounge with the three "assailants" after the alleged gang rape. In 2006, the Seventh Circuit reversed Adams's conviction based on ineffective assistance of counsel. In 2007, the prosecution dropped the charges, and Adams was released.

Edgar Coker: Dispute About Consent

In June 2007, Edgar Coker, 15 years old, was charged with rape, abduction, and breaking and entering to commit rape. Three days earlier, the mother of a cognitively impaired 14-year-old girl had arrived home to find Coker leaving, and her daughter pulling up her pants. The mother called the police and reported her daughter's disability rendered her unable to consent to sex. The victim reported Coker had broken in the home. On the same date, a detective took a statement from Coker, who stated the girl initiated sexual relations with him. Under threat the state would waive the case to adult court, the defense attorney negotiated a plea bargain. Coker would plead guilty to rape and breaking and entering, which resulted in confinement to a juvenile facility and lifetime sex offender registration.

Three months later, the victim admitted she fabricated the rape charge because of fear of punishment. Her mother notified Coker's family and attorney. The original trial court and an appellate court refused to vacate the conviction. However, a subsequent petition filed by public interest attorneys argued Coker's defense lawyer was deficient because he failed to review Coker's statement to the detective; interview Coker's brother, who had entered the house with him and could confirm there was no break in; and failed to review Coker's educational records, which would have demonstrated Coker had cognitive deficits like the victim. At a subsequent hearing, Coker's conviction was reversed, and the charges were dismissed.

Ralph Armstrong: Acquaintance Rape Charge With an Incapacitated Victim

In 1980, Charise Kamps, a University of Wisconsin student, was found murdered and sexually assaulted in her apartment. She had multiple injuries, indicating strangulation and sexualized assault with a blunt instrument ("Ralph Armstrong—National Registry of Exonerations," n.d.). The prior night she had been out with her friend Jane May, May's fiancé Ralph Armstrong, and others. Armstrong was also a student at the university; however, he had been recently released from prison in New Mexico for rape and other sex offenses. Armstrong reported he had been out with Kamps, May, and others, drinking and doing drugs. He had visited Kamps' apartment but had spent the night with May. Armstrong's brother, Steven, who was visiting at the time, was also questioned but was not considered a suspect. Armstrong was prosecuted, and the state produced two significant witnesses. One testified he saw Armstrong enter and leave Kamps' apartment around the time of the murder. This witness' recall was aided by hypnosis. The other witness was a crime analyst, who testified hair recovered from the scene was consistent with Armstrong's. Armstrong was convicted, and his appeals were denied.

When DNA testing became available, it was demonstrated the hairs were not Armstrong's, and Armstrong was awarded a new trial. Further postconviction investigation revealed the prosecutor had allowed potentially exculpatory evidence to be destroyed and had failed to notify the defense that two witnesses reported Armstrong's brother, Steven, had confessed to the crime after Armstrong's conviction. Steven Armstrong had since died. The charges against Ralph Armstrong were dismissed. He was returned to New Mexico, where he was wanted for parole violation. This acquaintance rape charge stemmed from secondary circumstantial and manufactured evidence (hypnosis and hair analysis), as in a stranger rape case.

Thus, in wrongful conviction where acquaintance rape is charged, three notable features were observed. One is a false accusation by a youthful complainant. The record suggests instances where immature complainants did not intend to make a formal charge, but after an informal disclosure the complainants were pressured to make formal charges. For instance, in the Dotson, Banks, Adams, and Coker wrongful convictions, the youthful complainants privately reported complaints and were then compelled by circumstances to make formal complaints. The second is official misconduct in the form of withholding exculpatory evidence (as in the Ralph Armstrong case). The third is the role of inadequate defense representation, as apparent in the Mark Clark, Jarrett Adams, and Edgar Coker cases.

WRONGFUL CONVICTION WHERE INTRA-FAMILIAL CHILD SEXUAL ASSAULT WAS ALLEGED

Child sexual abuse is not uncommon (Berliner, 2011; Deblinger, Mannarino, & Cohen, 2015; Fontes, 2005), and, as is the case with rape in general, child victims are more likely to be assaulted by someone they know rather than by a stranger (Berliner, 2011; DePanfilis, 2011). Typically, intra-familial child sexual assault allegations involve the initiation of sexual contact with minors who are not capable of consent (Fontes, 2005; Myers, 2013). Some cases involve force, or threat of force, while other cases involve nonforceful initiation into sexual activity (Smallbone & Wortley, 2001). In the context of sexual assault, family would mean the legally recognized family as well as people living as family members (broadly defined). Commonly, intra-familial child sexual assault involves allegations of perpetration by an adult male against a minor female, but perpetrator and victim status are not defined by gender (DePanfilis, 2011; Fontes, 2005). Allegations of intra-familial child sexual assault are often associated with marital and/or interpersonal conflict and divorce (Graham-Bermann & Howell, 2011). As is the case with acquaintance rape and stranger rape, allegations of intra-family child sexual assault can be intentionally false or mistakenly erroneous. Reports of intra-familial child sexual assaults require careful, informed assessment (Lamb, Hershkowitz, Orbach, & Esplin, 2008; Saywitz, Lyon, & Goodman, 2011), and many police, prosecution, and child protective agencies have specially trained units (Lyon & Ahern, 2011; Myers, 2013; Warren, 2013) for this purpose. The "child sexual abuse hysteria" (Nathan & Snedeker, 1995) associated with multiple wrongful convictions, primarily of family members and/or staff at child care centers, in the 1980s and 1990s is covered in Chapter 5. What follows is a selection of cases to illustrate features and processes found among confirmed cases of wrongful conviction in intra-family child sexual assault.

Amine Baba-Ali

In 1988, Amine Baba-Ali and his wife were divorcing. He was accused of the rape of his 4-year-old daughter during a visit at his Queens, New York, home. A physician (Nadine H. Sabbagh, MD) examined the child and testified Baba-Ali had assaulted the child "multiple times, breaking her hymen" ("Amine Baba-Ali—National Registry of Exonerations," n.d.). The child also testified, but she had no recall of being abused. Prior to the examination by Dr. Sabbagh, two other physicians had examined the child and found no evidence of abuse (Powell, 2014). These reports were not provided to the defense until the night before trial, and the defense did not subpoena the doctors. Baba-Ali was convicted of multiple counts at a bench trial in 1989. In 1992, his conviction was reversed based on ineffective defense representation and prosecutorial misconduct. During preparation for retrial, the prosecution had the child examined again. It was determined the child's hymen was intact, and there was no indication of abuse. The charges were dismissed. Baba-Ali had spent 3 years in prison, where he sustained a major injury from an assault. His career as an editor of technical books was ruined. He remarried, but as of 2014 he had not seen his daughter in 20 years.

Baba Ali's prosecution apparently stemmed from false rape charges and reflected a "no-crime case" wrongful conviction. The charge emerged in the context of a pending divorce. The physician's testimony the child had been assaulted several times was manufactured evidence. It cannot be determined with certainty whether the child sexual abuse allegation was intentionally false or whether Baba Ali's wife, and the medical expert, shared and reinforced each other's mistaken notion of a crime. In this case, the prosecution and the litigation process were ineffective in identifying a false allegation.

Jepheth Barnes

In 1995, Jepheth Barnes (age 51) was charged with the sexual assault of his 11-year-old stepdaughter. The accusation emerged 2 days after he separated from his wife, the mother of the child and a 13-year-old male child. The child was examined by an emergency room physician, who found sperm but noted it lacked motility, suggesting a sexual encounter prior to the time alleged by the child. An analyst from the South Carolina Law Enforcement Division testified the specimen was insufficient for a DNA profile to be generated, but Barnes could not be ruled out as the source. Further, the analyst indicated the statistical probability could not be estimated. Barnes was convicted in 1996 and sentenced to 16 years ("Jepheth Barnes—National Registry of Exonerations," n.d.). In 2002, a recent law school graduate began investigating Barnes' innocence claim. Dr. Ronald Ostrowski from the University of North Carolina conducted a review of the prior analysis and found Barnes was actually eliminated as the source of the rape kit contents. Further analysis revealed the material from the rape kit was matched to the complainant's brother, who was 13 years-old at the time the material was collected. The judge vacated Barnes' conviction and ordered a new trial. The prosecution elected not to try Barnes a second time.

The charges against Barnes were associated with marital discord. Whether the allegations were intentionally fabricated or merely mistaken cannot be established. The wrongful conviction was supported by invalid forensic evidence (manufactured) provided by a state expert. Postconviction investigation indicated the defendant was excluded as the source of biological residuals collected from the child. It was not necessarily a no-crime case since there was evidence the child may have been a victim of intra-familial sexual abuse, though not by the defendant.

Robert McClendon

Robert McClendon was charged with the abduction and rape of his 10-year-old daughter in 1990. The child reported she was forcibly taken from her Columbus,

Ohio, backyard, and her eyes were covered. She was then driven to an abandoned house, where she was raped ("Robert McClendon—National Registry of Exonerations," n.d.). After the assault, she was taken in a car to a convenience store. When the assailant went inside, the child fled and returned home. She did not tell her mother until the following day, when the mother observed her to be walking as though she had been injured. The child was examined at a hospital; it was confirmed she had been raped, and a rape kit was taken. Regarding the perpetrator, the child reported, "I think it was my dad, but I may be wrong because my eyes were covered" ("Robert McClendon—National Registry of Exonerations," n.d.). It was reported, however, that the child had only seen her father one time prior to the sexual assault. Pretrial, McClendon consented to a polygraph examination with an agreement the results would be admissible at trial. The polygraph examiner found McClendon's responses "could be a deliberate attempt at deception" ("Robert McClendon—National Registry of Exonerations," n.d.). Despite his alibi witnesses, Robert McClendon was convicted following a bench trial in 1991. He was sentenced to 15 years to life. McClendon's initial requests for DNA testing were denied. In 2007, with the assistance of the Ohio Innocence Project and the *Columbus Dispatch* newspaper, McClendon was one of several Ohio defendants who were provided pro bono DNA testing (*The Columbus Dispatch*, 2008). McClendon was DNA excluded as a contributor of crime scene semen in 2008 and subsequently exonerated. He had served 17 years in prison.

McClendon was wrongly convicted of an intra-familial child sexual assault that had many of the characteristics of a stranger rape with a capable victim. McClendon was effectively a stranger to his 10-year-old daughter, who had only seen him once before, and thus her ability to make a reliable identification was impaired. The misidentification coupled with the unreliable (manufactured) polygraph evidence sealed the conviction. Unfortunately, the police and prosecution investigation and the trial litigation were ineffective in correcting an erroneous identification, and the error was ratified for many years during postconviction deliberations.

Clyde "Ray" Spencer

In 1985, Ray Spencer was convicted of 11 counts of sexually molesting his daughter (5 years old), son (9 years old), and stepson (5 years old) in Washington State. Nineteen years later, he was exonerated via a governor's pardon and released (Chammah, 2017). Ironically, the child sexual abuse investigation was initiated by Spencer, a divorced police officer whose children visited with him. When he learned the children made allegations against him, he became distraught, was hospitalized, and eventually entered a no-contest plea after he was falsely informed he failed a polygraph. Postconviction investigation revealed the entire investigation was biased. The supervisor of the principal investigator was dating one of Spencer's former wives. This supervisor administered the polygraph. According to Spencer's son (in adulthood), to elicit accusations against Spencer, the principal investigator provided gifts and informed him the other siblings had already accused the father. Spencer's son recalled he eventually fabricated accusations to appease the investigator and his mother. Spencer's daughter, in adulthood, had no recall of abuse or making accusations against her father. However, the stepson maintained a belief he had been abused by Spencer. Suppression of exculpatory evidence, unreliable medical evidence, and inadequate defense representation were also apparent. In December 2017, Spencer settled the civil suit for 6 million dollars ("Ray Spencer—National Registry of Exonerations," n.d.).

The allegations against Spencer emerged in the context of marital discord/dissolution. Evidence was manufactured via biased and suggestive questioning of children false polygraph feedback, and there was personal bias on the part of members of the investigation team. Two of the children recanted the allegations in adulthood. The suppression of exculpatory evidence, plea bargaining in the context of severe penalties, and inadequate defense representation were also elements in the case.

Review of wrongful convictions where intra-familial child sex assaults were alleged reveals several recurrent features that warrant attention in the investigation and prosecution of these cases. The first is unreliable accounts of child abuse that emerged in the context of marital discord/dissolution (apparent in the Baba Ali, Barnes, and Spencer cases). In the Spencer case, child accusers recanted in adulthood. The withholding of exculpatory evidence and unreliable medical testimony were features in the Baba Ali, Barnes, and Spencer cases as well. Inadequate defense representation and plea bargaining in the context of severe conviction penalties were also elements in Spencer's wrongful conviction. The McClendon wrongful intra-familial child sexual assault conviction exhibited many of the features of a stranger rape with a capable witness' misidentification.

SUMMARY

Prior investigators (Connors et al., 1996; Gross et al., 2005) have noted there was a relationship between rape and wrongful conviction. Available data from the NRE and the IP indicate there is clearly a robust association between rape and confirmed wrongful convictions. The focus and analysis of this chapter has been on the features and characteristics of that relationship. The available data indicate when sexual assault perpetration is disaggregated, wrongful conviction is more common among stranger rapes than among acquaintance rape and intra-familial child sexual assaults, even though stranger rape occurs less frequently than acquaintance rape and intra-familial child assaults.

Drawing from the work of LeBeau (1987), a working definition of stranger rape was introduced. It was noted that the investigation of stranger rape presents unique challenges in terms of formulating motive and also with regard to reliable identification. In addition, the perception and response to stranger rape typically differs from the response to other rapes. These observations led to the formulation of a four-point stranger rape thesis to account for the range of special challenges encountered in the investigation of stranger rape. The stranger rape thesis suggests certain crimes, or subtypes of crime (stranger rapes), are more likely to elicit the common biases (tunnel vision, confirmation bias, ratification of error, outcome bias) observed in wrongful conviction investigations.

In addition, a distinction among stranger rapes was recognized with regard to the capacity of the victim to assist in the investigation (victim status). Terms and concepts were introduced to illustrate the investigation process, such as correct assessment of the relational aspect of an offense, black box investigation to denote the secrecy surrounding critical investigation procedures (witness identification, interrogation, and others), and manufactured evidence to indicate evidence that was created rather than discovered. Also, a continuum of intentionality was described to convey that the manufacture of evidence may range from the inadvertent to the intentional. These concepts and processes were illustrated with stranger rape wrongful conviction narratives. This chapter also included examples where wrongful convictions occurred in the context of acquaintance rape and/or intra-familial child sexual assault allegations, noting the role of different types of wrongful conviction risks. While there are overlapping features, there is value in recognizing the distinctions among these three broad types of sexual assault cases.

NOTES

1. The Garrett and Neufeld (2009) study focused on invalid scientific testimony and was also drawn from the Innocence Project data, which are largely stranger rapes.
2. The legal definition of rape varies considerably across US jurisdictions, including terms such as rape, aggravated sexual assault, sexual deviant conduct, oral copulation, and more (Johnson & Melendez, 2019).
3. Obviously, there may be exceptions, and most rapes, stranger or otherwise, are not reported to the police.
4. The Kassin et al. (2012) data did not rule out the role of prosecutor discretion in securing more evidence to support a (false) confession as compared to an (erroneous) identification.
5. William Jackson Neal, Jr., who arguably resembled Dail, was subsequently indicted for the 1987 rape and convicted in 2010 (WRAL.com, 2010). Similar spontaneous misidentifications by rape victims occurred in the Julius E. Ruffin (Newsome, 2007), Randall Lynn Ayers (NRE), Michael Mercer (IP), Kevin Byrd (IP), Vincent Moto (IP), Johnny Pinchback (IP), Josiah Sutton (IP), and Thomas Haynesworth (IP) cases (see Johnson & Melendez, 2019).
6. Ironically, in US interrogation, police are prohibited from fabricating a suspect's confession, but they are allowed to provide a fabrication that may elicit an ostensibly "true" confession. An interrogator with doubt about fabricating will proceed with the expectation the resulting incriminating statement will be ruled admissible; see *Arizona v. Fulminante* (1991).
7. Calvin Johnson, Jr., Bernard Webster, and Herman Atkins, as discussed in Chapter 3, were all wrongly convicted of rape, with evidence including multiple eyewitness misidentifications (M. B. Johnson, Griffith, & Barnaby, 2013). The

Willie Sanders prosecution also relied on multiple eyewitness misidentification, though Sanders was acquitted.

8. It is important to recognize the cross-racial challenge inherent in the identification was only one element of the racialized nature of the prosecution of Ronald Cotton. The other substantial race relevant aspects of this Black defendant, white victim, stranger rape prosecution are presented in Chapter 3.

9. For instance, the wrongful convictions of Calvin Wayne Cunningham from Virginia ("Calvin Wayne Cunningham—Innocence Project," n.d.); Charles Dabbs from New York ("Charles Dabbs—Innocence Project," n.d.); Willie Davidson from Virginia ("Willie Davidson—Innocence Project, n.d.); and Chad Heins from Virginia ("Chad Heins—Innocence Project," n.d.) were all associated with faulty assessment of the relational aspect of the offense.

10. For instance, examples include Penny Beerntsen in the Steve Avery case (Thompson, 2016); Jennifer Thompson in the Ronald Cotton case (Thompson-Cannino et al., 2009); Michelle Murray-Mallin in the Timothy Cole case (Kix, 2016); Ann Meng (Newsome, 2007) in the Julius Ruffin case; Tomeshia Carrington-Artis (WRAL. com, 2008b) in the Dwayne Allen Dail case; Nancy Roper in the Steve Titus case (Loftus & Ketcham, 1991); D. S. in the McKinley Cromedy wrongful conviction (*State v. Cromedy*, 1999); and numerous other unnamed capable victims of stranger rapes whose misidentifications led to wrongful convictions.

11. In 2005, Avery was convicted in an unrelated murder case, which was also covered in the documentary film *Making a Murderer* (Ricciardi & Demos, 2015).

12. While imprisoned, Danzinger suffered a disabling head trauma, which left him institutionalized for life (Falkenberg, 2001).

13. Kassin (2015) differentiated the "compliant" false confession, which the suspect recognizes is untrue, from the "internalized" false confession, where the suspect, for a period of time, actually believes the false confession.

14. The relevance of all-white juries for Black defendants is discussed in Chapter 3.

3

Race and Rape Prosecution
in US History

> (W)hen stern and sad-faced white men put to death a creature in human form who has deflowered a white woman . . . they have avenged the greatest wrong, the blackest crime.
> —UNITED STATES SENATOR BEN TILLMAN FROM SOUTH CAROLINA, to his Senate colleagues in 1907 (Davis, 1983, p. 187)

> You rape our women and are taking over our country.
> —DYLANN S. ROOF, avowed white supremacist, prior to firing shots that killed nine African Americans in a Charleston, South Carolina, Black church on June 17, 2015 (Sanchez & Foster, 2015)[i]

In 1979, Nate Walker fled the New Jersey authorities and assumed residence, under an alias, in California. Walker had been (mis-)identified, 4 months after the knifepoint rape, by an Elizabeth, New Jersey, white woman who was attacked in Newark in 1974. Walker was convicted at the 1976 trial, despite substantial evidence of his innocence (B. Braun, 2005; Sterling, 1986; *State v. Walker*, 1979; Leavy, 1987). Walker had an alibi supported by testimony and a time clock. Also, the victim reported the assailant was circumcised, with one testicle, while Walker was uncircumcised and with two testicles. A blood test could have eliminated Walker as the perpetrator, but apparent ineffective defense representation resulted in a failure to order the testing.

---

i. An early version of this chapter, titled—'Race and Wrongful Convictions: Toward Resistance and Racial Justice'—was presented (4/14/14) as an invited lecture at the California State University—Long Beach, Department of Africana Studies.

While serving his sentence Walker won an appellate court reversal on a legal technicality and was released on bond in 1978. Unfortunately, in 1979 the New Jersey Supreme Court reinstated his conviction and sentence (*State v. Walker*, 1979). Rather than return to prison, Walker left New Jersey for California, where he remained until apprehended by the FBI; he returned to New Jersey prison in 1982. In 1986, with the advocacy of Jim McCloskey and Centurion Ministries, the blood sample testing ruled out Walker as the contributor of the semen. He was finally released 11 years after the charges were made. Walker, armed with his account of his wrongful conviction, later became an effective lobbyist for the repeal of New Jersey's death penalty (personal interview with Nathaniel Walker, 2007).

Walker's case illustrates the familiar pattern of Black defendant, white victim stranger rape with misidentification resulting in wrongful conviction. It includes other common elements, such as the weapons effect, the defendant's discounted alibis, ineffective defense representation, and vulnerability related to prior criminal justice system exposure. Walker's case was not one of the familiar Jim Crow Era "legal lynching" cases or one of the late 20th Century DNA exonerations. It was a post–civil rights era wrongful conviction of a vulnerable Black defendant in a northern state, and as such the character of the racial bias was not readily apparent.

Recent research (Free & Ruesink, 2012; Murty & Vyas, 2010; Gross et al., 2005; Garrett, 2011; M. B. Johnson, Griffith, & Barnaby, 2013; E. Smith & Hattery, 2011) indicates African Americans are overrepresented among those wrongly convicted in the United States. This disproportion is apparent not only relative to African American representation in the general population but also with regard to race/ethnic differences in conviction rates. Among the first 250 DNA exonerations, 62% involved Black defendants (Garrett, 2011). Several researchers (Garrett, 2011; Gross, 2008; Gross et al., 2005) have pointed out the disproportionate representation of Black defendants among the wrongfully convicted is most pronounced among rape cases.

As elaborated in material that follows, during the pre–Civil War period, rape law functioned to reinforce the subordination of the enslaved (and "free") Black population. After emancipation, the narrative of the Black sexual predator was constructed and promoted to undermine support for Black political rights and enforced by terroristic violence (lynching and other assaults) against the entire African American population. The historical myth of Black sexual predation and criminality contributes to the ongoing risk of wrongful conviction faced by Black defendants charged with rape, especially in Black assailant/white victim cases, the highly infrequent type of rape for which there is a large concentration of wrongful convictions.

The current chapter examines historical aspects of race and rape prosecution in the United States where, in law, the definition and consequences for rape varied based on the race of the defendant as well as the race of the victim. There were statutorily separate sexual assault penalties based on the race of the complainant and defendant (Sommerville, 2004; Davis, 1983; Wriggins, 1983), with Blacks charged with the rape against white victims receiving the most vigorous prosecutions and severe sentencing. This legal foundation and the implied social judgments have persisted, with some variation, throughout major historical eras in US race relations. That is, from the Era of Race Based Enslaved Labor (pre-Civil War period), through the Era of Jim Crow Segregation (post-Civil War period to 1962), and continued to inform current post Civil Rights Era (1963-present) processes in a substantial portion of the more recent wrongful convictions in sexual assaults where Black defendant, white victim, "stranger rapes" predominate (M. B. Johnson et al., 2013; E. Smith & Hattery, 2011).

Through examining change in law and practice, as well as constancy in race and rape prosecution, the social-political construction of rape in law is apparent. Rape law and prosecution are about more than crime and punishment (or deterrence). These issues are also linked to the political disenfranchisement and subordination of the African American population (W. L. Patterson, 1951). This chapter provides a brief overview of race and rape law in early US history followed by the presentation of race and rape as informed by the more recent findings and literature on wrongful conviction and racial discrimination.

THE ERA OF RACE-BASED ENSLAVED LABOR: THE PRE-CIVIL WAR PERIOD

Prior to the Civil War, the legal subordination of the African descendant population in the United States operated directly through state power and the force of law. This was reflected in state slave codes that applied to enslaved Blacks, as well as free Blacks to varying degrees in different states. Slave codes held Blacks could not vote, serve on juries, testify in court against whites, learn to read, carry weapons, travel without passes, or raise their hands in self-defense against whites. These codes were established as early as 1690 and through limiting the rights and protections of the enslaved population (Mann & Selva, 1979) codified "white supremacy." Thus, entitlements and protections afforded to whites and enslaved Blacks (as well as free Blacks) were separate and unequal (Harris, 1994). While there were disputes within and among states about the status of African Americans, these disputes were clarified in the 1857 US Supreme Court *Dred Scott* decision, which held African Americans were "beings of an inferior order, and altogether unfit to associate with the white race, either in social or political relations, and so far inferior that they had no rights which the white man was bound to respect" (*Dred Scott v. Sanford*, 1856).

One of the signature features of the racially defined system of enslaved labor in the United States was the severe penalties (castration or death) designated specifically for sexual attacks on white women by Blacks. During the pre–Civil War period, the statutory and case law record indicates several southern, as well as northern, states delineated such penalties. Wriggins (1983) noted statutes in Alabama, Mississippi, Tennessee, Missouri, Arkansas, Pennsylvania, and Kansas with prescribed penalties of death or castration for enslaved or free Blacks, and mulattos, charged with sexual attacks on white women. During the early 1700s, castration was the punishment for only one crime in both Pennsylvania and New Jersey: the crime of rape on a white woman by a Black (Jordan, 1974, as cited in Mann & Selva, 1979). In Virginia, Blacks faced castration for several offenses until 1769, when the penalty was eliminated for all offenses but retained for only one offense, rape or attempted rape of a white woman.

While there was substantial legal focus on the notion of victimization of white women by Blacks, enslaved African women had no protection from sexual assault from white males. Curtis (1974, p. 22) used the term *institutional access* to characterize the freedom white men had to sexually exploit and assault enslaved Black women (also see Davis, 1983). The law regarded enslaved Black women as the property of their "owners," and rape laws did not protect enslaved women from the sexual demands of their owners or other white men.[1]

An example of how rape law was modified, while practice remained unchanged through historical eras, was provided by Partington (1965). The pre–Civil War Virginia statute indicates Blacks convicted of rape could be executed, while the maximum penalty for whites was 20 years. The post–Civil War, "race-neutral," statute left the penalty to the discretion of the jury. Under the race-neutral standard, the state of Virginia executed 56 people for rape and connected charges from 1908 to 1963. Each of the defendants executed was Black. The Virginia Supreme Court of Appeals responded to an allegation of racial bias by stating, "There is not a scintilla of evidence in the record to support this statement and it is contrary to fact" (Partington, 1965, p. 62).

Some have argued the severe penalties delineated for enslaved Blacks charged with rape of white women were indicative of widespread southern fears and anxieties about Black male sexual aggression. Sommerville (2004), however, has suggested the statutory record gives a false impression that enslaved Blacks charged with sexual assaults against white women were summarily condemned by white southerners and subjected to the ultimate punishments. Sommerville cites court proceedings and related sources that documented significant portions of white communities were often supportive of Black defendants[2] and were effective in preventing the imposition of the most severe penalties. Notwithstanding Sommerville's point that some white southerners were tolerant of Black male/white female sexuality, the statutory record is a clear indication of social judgments and prevailing law. The separate statutory penalties based on race of the defendant and race of the victim persisted in many US states until the Civil War and the Fourteenth Amendment, which was designed to ensure equal protection of law.

THE ERA OF JIM CROW SEGREGATION: THE POST–CIVIL WAR PERIOD

Following the Civil War, enslavement of the African American population was no longer supported by state power and the force of law.[3] However, during this period lynching emerged as a major instrument in the continued effort to subordinate the African American people relative to whites. Rape allegations and prosecution for rape, that is, the focus on Black rapists of white women, played a major role in instigating and supporting the lynching of Black citizens and terrorizing the African American community at large. Lynching took two principal forms: extralegal "mob lynching" and "legal lynching" via state judicial proceedings. These two forms of lynching typically coexisted within the same states, and the threat of mob lynching was often an element in precipitating legal lynching. The record also indicates the charge of rape against Black defendants and the resulting lynching served political aims within, and beyond, the confines of southern segregationist states.

MOB LYNCHING AND RAPE

With the defeat of the Confederacy in the Civil War, those in the slave-holding class in particular, and the white southern population in general, were deprived of their former control of state power and the force of law. During the Reconstruction period (1865–1877), separate criminal penalties based on race were removed from state laws consistent with the Fourteenth Amendment guarantee of equal protection of law. Federal troops remained in southern states to enforce federal law until 1877. With the withdrawal of federal troops, fatal assaults on Black citizens (lynchings) emerged as a key element of the extralegal violent subjugation of African American people (J. Allen, Als, Lewis, & Litwack, 2000; Patterson, 1951; Kinshasha, 2006).

Estimates of the number of African Americans lynched from the end of the Civil War until the 1950s range from 3,000 to 5,000 (Gibson, n.d.); Mann and Selva (1979) (citing Demaris, 1970) estimated 5,000 from 1865 to 1955. J. Allen et al. (2000), in *Without Sanctuary: Lynching Photography in America*, reported 4,742 lynching deaths from 1882 to 1968 (also see Pfeifer, 2004). The United States did have a history of lynching "outlaws" dating back to colonial times that was not connected to racial animosity. However, lynching acquired a racial character, became a "racist blood sport" (Muhammad, 2010, p. 60), in the south following Reconstruction. The lynching of African Americans was not limited to the old southern states, that is lynching occurred in New York (Pfeifer, 2004), Minnesota (Fedo, 2000), California (J. Allen et al., 2000), and many other than southern states.

The mob lynching of African Americans typically took the form of hanging via a noose, and/or burnings, with limitless combinations of brutality and sadism. Victims were commonly tortured in various ways prior to their death. The integral relationship of rape allegations to the lynching of Black men is illustrated by several cases. Wells (Duster, 1970) described an 1893 Texas lynching of a Black man, Henry Smith (Another Negro burned: Henry Smith dies at the stake, 1893), charged with the rape and murder of a child.[4] Wells' independent journalistic report indicated there was no evidence of rape, but the rumor was spread to facilitate the mob violence (Royster, 1997). Henry Smith was "tortured with red hot irons searing his flesh for hours before finally the flames were lit which put an end to his agony" (Duster, 1970, p. 84).

Similarly, J. Allen et al. (2000) reported Sam Hose was lynched on a Sunday afternoon in Georgia in 1899. Hose was stripped and secured to a tree. His ears, fingers, and genitals were cut off before he was doused with an accelerant and burned alive.[5] While the lynching victims and their families suffered most directly, lynching, by design, spread terror through entire African American communities, causing many families to flee the south, others to abandon active advocacy for equal rights and justice, and others to arm themselves in self-defense.[6]

Many unfamiliar with lynching think the mob attacks were clandestine and occurred under the cloak of night, which did occur in some instances. However, lynchings were often public displays, announced in advance, that took on the character of a festival and were witnessed by hundreds. The 1893 lynching of Henry Smith described by Wells (Duster, 1970) noted the event was announced in advance in local papers, special rail service was available for spectators, and school was dismissed so children could witness the spectacle. J. Allen et al. (2000) reported 2,000 white Georgians witnessed the 1899 lynching of Sam Hose. Hose had killed his employer, a landowner, after the escalation of a dispute about earnings due. However, the version that appeared in the local press reported Hose killed his employer in a sneak attack and thereafter raped the planter's wife. In addition, lynchings were frequently memorialized in photographs that were available for purchase as postcards celebrating the event (J. Allen et al., 2000).[7] These postcards were widely in use until 1908, when the US Post Office prohibited further distribution of lynching imagery in postcards (Lacayo, 2000).

Davis (1983) pointed out lynching was fundamentally political violence. It was essentially unheard of during slavery because of the monetary value of enslaved Africans. Lynching emerged in the aftermath of the Civil War as a form of political terrorism against the Black population. The initial justification was that it was necessary to prevent riot and insurrection by Blacks. White supremacist vigilantes (i.e., Ku Klux Klan) asserted lynching was necessary to prevent domination by Blacks. After Reconstruction, lynching continued with a new justification: It was necessary to protect and avenge white women from sexual attacks by the emancipated Blacks. Sommerville (2004) pointed out Thomas Dixon wrote two novels, The Leopard's Spots (1903) and The Clansman (1905), both of which depicted freed Blacks eager to sexually attack virtuous white women. The sexual assault of white women by Blacks was a major element in the hugely popular 1915 film adaptation of The Clansman titled, Birth of a Nation, which heroically portrayed the Ku Klux Klan as the protectors of white women from these attacks.[8]

The journalist Ida B. Wells challenged the accepted notion that lynching was a response to rapes committed by Black men (Giddings, 2008; Schiff, 2005; Duster, 1970). Wells' informed objections noted lynchings were executions without trials, executions conducted in a vile and depraved manner. Her published investigative work revealed that only a third of lynch victims were accused of rape (Royster, 1997; also see Davis, 1983), and among those charged many were demonstrably innocent. For example, white women who engaged in consensual sex with Black men were often coerced to charge rape when they were discovered (Duster, 1970). Also, independent investigation of the lynching of Sam Hose found the widow of the planter reported Hose acted in self-defense and denied she was raped (J. Allen et al., 2000). Wells also contributed to documenting the unspoken history of white male sexual assaults on Black women (Duster, 1970). Prior to Wells, most whites (as well as many Blacks) accepted the claim that lynchings were reactions to Black sexual assaults on white women (Muhammad, 2010).

Advocacy by Wells and many others[9] led to a decrease in lynching and the introduction of federal antilynching legislation. A bill was approved in the House of Representatives in 1922 but never passed the US Senate. Lynching, though with reduced frequency, persisted at least until the 1950s. In 2005, the US Senate apologized to the victims of lynching and their families for the failure to support antilynching legislation when it was most needed.[10]

One of the most widely publicized mob lynchings occurred in 1955 when 14-year-old Emmett Till was brutally murdered in Money, Mississippi.[11] Emmett had been raised in Chicago and was visiting relatives in Mississippi during the summer. It was alleged Emmett flirted, or whistled, at the 21-year-old, white female proprietor of a small grocery store (Blinder, 2018). Several days later, armed and under cover of night, the woman's husband and his brother abducted and brutalized Emmett before killing him with a gunshot and depositing his body in a local river. Emmett's body was returned to Chicago, where his mother (Mamie Till Mobley) bravely decided to have an open casket funeral so the world, via the press and media, could observe the severe brutality the teen had endured. In September 1955, the alleged perpetrators (Roy Bryant and J. W. Milam), were acquitted by an all-white male jury. The brutal lynching of Emmett Till was cited by Rosa Parks, and others, as a catalyst for the December 1955 Montgomery bus boycott (Theoharis, 2013). In a 1956 *Look* magazine interview, the two perpetrators, under the protection of double jeopardy, admitted committing the crime (Huie, 1956).

The record indicates mob lynching was political violence perpetrated against the African American population to suppress Black social, political, and economic advancement. How rape allegations became central to the interplay of social forces is illustrated dramatically in the 1921 white mob attacks in the Tulsa, Oklahoma, Greenwood Community known as "Black Wall Street." The mob violence by whites, with estimates of 39 to 300 deaths, was clearly an economically motivated attack on the successful African American businesses and community (Hirsch, 2002; Tulsa Race Riot Commission, 2001). Less well known is the role of sensationalist press coverage of a rumor alleging a Black young man had sexually assaulted a white elevator operator in precipitating the attacks. *The Tulsa Tribune* (1921) headline read "Nab Negro for Attacking Girl in an Elevator." The rape allegation was sufficient to justify the white mob violence that killed Blacks and burned Black businesses, homes, and hospitals.

Similarly, 2 years earlier in Omaha, Nebraska, a riot by whites resulted in the public burning of William Brown, a Black suspect in the alleged rape of a 19-year-old white woman. An atmosphere of economic competition was instigated by the racially segregated labor force. Tensions escalated as large numbers of Black workers migrated to Omaha to work in the meatpacking industry (For action on race riot peril, 1919; also see Lawson, 1977). The economic conditions combined with the rape allegations in the press to precipitate and legitimize the public murder of Brown and the burning of the Douglass County Court House. The political–economic motive was not sufficient to justify the mob executions and excessive violence that characterized the lynching of William Brown. However, the noble aim of protecting and preserving the honor of white women did provide sufficient ("moral") justification.

The allegation of rape caused many critics of lynching to pause because no one would risk defending "rapists" (which continues today). Thus, lynching was not only defended but also heralded by leading southern politicians, such as the US senator from South Carolina, Ben Tillman, who explained to his Senate colleagues in 1900, "We of the South have never recognized the right of the negro to govern white men, and we never will. We have never believed him to be the equal of the white man, and we will not submit to his gratifying his lust on our wives and daughters without lynching him" (as cited in Herbert, 2008). Thus, in the popular imagination (and subconscious) of many whites, via political rhetoric as well as literature and film, Black freedom and equal rights became associated with rape. The brutality of lynching verified the linkage because only the most lurid crime could have provoked such a brutal response.

Legal Lynching and Rape

Legal lynching is the term used to describe legal proceedings against African Americans that amounted to a formalized mob lynching. Wriggins (1983, p. 107) indicated legal lynching referred to criminal trials that were the "functional equivalent of lynching." In other words, Black defendants were given sham or show trials to provide a facade of legality. In this way, the political subordination of the African American population continued in the form of state criminal proceedings. Readily identifiable elements of legal lynching include mob intimidation, lack of due process, racially biased legal presumptions and doctrines, and racially biased sentencing practices (M. B. Johnson et al., 2013).

The 1931 Scottsboro, Alabama, trials are notorious illustrative examples of legal lynching. Conflicts and presumptions about race and rape were at the heart of the controversy surrounding the Scottsboro cases, which received extensive US and international press coverage (Aretha, 2008; Acker, 2007). Sagarin (1977) commented the Scottsboro trials were unique not due to the process or outcome but due to the scrutiny and attention the cases received. The Scottsboro trials illustrate how race defined the perception and prosecution of rape in the context of criminal proceedings.

The Scottsboro cases involved nine African Americans charged with the rape of two white women. The defendants ranged in age from 12 to 19 years old. These defendants had been riding as "hoboes" on a freight train that ran through Alabama and Tennessee. Reportedly in the course of a fight between Black and white hoboes, two white males were thrown off the train while two white women remained. The white males reported the fight to local authorities. The alleged Black assailants were arrested at a subsequent train station. Following the arrests, the two women reported they had been raped by the Black suspects. The rape allegations emerged in the context of the older woman's criminal liability for transporting the younger one across state lines for prostitution.[12] The Black suspects were held in jail and initially tried in Scottsboro, Alabama. As the rape charges circulated through the area, a lynch mob assembled near the jail (Aretha, 2008). In three limited trials completed in 2 days, each of the defendants, except the 12-year-old, was convicted and sentenced to death.

The Alabama Supreme Court upheld seven of the eight convictions, sparing only the 13-year-old. However, the US Supreme Court reversed all the convictions, noting the defendants were deprived of effective defense counsel (*Powell v. Alabama*, 1932). In subsequent trials, the defendants were convicted again. Noteworthy during the second set of trials, the younger of the two women testified there had been no rape or sexual contact at all, but she had agreed with the accusation at the insistence of the older woman. Despite this testimony, the defendants were again convicted and sentenced to death. The verdicts were reversed again by the US Supreme Court as a result of evidence Blacks were systematically excluded from the jury pool (*Norris v. Alabama*, 1935). In subsequent prosecution, charges were dropped against five of the defendants. One defendant was sentenced to death and three were sentenced to 75 years or more. None of the defendants was executed, but some served lengthy terms. In 2013, the Alabama Board of Parole posthumously pardoned the three defendants whose convictions had not been previously reversed or pardoned (Blinder, 2013).

Various elements of legal lynching are apparent in the Scottsboro cases. A lynch mob had gathered demanding the suspects be delivered for punishment (Aretha, 2008). Due process violations were the basis of US Supreme Court reversals noting the lack of effective defense representation (*Powell v. Alabama*, 1932) and exclusion of Blacks from the jury pool (*Norris v. Alabama*, 1935). Racial bias in legal presumptions was obvious in the jury charge issued by Judge William Callahan, noting, "There is a very strong presumption under the law that she [a white woman] would not and did not yield voluntarily to intercourse with the defendant, a Negro" (Sommerville, 2004, p. 217).[13] The death sentences initially imposed on the Scottsboro defendants were common for Blacks convicted of rape of white women. At that point, every Black defendant convicted of the rape of a white woman in Alabama had been sentenced to death (J. Goodman, 1994).

The record of disparate sentencing associated with legal lynching and rape charges is quite extensive. A report (Patterson, 1951) on rape and race sentencing in Louisiana prepared in connection with a Black World War II veteran charged with rape found there had been 39 executions for rape from 1900 to 1950. Two of the condemned were white; the other 37 were Black defendants (and African Americans represented 35.9% of the state population). Before Louisiana became a state (in 1812), separate statutory punishments had existed for rape, based on the race of the offender. This practice continued when Louisiana became a state and continued further after the passage of the Fourteenth amendment by charging Black defendants with "aggravated" rape punishable with death and white defendants with "simple" rape with lesser penalties (Patterson, 1951).[14]

Louisiana was not exceptional with this practice. Partington (1965) found the state of Virginia executed 43 men for rape and another 13 for attempted rape from 1908 until the time of his study. All of the men executed were Black. Examination of race of defendant and race of victim data further reveal adverse disparate sentencing faced by Black defendants. Wolfgang and Reidel (1973) reported 36% of the Black men convicted of the rape of white women (1945–1965) were executed, while only 2% of men convicted in the other three racial dyads were executed. Their analysis indicated legally relevant, other than racial, factors did not account for the strong race effects.

A 1964 study by the Florida Civil Liberties Union (Mann & Selva, 1979) found men convicted of intraracial rapes had a 4% or 5% execution rate, while Black men convicted of rape against a white female had a 54% execution rate. The study also noted, consistent with rape and race prosecution bias, white men convicted of rape of Black women had a 0% rate of execution. A 1967 report on rape convictions in Baltimore, Maryland, found that Blacks convicted of rape against whites received dramatically more severe sentences than defendants convicted in the other three perpetrator–victim race dyads (Negroes accuse Maryland bench, 1967). Consistent with these findings, US Department of Justice data indicate 89% of the men executed for rape in the United States from 1930 to 1968 were African American (Bureau of Prisons, 1969).

LaFree (1983) provided evidence of adverse disparate sentencing imposed on Black defendants convicted of rape of white women in the post–civil rights era. LaFree examined the rape charges in a large midwestern city from 1970 to 1975. The data indicated Black men accused of rape of white women were not more likely to be arrested or found guilty, and LaFree critiqued other research for failing to examine a range of relevant dependent variables. LaFree demonstrated the adverse outcomes experienced by Black defendants charged with sexual offenses against whites were apparent on multiple indicators (e.g., severity of charging, felony charging, sentence length, prison confinement) when compared to other defendant/victim dyads. This led LaFree to conclude "more powerful groups in society enforce sexual-property rules, in part, by the differential application of the criminal law" (LaFree, 1983 p. 853), illustrating the social political construction of rape law and prosecution.

The Scottsboro trials and associated appeals received worldwide press attention. In subsequent years, there were similar cause célèbre legal lynching cases (Willie McGee, 1945; the Groveland 4, 1948; the Martinsville 7, 1949) that received substantial US and international press coverage. Each of these cases involved Black defendants, in southern states, convicted by all-white juries of raping white women, with resultant death sentences (Heard, 2011; Martin, 1987; Rise, 1992). The NAACP (National Association for the Advancement of Colored People) and the Civil Rights Congress (though often at odds over tactics and philosophy) led legal challenges on behalf of the defendants (Martin,

1987). The legal arguments and advocacy highlighted racially discriminative due process violations and sentencing, particularly reserving the death penalty for Black defendants charged with rape against white victims. However, the legal appeals for these defendants met with only limited success.[15] These cases also were proving grounds for noteworthy legal advocates, such as Thurgood Marshall, who represented the Groveland defendants (G. King, 2012; Martin, 1987), and Bella Abzug, who participated in legal advocacy on the behalf of Willie McGee (L. S. Braun & Thom, 2007). The arguments that were advanced led, in time, to the abolition of the death penalty as a punishment for rape in *Coker v. Georgia*, 1977, discussed further in this chapter.

The Legal Lynching of George Stinney: The Power of the Black Rapist Narrative

Another illustration of legal lynching is provided by a case known for the execution of the 14-year-old defendant but less well known for the role of race and (alleged) rape in the outcome. In legal and criminal justice circles, the name George Stinney is recognized as the youngest person executed in the United States in the 20th Century (McVeigh, 2014). In 1944, following a day long trial, George was convicted of the murder of 11- and 8-year-old white girls in rural South Carolina. The bodies of the young girls were discovered on the "Black side" of the segregated mill town. The cause of death was blunt force trauma. A deputy reported George confessed following his arrest. The only evidence against him was the reported verbal confession. George had no access to his parents or legal counsel during his questioning by the police. After the purported confession, he was transported to the Columbia, South Carolina, jail, 50 miles from his home, ostensibly to prevent mob lynching. As reported by George's sister in a 2014 interview (McVeigh, 2014), their father was fired from his job, and the family was urged to leave town. George did not see his family until after he was found guilty by the all-white male jury. No transcript of the trial was preserved. His court-appointed defense counsel, who was a candidate in a local election, called no witnesses and failed to cross-examine the state's witnesses. While George was not formally charged with rape, the court allowed speculation at trial that rape was the motive in George killing the younger girl, with intent to rape the older one. The state's formulation of the crime was George did not rape the older child, but he killed her also.

Given the region, the history, and conventional interrogation practice during the pre–*Miranda* period (Leo, 2008), it seems evident the insertion of the rape motive helped seal the outcome. George, the young teen, was executed by electric chair less than 3 months after the girls' bodies were discovered. Seventy years later, his conviction was vacated with a ruling he did not receive a fair trial (Bever, 2014; also see McVeigh, 2014). There was also evidence George was innocent. There were alibi witnesses who were not allowed to testify at trial as well as evidence the child victims were killed at another location and deposited where they were found. It was highly unlikely George, less than 5 feet tall and weighing less than 100 pounds, could have moved the bodies (Bever, 2014). The legal lynching of George Stinney illustrates the power of the Black rapist narrative.

So, in the aftermath of the Civil War and the Fourteenth Amendment guarantee of equal protection of law, lynching (the "mob" as well as the "legal" variety) was a component of the broader quasi-legal strategy (along with the poll tax, literacy tests, and grandfather clauses) to maintain Black voter disenfranchisement. The narrative of the Black rapist (or Black criminality in general) was the socially constructed foundation for the recurring political violence. The widespread disenfranchisement of Black voters in southern states not only resulted in segregationist control of local and regional government (and juries) but also disproportionately increased representation of segregationist states in the federal government.

As a result of Black voter disenfranchisement, in Black majority or near-majority southern counties, the white voters in those districts had dramatically greater representation in the US Congress than white voters in the North or West. For instance, W. L. Patterson (1951) reported, "In South Carolina, it took 4,393 voters to elect a representative to Congress in 1946 whereas in Illinois it took 137,877 voters" (p. 142), with multiple similar contrasts among several southern versus northern congressional districts.[16] Thus, the racial animus apparent in the socially constructed specter of the Black rapist was not simply a matter of personal prejudice or social custom but actual political control and influence. Southern segregationist advocates and politicians equated Black voting and political participation with rape. As Davis (1983, p. 188) stated, citing the earlier work of Frederick Douglass and Ida B. Wells, "As soon as the propagandistic cry of rape became a legitimate excuse for lynching, former white proponents of Black equality became increasingly afraid to associate themselves with Black peoples struggle for liberation." Consequently, "The closer the black man got to the ballot box, one observer noted, the more he looked like a rapist" (J. Allen et al., 2000, p. 30).

So, with the transition from the Era of Race-Based Enslaved Labor to the post–Civil War period, though the law was modified and statutes became "race neutral" to correspond with equal protection requirements, often outcomes were in effect largely unchanged, and 89% of US defendants executed for rape between 1930 and 1968 were Black (Bureau of Prisons, 1969).

POST–CIVIL RIGHTS ERA: 1963 TO THE PRESENT

The dating of the post–Civil Rights Era is somewhat arbitrary. The year 1963 is used as a point in the decade when the civil rights of African Americans, that is, voting rights as well as protection from discrimination in housing and public accommodations, became recognized as a major national, rather than regional, issue. This was manifest in the historic March on Washington in August 1963. By this time, the mob lynching of African Americans had been virtually eliminated. Yet, there continued to be many noteworthy, highly publicized, criminal cases that involved race and rape allegations, even though major hallmarks of legal lynching had been largely eradicated. This period continues until the present. Though the transition from the Jim Crow Era to the post–Civil Rights Era was significant and substantial, available data indicate there remained an increased risk of wrongful conviction encountered by Black defendants facing sexual assault charges. A number of post–Civil Rights Era wrongful convictions, such as Edward Carter's 1979 misidentification in Michigan and Earl Washington's 1984 "false confession," wrongful conviction in Virginia, are barely distinguishable from the legal lynching endured by the Scottsboro defendants and the juvenile George Stinney.

This section describes some of the instructive post–Civil Rights cases in the context of the model of wrongful conviction risks and processes introduced in Chapter 2. This section also identifies many of the mechanisms that contribute to an increased risk of wrongful conviction for Black defendants charged with sexual assault during an era when overt racial discrimination was legally prohibited. In many ways, as was the case with the transition from the Era of Race-Based Enslaved Labor to the Jim Crow Era, legal procedures were modified, but outcomes were often unchanged.

In Chapter 2, the common pattern in the "manufacture" of unreliable evidence in wrongful rape conviction (the "black box") was presented with a focus on the process contingent on certain characteristics of the offense, that is, shaping unreliable identifications where victims and/or witnesses are available, and eliciting and scripting "false confessions" where the victim/witness is not available to make identifications. These features, common across wrongful rape convictions, are apparent in Black defendant cases along with the additional racialized elements (principally, coded racial messaging to elicit conscious and latent fears, cross-racial identification error, all-white juries, and racial bias affecting press coverage, the police, jurors, attorneys, trial and appellate judges, etc.).

Many of these elements are operative in two pre-*Miranda*, pre-DNA false confession cases that occurred in New York City in the mid-1960s. The time period and locale are relevant because many of the earlier contentious race and rape cases occurred in southern states with overt Jim Crow segregation. The George Whitmore case received considerable press attention (Vitello, 2012; Huff et al., 1996), while the wrongful conviction of 12-year-old juveniles from Brooklyn (*In the Matters of Gregory W. & Gerald S.*, 1966) was not reported widely. Both cases involved stranger rape and murder allegations. During the post–Civil Rights era, major northern urban areas (e.g., New York City and Chicago, Illinois) increasingly became a common location for wrongful conviction associated with police (mis)conduct (Gross & Shaffer, 2012; R. King, 2016; Drizin, 2013; Rosen & Schonder, 2012).

George Whitmore, 1963

The Manhattan police were working under pressure to close the double murder of high-status young white women. The police mistakenly linked Whitmore, a rape suspect in an unrelated Brooklyn offense, as the perpetrator of the double murder and influenced his misidentification. Whitmore was (wrongfully) convicted of the rape charge, but his trial conviction was properly set aside by the judge (Huff et al., 1996). The case includes many elements common in wrongful conviction in sexual assault: high-status (white) victims, a stranger assault, pressure on the police for arrests, a convenient (vulnerable) Black suspect, coercive interrogation, a false confession, police and prosecutorial misconduct, and evidence of juror racial bias.

On the day civil rights spokesman Martin Luther King, Jr., delivered the famous "I Have a Dream" speech in Washington, DC (August 23, 1963), two young white women were killed in their upper East Side apartment near Park Avenue. There was considerable hue and cry pressure for arrests (Vitello, 2012; Huff et al., 1996). There was no discernible progress in the investigation and the "career girls" murders (also known as the "Wylie-Hoffert case") remained in the press despite other major news items such as the September 15th bombing of the 16th Street Baptist church in Birmingham, Alabama, and the November 22nd assassination of President Kennedy.

In April 1964, police reported George Whitmore had been arrested for attempted rape in Brooklyn, was being questioned about a Brooklyn murder, and was carrying a photo of one of the career girls. After an 18-hour interrogation, without a break, Whitmore signed a 62-page confession (described as the longest in New York history). The Brooklyn District Attorney announced the career girls case had been solved. At arraignment, however, Whitmore revoked the confession and accused the police of trickery and assault during a prolonged interrogation. Further, the parents of the deceased victim stated the incriminating photo was not their daughter. By the time Whitmore was tried for the attempted rape in Brooklyn, it was clear to the Manhattan District Attorney that Whitmore's confession to the career girls murders was false, and there was another suspect. However, this knowledge was concealed to facilitate the Brooklyn rape prosecution. It was also learned Whitmore's identification as the Brooklyn rapist was tainted by the witness being informed he was a suspect in the career girls murder. In addition, despite a contrary FBI report, the Brooklyn District Attorney, in his closing remarks to the jury, referred to a button taken by the victim from the assailant as evidence of Whitmore's guilt. Whitmore was convicted of the attempted rape, but the judge set aside the verdict after interviewing jurors about racist remarks made during deliberations. A man by the name of Richard Robles was later convicted of the career girls murder (Huff et al., 1996). Whitmore's case was cited in the landmark US Supreme Court *Miranda* decision as an example of a false confession (Vitello, 2012), and the facts of Whitmore's case became the basis for the pilot episode of the long-running Kojak television series.

Gregory and Gerald, 1964

In 1964, two white women, described as "aged domestics" in the New York Court of Appeals ruling (*In the Matter of Gregory W. and Gerald S.*, 1966), were sexually assaulted in Brooklyn. One victim was killed during the attack. The survivor reported she could not make an identification, but given the assailant's strength and voice she believed it was a Black male in his late teens or early 20s. Two 12-year-olds were questioned, "confessed," and adjudicated delinquent in juvenile court. The trial court's ruling was upheld in state appellate court but later reversed by New York's highest court. The Gregory and Gerald case shares features of other Black defendants wrongfully convicted of sexual assault: white victims of stranger rape with the resulting pressure on police for arrests, vulnerable Black suspects, coercive interrogation, false confession, and trial conviction.

Two weeks after the assaults, young Gregory was questioned by police for an hour in an unrelated matter. This was followed by questioning by two detectives investigating the rapes and murder. Gregory's parents were at the precinct during some of the questioning but not in the room during interrogation. According to the detective's testimony, the questioning of Gregory began at 8:00 p.m., and Gregory provided a full confession by 1:00 a.m. The juvenile was then taken to the crime scene for a "reenactment." This was followed by another 6–7 hours of questioning until he named an accomplice, Gerald. Gerald was then picked up at 8:00 a.m. and confessed after hours of questioning. At 5:00 p.m. that evening, a district attorney arrived with a stenographer and took formal statements. The youth were then held in juvenile detention. The following day, the detective learned Gregory was in a locked psychiatric unit at the Brooklyn (Kings) County hospital at the time of the offenses. The detective went to the juvenile detention the night before the court hearing and secured a supplemental "confession" from Gregory that he had escaped from the hospital, committed the crime, and reentered the locked hospital unit without detection.

Despite a psychiatrist's testimony, Gregory's incriminating statements were allowed as evidence, and he was adjudicated delinquent for the offenses. In a 3–2 decision, the trial adjudication was affirmed by the appellate court. However, the New York State highest court reversed the ruling, noting the incriminating statements lacked reliability with regard to known facts of the offense and were involuntarily obtained.

It is not apparent from the record whether Gregory and Gerald were particularly large for their age, but it is difficult to imagine 12-year-olds committing the charged offenses (burglary, murder, rape, and sodomy). The allegations become even more remote with the supplemental confession, including the escape and reentry to a locked hospital ward without detection. In reversing the trial adjudication, the NY State Court of Appeals cited the 1947 US Supreme Court *Haley v. Ohio* decision noting, "Age 15 is a tender and difficult age for a boy of any race" (*In the Matter of Gregory W. & Gerald S.*, 1966, p. 6.). The trial court and appellate judgments against the 12-year-olds are consistent with racial bias against Black juveniles, who are commonly perceived to be more predatory and less innocent than white youth (Goff, Jackson, Di Leone, Culotta, & DiTomasso, 2014). This is illustrated in the other cases, such as the George Stinney execution noted previously and the preadolescents charged in the Ryan Harris stranger rape/murder (Kotlowitz, 1999) and further elaborated by Drizin (2013).

Nate Walker, 1974

The wrongful rape conviction of Nate Walker was presented to open this chapter. Walker's wrongful conviction involved stranger rape and delayed cross-racial mis-identification complicated by weapons focus. Walker was a vulnerable Black suspect with prior criminal justice exposure whose alibis were discounted and who received ineffective defense representation. In such a case, the witness/victim is susceptible to inadvertent and/or intentional suggestion from police investigators during black box witness identification procedures: Law enforcement officers, under pressure to close the case, may convey their idea that a potentially dangerous suspect should be convicted. While the formal legal record does not include evidence of racial bias in his wrongful conviction, the mechanisms of race bias in the post–civil rights era are typically covert and hidden, as elaborated in the material that follows.

Coker v. Georgia, 1977: The Death Penalty for Rape

Another significant development in race and rape prosecution was the US Supreme Court 1977 *Coker v. Georgia* ruling. The appeal on Coker's behalf did not assert innocence. Counsel for the African American defendant, argued the State of Georgia, exhibited a pattern of racial bias in sentencing for rape. The US Supreme Court agreed to hear the appeal limited to the question of whether execution for rape violates the Eighth Amendment prohibition of "cruel and unusual" punishment. The Supreme Court decided death was an inappropriate penalty for the rape of an adult woman, thus avoiding any ruling on the matter of racial bias in sentencing (as a Fourteenth Amendment equal protection claim). Ogletree (2006; as well as Baldus & Woodworth, 2003) argued the high court had avoided the issue of racial bias in death sentencing for rape in earlier decisions, such as *Maxwell v. Bishop* (1970), where the Black defendant was also sentenced to death for a rape, without fatality, of a white woman. In *Maxwell*, as in *Coker* later, the Supreme Court granted relief on other grounds, and racial bias in sentencing for rape remained unexamined by the Supreme Court.

The William Bernard Jackson Conviction, 1977: "The Grandview Rapist"

In 1977, an all-white jury sentenced African American defendant William Bernard Jackson to 14–50 years in prison for two separate stranger rapes (Jackson, 1983). At trial, two white rape victims identified Jackson as their attacker (Ohio doctor accused of 36 rapes, 1982). After serving 5 years in Ohio State prison, Jackson was released and subsequently exonerated. William Bernard Jackson's release was the result of the arrest of Dr. Edward F. Jackson (no relation), whose indictment included 36 counts of rape. Dr. Edward Jackson was described as a "prominent"

Columbus physician, married, and the father of two children (Associated Press, 1983). According to police, he was also the long-sought "Grandview rapist," who used a ski mask, gloves, flashlight, and rope in his attacks on women in the Grandview section of Columbus. According to the press (*The New York Times*, 1982), William Bernard Jackson acknowledged the indicted Dr. Jackson did resemble him. William Bernard Jackson's wrongful rape conviction highlights Black defendant vulnerability to cross-racial misidentification (including multiple eyewitness misidentification), as well as vulnerability associated with an all-white jury. In addition, the investigation was tainted by the creation of a composite sketch (Jackson, 1983), a process that can undermine subsequent reliable identification (G. L. Wells & Hasel, 2007).

Willie Sanders, 1980: The "Brighton Rapist" Prosecution

The Willie Sanders case is noteworthy for the *Boston Globe's* (Klibanoff, 1980a, 1980b, 1980c, 1980d) detailed press coverage, which underlined the wrongful conviction risks in the cross-racial, stranger rape prosecution. Though Sanders was prosecuted vigorously, he was not convicted. During the winter of 1978–1979, at least eight white women were victims of rape, or attempted rape, by a Black assailant in the Brighton section of Boston. Given the method of attack and assailant descriptions, this was considered to be serial perpetration by a single rapist, called the "Brighton Rapist" (Klibanoff, 1980a; The Willie Sanders Defense Committee, 1980). The attacker was described as a thin Black male, approximately 5'6", about 25 years old, with a stubble beard and pockmarked face. Willie Sanders became a suspect because he worked for a building management company where some of the assaults had occurred. However, Sanders was 39 years old with a smooth complexion (The Willie Sanders Defense Committee, 1980).

A warrant for Sanders arrest was issued on December 28, 1978. However, he was not arrested until February 1, 1979, while the district attorney and police officials were meeting with hundreds of complaining citizens about the series of rapes. During the interval between the issuing of the warrant and Sanders's arrest, three more sexual assaults occurred. Four of the eight women attacked subsequently identified Sanders. Sanders sought to have the four cases combined, but the court denied his request, and the district attorney proceeded with the strongest case, the Christmas Day rape of 1978. The district attorney attempted to systematically exclude Black jurors. but a defense challenge resulted in a ruling against the district attorney and a final jury of 12 with two Black and two Latino members (The Willie Sanders Defense Committee, 1980) was seated. At trial, Willie Sanders' family provided alibi testimony regarding his whereabouts on Christmas Day, and three victims of the Brighton rapist testified Sanders was not the attacker.

The circumstances of Sanders's identification illustrate the police reliance on black box identification methods to "manufacture" evidence. The victim of the Christmas assault provided a description of the rapist and reported he appeared to be familiar with the basement area of the building where she was taken and attacked. The investigating officer learned, via telephone contact with the building management, that a "painter" (Sanders) fit the general description and was employed there. The rape victim sat with the investigator during the phone call. The investigator was told about the painter and relayed the information to the victim (Klibanoff, 1980a). The officer obtained a 1971 photo of Sanders, from a gun possession charge that was dismissed (Klibanoff, 1980b). The following night, the officer presented the victim with 20 photos, of which she picked 3 that could not be eliminated as her attacker. According to the victim's testimony, she stated the Sanders photo was "too heavy," "too fat," and "too old" (Klibanoff, 1980b). She was then told by an officer, "That's the painter," and she subsequently rated his photo above the other two. Several days later, the Christmas victim was shown a composite sketch produced by an artist in consultation with another victim. The Christmas victim then decided the composite sketch was the painter and made a definitive identification. However, the other victim, whose description produced the composite sketch, testified at trial that Sanders was not her rapist (Klibanoff, 1980b). This was how Sanders first identification was produced. The other three identifications all occurred after Sanders' arrest photo was presented in the media.

The jury acquitted Sanders of the Christmas rape. The district attorney proceeded with the three other cases without a conviction (Man's 4th rape case ends in acquittal, 1980). In addition to the biased identification procedures, there were other irregularities apparent in the prosecution. Crime scene biological evidence was not properly preserved, a potentially exculpatory fingerprint was destroyed by police, and there were numerous inconsistencies and clearly inaccurate testimony by police witnesses at trial as well as before the grand jury (Klibanoff, 1980d). The Sanders case demonstrates how multiple eyewitness misidentifications, a feature in several wrongful convictions in sexual assaults,[17] can be produced (Skagerberg, 2007).

Sands (1981) commented the Sanders case, highlighted the various ways the police shaped the rape victims' identification of Sanders. Sands observed the traumatized rape victim's behavior in court and suggested she appeared quite dependent and vulnerable to manipulation by police and prosecutors. Sands elaborated an alternative feminist perspective, critical of the alliance among feminists, police, and prosecutors who initiated the rape law reform movement (as presented in Chapter 1). Sands recognized Black on white rapes were investigated less carefully, prosecuted more vigorously, and sentenced more severely than intraracial rapes. She noted convicting any Black man would not result in protecting women from sexual assault. Other major feminist scholars (Davis, 1983; Wriggins, 1983; Estrich, 1987; J. D. Hall, 1983; Crocker, 2001; Gruber, 2009; McGuire, 2010; Gray, 2015) have expanded on this perspective.

WRONGFUL CONVICTION LITERATURE ON RACE

By the early 1990s, a substantial research literature on wrongful conviction had emerged. Several contributors cited the role of race and racial bias as a contributing factor to wrongful criminal conviction. Radelet, Bedau, and Putnam (1992) devoted two chapters to race bias and referred to "the ugly way white racism has corrupted criminal justice for blacks" (p. 114). Regarding sexual assault, Radelet et al. underlined the "catastrophic" (p. 136) consequences for Black defendants charged with rape. Huff et al. (1996), in a section called "Race as a Factor," noted "prejudices of police, prosecutors, and jurors" (p. 80) and also referred to the adverse consequences for Black suspects associated with erroneous cross-racial identification. Gross (1996), in a footnote to a discussion of wrongful conviction in capital cases, referred to the history of false allegations against Black defendants charged with rape of white victims (citing Bedau & Radelet, 1987; and Wolfgang & Reidel, 1973).

Scheck et al. (2001), in *Actual Innocence*, devoted a chapter to racial bias, presenting the case of Calvin Johnson Jr., a Black defendant charged in separate stranger rapes of two white women in Atlanta, Georgia. Johnson (who was later exonerated) was convicted of the case when he faced an all-white jury but acquitted in the other case, when there were Blacks on the jury. Regarding the conviction, Scheck et al. noted, "The black alibi witnesses had been rejected and the white identification witnesses had been accepted" (p. 271). Also, the Scheck et al. chapter on "False Confessions" focused on the Robert Miller capital prosecution in Oklahoma, where the Black defendant (Miller) faced an all-white jury, and the prosecutor introduced the notion of Blacks as sexual predators in his closing statement (also see S. L. Johnson, 2001).

Parker, Dewees, and Radelet (2001) authored a chapter, "Racial Bias and the Conviction of the Innocent," that described the overt racial bias in the prosecution of Clarence Brandley, charged with the stranger rape and murder of a white teen (also see Radelet et al., 1992). Parker et al. (2001) suggested a host of overlapping individual-level factors (racial bias, cross-racial misidentification, stereotyping, easy target status) as well as structural factors (the power threat hypothesis and urban disadvantage) are likely contributors to adverse outcomes for African American defendants.

Gross et al. (2005) also reported the disproportionate representation of Blacks among the wrongfully convicted as well as noting the disproportion was most striking with regard to rape exonerations. Gross et al. stated bias and discrimination likely play a role and also cited indicators Black juveniles may be subject to more coercive interrogation when compared to white juveniles. However, Gross et al. indicated "the most obvious explanation" (p. 458) was cross-racial identification error. In a later report, Gross (2008) stated, "Black men accused of raping white women face a greater risk of false conviction than other rape defendants," again attributing it to cross-racial identification error.

Taslitz (2006) indicated race is likely a substantial risk factor in wrongful conviction and called for more research on the question. Taslitz drew from the Parker et al. (2001) distinction between individual, psychological factors versus structural factors contributing to adverse racial bias. Taslitz focused on the psychological contributors, reasoning that broader structural change would not be achieved in the near term. Among the psychological factors, Taslitz noted the significance of cross-racial identification, citing the decades of research demonstrating the effect (Meissner & Brigham, 2001). Taslitz suggested the same "selective inattention" by whites that contributed to cross-racial identification error (or "own-race bias") was likely operative throughout the criminal investigation and guilt determination process, citing psychological and other research on race bias, prejudice, and stereotyping at various stages in criminal procedure.

Garrett (2011) as well reported on the disproportionate number of Black and Latino defendants among DNA exonerees, noting the numbers exceed the proportion of minorities among those convicted of rape and murder. Garrett raised the question, "Is being black a risk factor for being wrongly convicted?" (p. 73). Further, Garrett (2011, p. 73) stated, "There is a long history of discrimination surrounding charges of rape involving white victims and black men. There is also some evidence that prosecutors may pursue more serious charges in cases involving white victims and black men . . . [and] evidence white jurors may be less sympathetic to black defendants."

More recently, Gross, Possley, and Stephens (2017) specifically addressed the matter of race and wrongful conviction and noted varying forms of race bias and discrimination found to be operative in the conviction of innocent Black defendants. Gross et al. identified explicit and intentional racism, which they suggested was less common than widely held unconscious or implicit racial biases. They also suggested a form of institutional discrimination was likely common where "[people] are prone to going along with accepted practices" (p. 10). In addition, Gross et al. described "racially tainted official misconduct" (p. iii) in instances where the harm endured by Black suspects was not likely to be perpetrated on whites.

Before presenting additional research on race as a risk factor in wrongful conviction, the structural contributors advanced by Parker et al. (2001), and intentionally omitted by Taslitz (2006), warrant discussion. By structural contributors, Parker et al. referred to forces operating independent from individual racial prejudice or bias, such as the "power threat hypothesis" and "urban disadvantage." As presented by Parker et al., Blalock's (1967) power threat hypothesis suggests as the relative size of a minority group grows, the majority group will perceive threat and react by limiting access to economic and political resources. Thus, to the degree that whites are threatened by a perceived increase in the presence of Blacks, the criminal justice system can become an instrument in this reaction, in the form of increased surveillance, arrests, and guilt determinations by courts and jurors. This perspective is deemed structural because it is not reliant on individuals' specific racial prejudice or animosity.

Parker et al. (2001) cited Wilson's (1978) *The Declining Significance of Race*, and subsequent work (Wilson, 1987), in describing urban disadvantage as a contributor to wrongful conviction. In the 1970s and through the 1980s, poverty in the United States became increasingly concentrated in certain neighborhoods in urban centers. Shifting economic forces led to the wholesale loss of unskilled and semiskilled jobs in sectors of the economy where African Americans (especially males) had been employed for generations. These factors led to deterioration in housing, schools, recreation facilities, and community stability. This resulted in a continued exodus of middle and stable working-class elements from these neighborhoods.

Even without personal racial bias, racially disparate outcomes were produced where increases in certain types of crime, increased police surveillance, increased arrests, and available ameliorative resources for defendants of lower socioeconomic status were scarce at best. This resulted in profound socioeconomic disadvantage that was not reliant on individual racial bias or discrimination. Parker et al. suggested that within the concentrated poverty conditions of these communities the largest concentrations of wrongful convictions are likely to occur. Defendants in these circumstances are vulnerable and "easy targets" for prosecution in general and misconduct in particular. This perspective converges with the notion of race as a proxy for socioeconomic status presented in Free and Ruesink's (2012) discussion of wrongful conviction of African American men and is an essential aspect of what Alexander (2010) referred to as "mass incarceration in the age of colorblindness."

While wrongful conviction researchers have recognized race as a contributing factor in wrongful conviction, race bias has primarily been formulated (with the exception of Parker et al., 2001, and Gross et al., 2017) as overt prejudice on the part of individual system actors (often in southern states) and has not entertained notions of structural/systemic race bias or "implicit racial bias." Clearly, there are cases where individual prejudice and racial animus contributed to the framing of Black suspects such as Clarence Brandley (Parker et al., 2001) and Walter McMillian (who was framed for murder in Alabama because he was involved in a love triangle with a white woman; see Gross, 1996; Stevenson, 2014). However, the post–civil rights cases are not associated with the overt discrimination features found in the legal lynching cases (M. B. Johnson et al., 2013). As suggested by Free and Ruesink (2012), wrongful conviction in the recent post–civil rights era reflects more than failures on the part of individual system actors but rather "properties inherent in the criminal justice system" (p. ix), that is, the failures or errors are ratified, rather than corrected, by the system (the judge, jury, or appellate process).

MORE RECENT STUDIES AND DEVELOPMENTS

A series of recent studies examined the wrongful conviction of Black defendants with attention to rape cases (E. Smith & Hattery, 2011; M. B. Johnson et al., 2013; Olney & Bonn, 2014; Gross et al., 2017). The authors noted African Americans are overrepresented among the wrongfully convicted, and this overrepresentation is more pronounced among those wrongfully convicted of sex offenses (also see Garrett, 2011; Free & Ruesink, 2012; Gross et al., 2005; Gross, 2008).

E. Smith and Hattery (2011) examined race and exoneration by contrasting conviction rates and exoneration rates. They reported Black defendants are 40%–50% of the incarcerated yet 70% of those exonerated, suggesting an increased risk of wrongful conviction endured by Black defendants. Among DNA exonerations (Innocence Project data) for murder and rape, where race of the defendant and victim were reported, 84% of the cases involved a Black defendant and a white victim. E. Smith and Hattery reported Black men committed 16% of the rapes against white women, while this crime configuration resulted in 68% of the wrongful convictions, thus suggesting erroneous conviction is not random but rather distributed to the detriment of Black defendants. E. Smith and Hattery discussed the role of the commonly cited legal factors contributing to wrongful conviction and also noted the historical role of the "myth of the Black rapist" (p. 88) and lynching in the United States. These findings suggest there is a systematic way race operates to the detriment of Black defendants charged with rape against white victims. The mechanisms associated with this outcome are likely complex and are discussed further in this chapter.

Olney and Bonn (2014) examined legal factors and race among exonerees convicted of murder or sexual assault derived from National Registry of Exonerations data (Gross & Shaffer, 2012). This sample encompassed exonerations reliant on DNA as well as those independent of DNA. Olney and Bonn found DNA increased the chances of exoneration for defendants across three race/ethnic groups (whites, Hispanics, or Blacks). However, the time from conviction to exoneration was longer for Blacks than for whites or Latinos. Also, Black defendants were more likely to benefit from DNA in their exonerations as compared to whites or Latinos. Black ethnic identity uniquely increased the likelihood a convicted defendant would be exonerated even while controlling for the presence of DNA (thus demonstrating wrongful conviction risk associated with African American status). Olney and Bonn did not examine defendant/victim ethnicity dyads.

M. B. Johnson et al. (2013) conducted a descriptive study of Black defendants (35 from 1964 to 2011) wrongfully convicted of sexual assaults against white victims. There was a focus on identifying "risk factors" for wrongful conviction and determining if the overt racial bias observed in early legal lynching cases (i.e., Scottsboro) was apparent in more recent cases. Johnson et al., noted the common finding of a convergence of risk factors in each case, with eyewitness misidentification being the leading contributor (apparent in 22 of the cases). Among cases where victim death or incapacitation interfered with identification, coerced false confessions were a primary source of evidence (10 cases). Overt racial bias of the legal lynching variety (lynch mob intimidation, effective denial of defense representation, exclusion of Black jurors, and racist jury instructions) was not apparent, but the authors noted Black defendants experienced vulnerability associated with cross-racial misidentification, coercive interrogation, and all-white juries. The authors suggested the more recent (post–civil rights) Black defendant vulnerability to wrongful conviction, reported by several researchers (Gross et al., 2005, 2017; E. Smith & Hattery, 2011; Garrett, 2011; Olney & Bonn, 2014), is complex and distinct from earlier legal lynching cases.

In a subsequent commentary, M. B. Johnson (2013) noted the risk of wrongful conviction was not connected to sexual assault (per se) but, rather, more directly linked to stranger rape prosecution. This was characteristic of 34 of the 35 cases. Thus, while the Johnson et al. study was limited in scope (Black defendants wrongly convicted of sexual offenses against whites), within that scope the increased wrongful conviction risks associated with stranger rape and the distinct "victim status paths" (as presented in Chapter 2 and Figure 2.2) were apparent.

Given the focus of this chapter on race and rape in US history, illustrations are provided next of Black defendants who were wrongfully convicted of sexual assaults during the post–civil rights period. The pattern of wrongful conviction in sexual assault, particularly stranger assaults, is apparent with defendants across race/ethnic groups. In addition, there is evidence of further risk for Black defendants, most pronounced in white victim cases. This wrongful conviction risk takes the form of misidentification where there is a surviving and capable victim and coerced false confession where the victim is deceased or not capable of making (or ruling out) an identification. These misidentifications and coerced false confessions are the product of black box investigation methods described in Chapter 2. These two sources provide the primary evidence in wrongful prosecutions and are frequently supplemented by secondary forms of evidence (incentivized testimony from informants, unreliable expert testimony from lab analysts, and others), which are also unreliable.

POST–CIVIL RIGHTS MECHANISMS OF RACE BIAS

The mechanisms responsible for the adverse outcomes for Black defendants in the post–civil rights era are complex, and relegated from view, as compared to the more overt indications of adverse racial bias apparent in the earlier legal lynching cases (lynch mob intimidation, overt denial of due process, racially biased legal doctrines, and disparate sentencing). While it can be readily inferred from empirical sources (E. Smith & Hattery, 2011; Olney & Bonn, 2014; Garrett, 2011; Gross et al., 2005, 2017; Gross & Shaffer, 2012) that Black defendants experience unique risks of wrongful conviction, it is often not possible to substantiate racially biased contributions in individual criminal investigations, prosecutions, or trials. Such substantiation would require knowledge of the motivation of various actors. Parties who act with racial bias are not likely to make such bias public. Moreover, parties who act with such bias may not even be aware of their racial bias (Dovidio, Kawakami, Johnson, & Howard, 1997; Dovidio & Gaertner, 2004; Goff, Eberhardt, Williams, & Jackson, 2008). In addition, as noted in Chapter 2, common processes in the development of evidence such as custodial interrogations (Kassin, 2015) and witness identification procedures (Lampien, Neuschatz, & Cling, 2012) are not recorded. Exchanges between the prosecution and informants are not transparent (Neuschatz, Jones, Wetmore, & McClung, 2012). In-camera judge and attorney conferences are off the record, and, of course, jury deliberations are confidential.

Several scholars and researchers addressed the adverse criminal justice outcomes for African Americans that emerged during the post–civil rights period. The terms *race*, *racism*, and *race bias* have been used and operationalized differently in various presentations. Early in this period, Kovel (1970) provided a seminal formulation regarding manifestations of white racism in the US context. Kovel introduced the term "aversive racism" (p. 32) to broadly differentiate the character of white racism in the US north from the "dominative racism" more common in former Confederate states. Kovel also used the term "modern racism" (p. 34) to further elaborate how aversive racism had become the primary type of racism while the dominative type represented a regression that emerges where the existing racial order is threatened. Drawing from Kovel, Dovidio and others (Dovidio et al., 1997; Dovidio & Gaertner, 2004, 2008) presented a line of empirical research demonstrating aversive racism in various contexts. Dovidio and Gaertner (2004) noted many whites reject overt racist beliefs and express racial egalitarianism, but their behavior is influenced by negative stereotypes about Black people, and "discrimination will occur when an aversive racist can justify or rationalize a negative response on the basis of some factor other than race" (p. 8). This has obvious implications for juries as well as other parties (investigators, judges, attorneys, the press, and the public). As further elaborated by Cohn, Bucolo, and Sommers (2012), aversive racists are more likely to express adverse implicit racial bias toward Blacks when the social norms are ambiguous, where the adverse impact can be justified as unrelated to race, and where their behavior will not be interpreted as racially motivated.

Recognition that racism, in various forms, commonly operates to the detriment of Black defendants does not deny or diminish the adverse risks affecting white defendants charged with sexual assault. However, prosecutors use racial bias to make their case against Black defendants (as described by M. B. Johnson, 2001; also see S. L. Johnson, 1993). They use it in how they formulate their case, and they use it in how they present their case. Likewise, police investigators use it in investigating cases, as well as in decisions during questioning of witnesses and interrogation. They are likely to take greater liberties with defendants perceived to be "easy targets" because of their race/ethnic group, socioeconomic status, or where they live. So, clearly racism or race bias operates to the detriment of Black defendants. Investigators and prosecutors use it because it can be effective in achieving a conviction. It no doubt contributes to the unique vulnerability generally faced by Black defendants. Certainly, white defendants (and defendants from other race/ethnic groups) encounter risks of wrongful conviction, but obviously race bias is not used to the detriment of white defendants—that is what racism, in the US context, is. However, criminal investigators and prosecutors find other vulnerabilities to exploit with white defendants, as illustrated in the Deskovic, Krone, and the Beatrice 6 wrongful convictions presented in Chapter 2 and the Norfolk Four wrongful convictions presented in Chapter 4.

The contributions of Kovel (1970), Dovidio, Goff et al. (2008), Cohn et al. (2012), and others in distinguishing the public, private, and behavioral manifestations of race bias have been extremely valuable. However, race bias operates as not only personal traits (racial prejudice) among individuals but also social policy, as noted in the work of Parker et al. (2001), Alexander (2010), and others (see Harris, 1994).

THE BLACK DEFENDANT/WHITE VICTIM DYAD
IN WRONGFUL CONVICTION IN SEXUAL ASSAULT

As noted in the Introduction and Chapter 2, the disproportion of Black defendant/ white victim cases among wrongful convictions in sexual assault has been noted by several investigators (Gould & Leo, 2010; Garrett, 2011; Gross et al., 2005; E. Smith & Hattery, 2011). Garrett (2011, p. 73) noted the, "long history of discrimination surrounding charges of rape involving white women and black men," as well as evidence more serious charges are filed in Black defendant/white victim cases. E. Smith and Hattery (2011) referred to the historical role of the myth of the Black rapist, as presented previously in this chapter.

Harper Lee's (1960) Pulitzer Prize–winning novel, *To Kill a Mocking Bird*, was clearly a literary rebuttal to the myth of the Black rapist. In 1962, the novel became an Academy Award–winning motion picture, a product and contributor to the emerging post–civil rights era. The wrongful conviction narrative from *To Kill a Mockingbird* involved false rape charges. It was a critique of the myth of the Black rapist, in illustrating the white woman's pursuit of the Black man prior to crying rape. False rape charges are associated with wrongful conviction in "acquaintance rape" as depicted in *To Kill a Mockingbird*, but wrongful conviction in sexual assault in general and among Black defendant/white victim cases in particular is primarily associated with stranger rape. The centrality of stranger rape in wrongful conviction of Black defendants charged with sexual offenses against white victims has not received adequate attention (M. B. Johnson, 2013). By and large, wrongful conviction researchers (Gross et al., 2005; Neufeld & Scheck as cited in Connors et al., 1996) have attributed the predominance of sexual assault cases among wrongful convictions to the presence of DNA residuals to establish innocence and identification errors. There has not been adequate attention devoted to differential investigation motives and pressures (i.e., the stranger rape thesis) that likely impact the identification process and drive interrogation practice. As noted and illustrated in the historical sources, the Black defendant/white victim aspect of a crime adds to the "moral outrage" perception of an offense. This affects the police, the community, and the press, and contributes to a more intense and aggressive investigation.

Obviously, there were, and are, instances where Black assailants did in fact rape white women. This is clearly apparent in the multitude of cases where Black defendants were wrongly convicted in sexual assaults against white victims (M. B. Johnson et al., 2013). In virtually all these cases, the victims had indeed been attacked by Black assailants, but an innocent defendant, rather than the actual perpetrator, was convicted. While these cross-racial cases frequently generate substantial public attention, they are statistically quite rare in comparison to the dramatically more common intraracial sexual assaults.

There is a rather limited post–civil rights literature on the topic of the Black rapist and white victim, and this literature does not entertain the matter of wrongful conviction. Not long after Harper Lee's rebuke of the myth of the Black rapist, the myth was rekindled by Eldridge Cleaver's memoir, *Soul on Ice* (1968). Written while imprisoned in the state of California, Cleaver revealed he raped white women in what he previously regarded as " defying and trampling upon the white man's law. . . . I was defiling his women" (p. 14). Cleaver's memoir was well received, widely read, and while it is an exaggeration to say it resurrected the myth of the Black rapist (because the myth never really died), *Soul on Ice*, along with the press attention devoted to actual cases of Black rapists of white victims (e.g., defendant Ehrlich Anthony Coker in the US Supreme Court *Coker v. Georgia*, 1977, ruling and the notorious "Willie" Horton) continued to breathe life into the myth.

Scholarly research on "the Black rapist" has also been scarce. Agopian, Chappell, and Geis (1977) considered whether Black offender/white victim rape might be increasing given the increased social interaction between race/ethnic groups. The researchers noted it was difficult to determine if divergent findings from several studies were the result of regional variability, cohort specifics, a genuine increase, or some combination of these. The authors also noted the limitations of reliance on police data due to differential reporting and police response.

LeBeau (1985) also examined rape and race and noted that while rape was predominately intraracial, there were data to indicate Black offender/white victim rape was the most common form of interracial offending reported. LeBeau also cited sources that suggested an increased incidence of Black offender/white victim rape in western regions of the United States, which was referred to as "The West Phenomenon" (p. 127). LeBeau noted that crime victimization surveys may elicit valuable data on rates of victimization while masking the serial nature of a single offender's multiple attacks.

A more recent examination of available data on rape and sexual assault offending noted the importance of distinguishing acquaintance from stranger rape (Garland, 2009). Stranger rapes are more likely to be reported to law enforcement than are acquaintance rapes, and when reported they are more likely to be prosecuted. Garland cited D. E. H. Russell's (1984) finding that Black rapists more likely commit stranger assaults, and white rapists are more likely to assault acquaintances. Garland suggested the increased victimization cited among Black female victims may be an artifact of the predominant stranger rape victimization, while the acquaintance rape victimization of white victims remains unreported. While Russell's findings are dated, the methodologically rigorous approach used in her data collection (a large random community sample, face-to-face in-depth interviews by trained assistants, who were matched by race and ethnicity to the subjects) may have overcome some of the limitations of law enforcement and crime survey data.

The matter of reliable group differences among Black versus white (or other race/ethnic groupings) of rapists, with regard to perpetration rates, stranger versus acquaintance perpetration, or serial versus single perpetration remains unclear. However, the Black defendant/white victim dyad is an outstanding feature in the US history of race and rape prosecution and highly overrepresented among confirmed wrongful convictions in sexual assault.

The disproportionate vulnerability of Black defendants to wrongful rape conviction is apparent where Garrett (2011), citing DNA exonerations, noted 75% of rape exonerees were Black or Latino while 30% of rape convicts were Black or Latino (citing Rosenmerkel, Durose, & Farole, 2009). Similarly, Gross and Shaffer (2012), examining both DNA-reliant and other exonerations, found 25% of defendants convicted of sexual assaults were Black, while 63% of defendants exonerated for sexual assault were Black. The race dyad data further underlines the vulnerability of Black defendants. As reported in Chapter 2, Gross et al. (2005) reported the Black defendant/white victim dyad accounted for 5%–6% of all rapes but 49%–50% (39 of 80) of all rape exonerations. And, Garrett (2011) reported, 49% (84 of 171) of rape exonerees were Black defendant/white victim cases, while 10% of sexual offenses were interracial (citing Greenfield, 1997). Likewise, E. Smith and Hattery (2011), examining Innocence Project data, reported Black men committed 16% of the rapes against white women, while this crime configuration results in 68% of the wrongful convictions, indicating this infrequent offense dyad accounts for a disproportionately large amount of wrongful convictions.

CROSS-RACIAL IDENTIFICATION

Gould and Leo (2010, p. 856) commented, "A common pattern of error is when a white woman is raped by an African American or Hispanic man and unintentionally identifies an innocent person as the perpetrator." As suggested by Gross (2008; Gross et al., 2005) cross-racial misidentification maybe the most obvious or simplest explanation for the current increased risk of wrongful conviction among African American defendants. However, the focus here is on the context in which cross-racial misidentification occurs.

As presented previously in this chapter, biased and racially motivated prosecutions against Black defendants in rape cases have a long and complex history in the United States. Cross-racial misidentification merely refers to an increased likelihood of error in identification when witnesses are from ethnic/racial groups different from the suspect (also referred to as own-race bias; Meissner & Brigham, 2001; Brigham, Bennett, Meissner, & Mitchell, 2006). This is an area where the common lay conception 'they all look alike" is consistent with findings from controlled research. Beyond the basic finding, much of the research indicates cross-racial misidentification, in the US context, is more common and more pronounced among whites in identifying Blacks than the reverse (Meissner & Brigham, 2001; Slone, Brigham, & Meissner, 2000), which has obvious implications when considering the role of cross-racial misidentifications in wrongful conviction. Even though the notion of cross-racial identification error has intuitive appeal in criminal cases, it likely collides with an alternative lay notion, that a victim of a highly personalized attack, such as a rape, would certainly be able to identify her attacker and a resultant reluctance to doubt such identification.

Even prior to the extensive research by psychologists, cross-racial identification error was recognized among lawyers and legal scholars. S. L. Johnson (1984) noted Borchard (1932), in his landmark work, identified two cases where cross-racial misidentification led to wrongful convictions. Wall (1964), in *Eye-witness Identification in Criminal Cases*, stated, "In general, there is much greater possibility of error where the races are different than where they are the same. Where they are different, there is more likelihood of error where the subject belongs to a minority group and the witness to a majority group than there is in the opposite situation (p. 122)." Judge Bazelon suggested the matter of cross-racial misidentification has been neglected because the adverse effects primarily visit minorities (as cited in S. L. Johnson, 1984).

As noted by Connelly (2015), and consistent with data presented in Chapter 2, a substantially large percentage of documented wrongful convictions involved cross-racial identification error. The common terminology that refers to these outcomes as "errors" suggests an encapsulated erroneous judgment by a witness, often a crime victim. In that way, it fails to focus attention on the role of the law enforcement formulation of the offense, the use of biased identification procedures, the preventable sources of error (Lampien et al., 2012; Cutler & Kovera, 2010), and profound racial dynamics that influence the investigation and prosecution in many criminal cases. As illustrated in several cases presented in Chapter 2, often the police identification procedures not only failed to recognize an unreliable identification but also actually operated to make an erroneous impression appear to be an accurate and confidently held identification. In some cases, it was only when the victim/witness intimately involved came forward to provide their anecdotal accounts did the more complete picture emerge (Thompson-Cannino et al., 2009; Kix, 2016).

Connelly (2015) focused on cross-racial identification and wrongful conviction, and noted DNA exonerations as reported on the Innocence Project website indicated 72% of the total cases ($N = 321$) involved misidentifications, and 40% of the total number of defendants were misidentified in cross-racial contexts. Connelly cited the social science research noting the clear consensus cross-racial or own-race bias exists yet jurors tend to rely on eyewitness accounts even when doubt is warranted. Further, Connelly pointed out guidance from the US Supreme Court is inadequate. The leading case, *Manson v. Braithwaite*, 1977, focused on suggestive police practices and thus did not consider identification error stemming from cross-racial identification (or other event-related, "estimator," factors).[18] As pointed out by Connelly, the New Jersey Supreme Court advanced the jurisprudence in this area. A special master was appointed to review the empirical research on the reliability of eyewitness identifications (Gaulkin, 2010). In the subsequent *State v. Henderson* (2011) ruling, the New Jersey Supreme Court found the *Manson* guidelines to be lacking in that (among other things) three of the five *Manson* factors to assess reliability were dependent on witness self-report. As a result of the ruling, New Jersey adopted a four-step process for evaluating disputed identifications, including a pretrial hearing where the defense can present expert witness testimony related to both system and estimator factors affecting reliability.

ADDITIONAL POST–CIVIL RIGHTS MECHANISMS OF RACE BIAS

Drawing from Georges-Abeyie's formulation, K. K. Russell (2001) described the pre–civil rights legal acceptance of race discrimination (i.e., during the enslavement and Jim Crow eras) as "grand apartheid" and refers to post–civil rights era discrimination as "petit apartheid," meaning, "the myriad ways that covert racial discrimination operates within the justice system" (p. 3). Russell elaborated three inter-related characteristics of petit apartheid legal processes:

1. They occur out of public view and thus are hidden.
2. They are concentrated where law enforcement authorities have relative discretion.
3. They are derived from, and reinforce, racialized conceptions of deviance.

Russell's description of petit apartheid legal processes outlines the criminal justice and legal "spaces" wherein overt and implicit racial biases can operate.

Likely the most influential work to address the post–civil rights racial bias facing Black Americans has been Michelle Alexander's (2010) *The New Jim Crow*. The subtitle, "*Mass Incarceration in the Age of Colorblindness*," highlights the irony of increasing African American incarceration when racial discrimination was legally prohibited. Alexander described the "tough-on-crime" law enforcement environment that emerged in the aftermath of the Civil Rights Movement, particularly the so-called War on Drugs. According to Alexander, this took the form of social policy that reinstated a race-based social caste system as pervasive as the earlier southern Jim Crow laws. Alexander pointed out that while illegal drug abuse is no more common among Blacks than whites, racially different patterns of police surveillance and arrest, and race bias in sentencing, produced dramatically higher rates of incarceration among African Americans as compared to whites. Similarly, federal legislation that penalized crack cocaine (use and distribution) more severely than powder cocaine illustrates racially differential targeting of legislation. While Blacks were subjected to the more severe consequences for illegal drug use, including post–civil rights provisions that deprived the convicted of housing and education benefits and often voting rights, driving while intoxicated with alcohol, the form of illegal substance abuse associated with the most fatalities and where whites predominate, has the least severe penalties.

Drawing from the contributions of Kovel, Dovidio, Goff, Russell, Alexander, Parker et al., and others, a range of interacting and overlapping mechanisms of post–civil rights race bias affecting wrongful conviction is apparent. These mechanisms can be described as

1. Structural/systemic (including disparate impact legislation)
2. Adverse race bias (both explicit and implicit) practiced covertly and in informal procedures (the petit apartheid notion)
3. Solely implicit race biases operative in formal and informal procedures, which are often manipulated and inflamed by coded ("dog-whistle") messages that can distort the investigation and evidence review process and result in disparate outcomes including wrongful conviction

An illustration of the covert, relegated from view, operation of post–civil rights racial bias adversely affecting Black defendants is provided in *Foster v. Chatman* (2016a). In 1987, African American defendant Timothy Foster was convicted of killing an elderly white woman and sentenced to death by an all-white jury in Georgia. It is relevant to note Foster was 18 years old at the time of the offense, and he was also accused of sexually assaulting the victim. Pretrial prosecutors struck all four prospective Black jurors and then urged the jury to impose a death sentence "to deter other people out there in the projects" (*Foster v. Chatman*, 2016b). The trial judge accepted the prosecutors "race-neutral" explanation for striking the Black jurors. However, in 2016 the US Supreme Court found those peremptory strikes to be unconstitutional exclusion of jurors based on race. Foster's claim of discrimination was supported by the discovery of prosecutors' original notes that highlighted the names of Black potential jurors with circles drawn around the word *black* as well as related racially derogatory handwritten comments (Liptak, 2016).

STRANGER RAPE WITH SURVIVING, "CAPABLE" VICTIM, AND EYEWITNESS MISIDENTIFICATION

In the Introduction and Overview, Edward Carter's wrongful conviction was reported as an example of stranger rape, with a surviving capable victim, and cross-racial misidentification. Beyond the risk associated with cross-racial eyewitness misidentification, the racial bias in Carter's case was likely structural/systemic, covert, and informal. That is, as a consequence of racially differential policing, as an African American Carter was more likely to have a prior criminal record and be dependent on the public defense system. The resulting inadequate defense representation was structural (in that public defense is commonly overburdened) and also discretionary; that is, it is determined covertly by the counsel and not on the record or public. Among the cases described next, several are well known in the wrongful conviction literature and framed here to highlight the obstacles inherent in stranger rape investigation and the risks for Black defendants. Drawing from the distinction in victim status paths introduced in Chapter 2, cases with surviving capable victims and misidentification are presented, followed by cases with incapacitated victims and coerced false confessions. Cases that diverge from these two paths are also presented.

Timothy Cole: The "Tech Rapist" Prosecution

In 1985, Michelle Murray-Mallin, a white Texas Tech student, survived a knife-point stranger rape in Lubbock, Texas. The press reported she was the fifth victim of the "Tech Rapist," a knife-wielding, African American perpetrator who abducted women using a car (Shaw, 2011). A female detective, acting as a decoy, spoke to Timothy Cole near the crime scene 2 weeks after Murray-Mallin's assault and determined Cole was a suspect (Kix, 2016). Murray-Mallin chose Cole's photo from a spread where Cole's was the only frontal view and only color photo (Schwartzapfel, 2012). The photo spread was administered by the same detectives who conducted the stakeout. The following day, Murray-Mallin identified Cole in a live lineup and received positive feedback from the detectives (Kix, 2016). The prosecution supplemented the victim's in-court identification with less–than-scientific hair analyst testimony. The defense presented evidence the assailant smoked cigarettes, while Cole, who was asthmatic, did not. Also, several defense witnesses testified to support Cole's alibi. The judge ruled evidence of rapes continuing after Cole's arrest was inadmissible as well as fingerprints from earlier rapes that did not match Cole (*Timothy Cole—Innocence Project*, n.d.). Cole was convicted by an all-white jury in 1986. His appeals for relief were denied. In 1995 twice-convicted sex offender Jerry Wayne Johnson wrote a letter to the district attorney confessing to the rape of Murray-Mallin and noting Cole was innocent. The letter went unanswered (Schwartzapfel, 2012). In 1999, Cole died in prison from complications related to asthma, without knowledge of Johnson's confession. Johnson continued to write letters, and in time Cole's family and the Texas Innocence Project learned of Johnson's admission. Subsequent DNA testing excluded Cole and confirmed Johnson was the perpetrator. Cole was posthumously exonerated in 2009 (Shaw, 2011).

Cole was clearly vulnerable due to cross-racial identification error. However, cross-racial identification only means the identification had decreased reliability. In Cole's and similar cases, the police interviewing process (the black box procedures) not only failed to detect an erroneous identification but also made an unreliable identification appear accurate. That is, Cole's color, frontal photo stood out from the others, suggesting the perpetrator was among the photos presented, and it was Cole. The exposure to Cole's photo primed the witness for misidentification of Cole in the live lineup. It is also likely the officers' belief Cole was the perpetrator was communicated to Murray-Mallin, intentionally or inadvertently, during the identification procedure. The witness received positive feedback, which likely increased her confidence in the erroneous identification. As noted in Chapter 2, the sense of "moral violation" connected to stranger rape results in greater pressure on the investigating authorities, pressure on both the agency for results and internally generated pressure experienced by officers who want to

right a profound wrong and bring justice to the victim. Cole faced additional race
bias–related risk due to the all-white jury (discussed in the material that follows).
The degree to which racial bias (explicit or implicit) was a factor in the press and
public pressure on the police authorities, the individual police conducting the investigation, the jurors in general, the jurors in dismissing the alibi evidence, the
judge in general and in specific rulings, is a covert matter where such bias would
not be on the record. However, it is likely such bias existed and was substantial.

Herman Atkins

Herman Atkins was charged in a stranger rape that involved robbery and related
counts from a 1986 offense. He was convicted by a Riverside County, California,
jury in 1988 (Weinberg, 2003; *Herman Atkins—National Registry of Exonerations*,
n.d.). The victim was a young white woman working as a clerk in a shoe store. She
reported an African American man entered the store and, after looking at shoes,
produced a handgun and forced her to the rear of the store, where she was raped
and robbed. The perpetrator wiped ejaculate on the victim's sweater. The victim
was examined at a hospital, and her sweater was preserved as evidence.

The victim was questioned by police and shown photos but failed to identify
the assailant. However, during further questioning, she observed Atkins' photo in
a wanted poster connected to an unrelated offense. She then identified Atkins as
her assailant. She subsequently identified Atkins in a photo array that included the
same photo as well as in a lineup where all the other suspects were white (Weinberg,
2003). In addition to the victim's identification, the prosecution produced another witness who identified Atkins from the wanted poster as someone she
observed in the vicinity prior to the attack. At trial, the state relied on the witness
identifications as well as a crime laboratory serologist who examined specimens
from the sweater and evidence from vaginal swabs. He testified that only 4.4%
of the population could have produced the semen and Atkins was in this group.
The prosecutor asserted to the jury that the serologist's evidence corroborated the
witness accounts. Atkins's defense was mistaken identification. He testified on his
own behalf, and his wife testified he was not in Riverside County at the time of
the offense.

Atkins was found guilty by an all-white jury and was sentenced to 47 years
in prison. His initial appeals were dismissed. In 1993, the Cardoza Law School
Innocence Project accepted the case; however, it took four years for a hearing,
and the request for DNA testing was denied. In 1999, a subsequent motion was
granted, and testing by two separate laboratories indicated Atkins was not the
source of the semen. Atkins' conviction was vacated, and he was released in 2000.

As was the case with Timothy Cole, Herman Atkins's vulnerability was related
to challenges presented by cross-racial identification in the context of stranger
rape. It is critical to recognize the role of the black box identification methods in
reinforcing the erroneous identification. The repeat presentation of the wanted
poster photo in the subsequent photo spread, the live lineup where Atkins was

the only Black suspect, and the biased identification by the second witness all affirmed the erroneous identification and increased the witness' confidence in her selection. Stated differently, the victim likely made an honest mistake, but the police investigation (black box methods) made the honest mistake appear to be an accurate identification. The low-reliability identification was shaped and reinforced by the identification procedures and thus appeared certain.

In a stranger rape where an innocent victim has been attacked and violated, a defendant's denials and alibis will be dismissed, and the victim's account will be accepted. In cases with a Black defendant and white victim, these elements are magnified, especially in the eyes of an all-white jury burdened with overt and implicit notions about Black criminality and sexuality. The multiple eyewitness misidentification element in the Atkins case further highlights the black box flaws and the systematic character of error. Multiple misidentification is also apparent in wrongful rape convictions of Black defendants Calvin Johnson Jr., Bernard Webster, and James Waller (M. B. Johnson et al., 2013). The Innocence Project (2009) reported 38% of DNA confirmed misidentifications included the same misidentification provided by more than one witness.

McKinley Cromedy

In August 1992, a white female Rutgers University student (D. S.) was raped and robbed in her apartment by an African American assailant (*State v. Cromedy*, 1999). She made a police report, the crime scene was assessed for fingerprints, and a medical examination rape kit was taken. Five days after the attack, D. S. was shown mug shots, including McKinley Cromedy's photo, but made no identifications. Eight months later, she saw a man on the street she believed was the perpetrator. The police were notified and immediately detained the suspect (Cromedy). In a "show-up," D. S. confirmed the identification from behind a one-way mirror 15 minutes later. At trial Cromedy's defense counsel argued for special cross-racial identification caution for the jury. The judge refused, and Cromedy was convicted. On appeal the New Jersey Supreme Court reversed trial and appellate court rulings, noting the cross-racial instruction was appropriate given the facts (the prosecution relied entirely on the victim's delayed identification; the available forensic evidence did not link Cromedy to the offense; *State v. Cromedy*, 1999). Prior to the new trial, the prosecutor had DNA analysis of the rape kit, which ruled out Cromedy as the rapist. With his innocence established, Cromedy was released in 1999.

Like Cole and Atkins, Cromedy was vulnerable due to the cross-racial character of the identification. In Cromedy's case, the misidentification was a product of the victim's initial exposure to Cromedy's photo among the mug shots. This no doubt led to D. S.'s mistaken impression Cromedy was the rapist when she saw him 8 months later (referred to as "unconscious transference" in the misidentification literature; Cutler & Kovera, 2010). The police-arranged show-up identification made the erroneous identification appear reliable. The degree to which racial bias was a factor in the pressure on the police force (Black defendant/white victim offense, empathy for the victim, and press coverage), the individual officers conducting the investigation, the jurors in general, the trial judge in general and in specific rulings, the appellate court judges in confirming the trial verdict, cannot be substantiated but is likely. In this ruling, the New Jersey Supreme Court set a precedent indicating a cross-racial jury instruction was required where the iden- tification was not corroborated by other independent evidence. More recently, in *State v. Henderson* (2011), the New Jersey Supreme Court further elaborated procedures to reduce unreliable eyewitness identifications.

Ronald Cotton/Jennifer Thompson

The wrongful conviction of Ronald Cotton in the stranger rape of Jennifer Thompson is another example of the surviving capable witness and resulting misidentification. The inherent stranger rape risks and the role of the black box identification procedures were presented in Chapter 2. While the cross-racial identification challenge was an obvious feature in the case, it was conspicuously absent from a *60 Minutes* broadcast segment (Finkelstein, 2009). There were also more substantial racial dynamics in the prosecution. Even prior to Ronald Cotton's misidentification by Jennifer Thompson, he was known in the community as a young Black man who "liked white women" (Thompson-Cannino et al., 2009, p. 44) because as a juvenile he pled guilty to breaking and entering with intent to rape his 14-year-old white girlfriend. Racial fears and anxieties were heightened further when, 2 weeks after Jennifer Thompson's stranger rape by a Black male, another young white woman (Deborah Sykes) was raped and murdered by a Black man in a stranger assault in a nearby North Carolina community.[19] Further, race continued to play a role after Cotton's first conviction was reversed. The state chose an African American prosecutor for the retrial, who used his preemptory challenges to seat an all-white jury and secure Cotton's second (wrongful) con- viction. These racialized features were not part of the formal legal record yet no doubt contributed to overt and implicit adverse racial bias.

Bernard Webster

Several other wrongful convictions of Black defendants in stranger rapes are con- sistent with the observation of unreliable identification by a capable surviving victim. A white schoolteacher was raped in her Towson, Maryland, apartment during the summer of 1982. It was reported the attacker hid in a closet prior to the surprise attack, where he covered the victim's head with a robe, reported he had a gun, and raped her (*Bernard Webster—Innocence Project*, n.d.; *Bernard Webster— Northwestern School of Law*, n.d.). The assailant was described as a Black male with a dark complexion. A rape kit was taken. Three other witnesses described seeing a man who fit the description in the vicinity the day of the assault. They each selected Webster from a photo array. Two of these witnesses described the man as 5 feet, 8 inches, though Webster was 5 feet even. In addition, at trial the state presented misleading blood-typing evidence favorable to the prosecution (Police view chemist's work, 2003). Webster presented two alibi witnesses, yet he was convicted in 1983. In 2002, the Maryland Office of the Public Defender had the samples from the offense tested, and Webster was eliminated as the source. Subsequently, the crime scene DNA was matched to a man who was convicted of a 1988 rape (Gowen, 2002).

The DNA exoneration of Bernard Webster (and others noted previously) demonstrates multiple eyewitness misidentification as a product of black box investigation methods, though precisely how this occurs typically is not recorded. In some cases, such as in the Willie Sanders prosecution, adept defense representation is able to demonstrate the biased interviewing methods that produce multiple-witness misidentification. In other cases, it is postconviction investigation and discovery that expose the faulty investigation procedures (G. L. Wells & Hasel, 2007). In many other cases, because black box investigation procedures are done in secret, the methods can only be inferred.

The manifestations of post–civil rights race bias in Bernard Webster's wrongful conviction are consistent with accounts reported previously in this chapter. A Black defendant/white victim, home invasion, stranger rape would undoubtedly produce considerable press and public pressure (moral outrage) on the law enforcement authorities and pronounced sympathy for the victim. Webster was also vulnerable due his prior arrest (for theft of a pocketbook) and his limited education (Associated Press, 2002). Explicit or implicit racial biases made it easy for the prosecutor to cast doubt on Webster's alibi witnesses, and such racial bias would not be in the official legal record.

Several other Black defendants were wrongly convicted in stranger rapes where they were misidentified by capable victims/witnesses. Often, this occurred in cross-racial misidentifications (M. B. Johnson et al., 2013), but there are other cases where the misidentifications were made by Black victims/witnesses (e.g., Robert McClendon, described in Chapter 2; as well as Alan Newton, Gene Bibbons, Ronnie Bullock, and others).

STRANGER RAPE, INCAPACITATED VICTIM, COERCED FALSE CONFESSION

As noted in Chapter 2, when the victim of a stranger rape is also murdered, or otherwise incapable of making or ruling out identifications, wrongful convictions are often associated with black box investigation reliant on coerced false confessions. Because police are permitted to lie and use deception during criminal interrogations in the United States, and interrogations are commonly conducted in secrecy (M. B. Johnson, 2005; Leo, 2008), there is reason to believe Black suspects are likely subjected to more harsh and punitive interrogation than white suspects (Gross et al., 2005; M. B. Johnson, Citron-Lippman, Massey,

Raghavan, & Kavanagh, 2015) as a manifestation of what Gross et al. (2017) referred to as "racially motivated official misconduct." This is consistent with K. K. Russell's (2001) formulation of petit apartheid legal processes practiced where police have relative discretion, hidden from public view, and reinforce racialized conceptions of deviance.

The Central Park Five: Stranger Rape, Black Box Investigation, and Race Bias

The stranger rape risk and the accompanying reliance on secretive black box investigation methods in the Central Park Jogger investigation and prosecution were presented in Chapter 2. This prosecution is also widely known for the obvious racial dynamics (Duru, 2004; Burns, 2011; M. B. Johnson, 2005) that influenced the investigation and erroneous formulation of the offenses but were not part of the official legal record (Duru, 2004). The erroneous investigation and prosecution of the Central Park Five defendants illustrates the post–civil rights era racial bias the defendants faced.

The 1989 rape and life-threatening assault on a high-status, white female jogger in New York's Central Park resulted in dramatic press and media attention. The fact this crime occurred on a night when groups of Black teens from Harlem were committing attacks on others on the northern end of Central Park created substantial pressure on the New York Police Department (NYPD). A well-known New York businessman, Donald Trump, purchased ads in city newspapers calling for the reinstatement of the death penalty (Sullivan, 1992). This was a reflection of, and a contributor to, a sense of urgency distinct from that associated with other New York murders or rapes (Burns, 2011). Aggressive interrogations led to so-called verbal and written confessions, and videotaped incriminating statements were secured within 36 hours of the discovery of the incapacitated jogger. She was medically unable to make (or rule out) an identification of an assailant(s) (Burns, 2011; Sullivan, 1992). With the confessions secured, supplemental, less-than-scientific, opinion from a hair analyst (Burns, 2011) was obtained to support the district attorney's case. This evidence from the state was sufficient to win convictions in the two separate trials faced by the five defendants in 1990. So, where the victim/witness was incapacitated due to severe injuries, aggressive black box investigation via secret interrogations of vulnerable suspects produced multiple false confessions and five wrongful convictions.

Duru (2004) described the post–civil rights legal and social landscape that did not allow in-court expression or reliance on racial stereotypes or presumptions. Thus, explicit racial bias was not part of the formal legal record, consistent with K. K. Russell's (2001) formulation. However, Duru cited Lawrence (1987) indicating prevailing myths about Black male sexual prowess and inherent criminality meant "black men charged with rape continue to face an uphill battle in asserting innocence" (p. 1345). Further, Duru asserted that while these elements were absent in an explicit form during the Central Park Five trial proceedings, the pretrial and trial public discourse in the press and media were filled with racially biased stereotypes and animal metaphoric references to the defendants. Press reports and commentary described the youthful defendants in the most vile terms even though there were no indicators of prior criminal offending. The widely harbored racialized fears and anxieties, active and latent, conscious and unconscious, meant racialized messages could be conveyed efficiently by insinuation and innuendo such that the notion that any of the defendants might be innocent became highly remote. This widely accepted presumption of guilt is illustrated in the title of a journalist's book, *Unequal Verdicts: The Central Park Jogger Trials* (Sullivan, 1992) published 2 years after the defendants' trials. The book focused on the divergent nature of the trial convictions: Only one of the five defendants (Kevin Richardson) was convicted of attempted murder, and also one defendant (Kharey Wise) was acquitted of rape. Sullivan's book length account never considered that any of the defendants were innocent.

The wrongful conviction of the Central Park Five juvenile defendants is indicative of the racial stereotype of Black adolescents as especially predatory offenders (Goff et al., 2014), noted previously in describing the wrongful convictions of Gregory and Gerald, as well as George Stinney. The adherence to this presumption is in line with the observation by Gross et al. (2005, p. 550), "It may be that police officers are more likely to use coercive interrogation tactics on black juveniles than on white juveniles." As presented by Garrett (2010), the DNA exoneration of innocent defendants makes it clear their detailed incriminating admissions were scripted by police interrogators.

The Ollins, Ollins, Saunders, and Bradford Chicago Prosecution

Three years earlier than the attack on the Central Park Jogger in New York, the brutalized body of a white medical student (Lori Roscetti) was discovered near a housing project in a Chicago Black neighborhood. She had been raped. The case went cold for 3 months, and the police were under considerable pressure (Possley & Mills, 2001) for arrests. The Chicago police consulted with FBI criminal profiler Robert Ressler, who directed investigators to seek "black youths, somewhere between three and six males, ranging in age from 15 to 20, who would have previously been in jail and who lived close by the scene of the abduction" (Ressler & Shachtman, 1992, p. 166; also see Possley & Mills, 2001). In his memoir, *Whoever Fights Monsters*, Ressler and Shachtman (1992) celebrated his role in the apprehension of the suspects who, it turns out, were innocent. Equipped with Ressler's criminal profile, along with reward money as incentives, the Chicago police secured "confessions" from Marcellius Bradford and Calvin Ollins (aged 17 and 14, respectively) which were used in the "successful" prosecution of the teens as well as Larry Ollins and Omar Saunders (aged 16 and 18, respectively). The content of the confessions were markedly similar to Ressler's formulation of the offense.

After serving 13 years in prison, Calvin and Larry Ollins and Omar Saunders were cleared by exculpatory DNA and revelations concerning the fraudulent nature of the trial serological testimony by laboratory analyst Pamela Fish (Possley & Mills, 2001; Garrett & Neufeld, 2009). Bradford reported his confession was the result of repeated assaults while he was restrained. Calvin Ollins reported he was told he could go home if he signed the admission. Both juveniles who confessed reported they were instructed to study the police version of the offense and repeat it in their statements. In addition, Bradford's false confession and subsequent testimony for the state was provided in exchange for a lesser sentence. The testimony was embellished at trial to correspond to the state's (flawed) formulation of the offense (Possley & Mills, 2001). That is, Bradford testified he covered his hands with paper bags to avoid leaving fingerprints and instructed the other offenders not to ejaculate to explain the lack of physical evidence. To support and supplement the confessions, the prosecution obtained secondary evidence, incentivized testimony from two other witnesses, one seeking reward money and the other to avoid prosecution for the attack on the medical student. DNA testing of crime scene semen established the brutal attack on Roscetti was perpetrated by adults, not juveniles (Possley, Ferkenhoff, & Mills, 2002). Again, as noted by Garrett (2010), the DNA exoneration of defendants who had provided detailed false confessions indicates the confession content was provided by the investigators.

Bivens, Dixon, and Ruffin Capital Prosecution in Mississippi

Black assailant/white victim stranger rape, incapacitated victim, and reliance on coerced confessions were also apparent in the exoneration of Phillip Bivens, Bobby Rae Dixon, and Larry Ruffin. In 2010, Dixon and Bivens were exonerated for the May 1979 rape and murder of Eva Gail Patterson of Hattiesburg, Mississippi (Robertson, 2010; Associated Press, 2010). Mrs. Patterson was the victim of a nighttime home invasion while her husband was working offshore. The only witness was her 4-year-old son (Luke), who reported a lone assailant.

Larry Ruffin, a 19-year-old on leave from a halfway house at the time, was an initial suspect. Ruffin was questioned days after the attack and reportedly made several admissions to the rape and murder. However, he subsequently recanted and alleged police coercion in eliciting the admissions. A year later, prior to Ruffin's trial, the police obtained a statement from Dixon, who had also been a resident of the halfway house. Reportedly Dixon indicated he was with Ruffin when Ruffin committed the offense. Dixon pled guilty to avoid exposure to the death penalty and reportedly indicated Phillip Bivens also participated. Bivens was arrested in his home in California. He had been visiting Mississippi at the time of the offense. After being returned to Mississippi, Bivens also agreed to plead guilty and testify for the prosecution to avoid exposure to the death penalty.

At trial in 1980, Dixon contradicted his earlier report and testified that he had never seen the victim and was not with Ruffin or Bivens. Ruffin was convicted, spared the death penalty, and sentenced to life. Dixon and Bivens were also given life sentences. In 2010, the Innocence Project of New Orleans obtained authorization for DNA testing of the available sample. It was matched to a man (Andrew Harris) serving time for another sexual assault of a person who had been a neighbor of Mrs. Patterson (Acker, 2013). Bivens was released. Dixon had been released on medical parole earlier due to lung cancer. Ruffin had died of a heart attack in prison 8 years earlier.

The Bivens, Dixon, and Ruffin wrongful conviction follows the familiar pattern of the Black defendant/white victim stranger rape with an incapacitated victim. The resultant black box investigation, reliant on coercive interrogation, included the threat of execution. This is one of a series of cases where innocent rape defendants pled guilty (M. B. Johnson & Cunningham, 2015). The case illustrates the length the prosecution would go in inventing a multidefendant, multistate formulation of an offense when a witness reported a lone assailant. It raises the question whether this would occur with a white defendant or an intraracial offense.

Earl Washington

In 1982, a young white woman (Rebecca Lynn Williams) was raped and murdered in her Virginia home. She survived long enough to report the assailant was a Black man she did not know (Leo, 2008). Eleven months later, Earl Washington, an intellectually limited laborer, was arrested in an adjoining county for assault and burglary of one of his neighbors. During the initial questioning, Washington reportedly confessed to the assault and theft. He thereafter confessed to several other crimes, including three he clearly had not committed. He subsequently confessed to the murder of Rebecca Williams but not to rape. However, the officer questioning Washington did not know about the rape.

The following day, Washington was questioned by an officer (Harland Hart) knowledgeable about the attack on Williams as well as a state police officer (Curtis Wilmore). These interrogations, as well as the prior questioning, were not recorded. After an hour of questioning, Wilmore prepared a written statement which included Washington's confession to the rape and murder of Rebecca Williams. The officers noted the confession was a clear indication of guilt because it included detail of the offenses that only the perpetrator would know ("specialized knowledge"). However, the content of the incriminating statement was inconsistent with key crime facts (e.g., the size and race of the victim, the manner of entry to the home, and the number of stab wounds).

Eight months later, consistent with the prosecutor's insistence the confession could only have been produced by the guilty party, Washington was convicted and sentenced to death (Leo, 2008). During his 17 years of imprisonment, Washington's conviction was affirmed in eight separate appeals, and courts routinely cited the detail in his confession statement that would only be known by the guilty party. As a result of initial DNA testing in 1993, and more sensitive DNA testing in 2000 (which was matched to a convicted rapist), Washington's death sentence was commuted, and he was eventually pardoned. Subsequent civil litigation found Officer Wilmore fabricated the content of Washington's confession and resulted in a multimillion-dollar award for damages (Washington, 2006). Wilmore's black box interrogation provided an opportunity for the investigator to insert crime details into an admission attributed to Washington. The racial bias in the investigation and prosecution is not apparent in the formal record, but whether Wilmore would have gone to this length with a white defendant or a same-race sexual assault is a reasonable question.

MULTIPLE FALSE CONFESSIONS: THE DIXMOOR FIVE AND ENGLEWOOD FOUR

Multiple false confessions (along with multiple eyewitness misidentifications) are dramatic examples of manufactured evidence. In a typical wrongful conviction, the prosecution failed to correctly identify the actual offender and also erroneously convicted an innocent party. In the multiple cases, each innocent defendant convicted reflects additional substantial error. In addition to the Dixmoor Five and Englewood Four cases described in this section and the Central Park Five defendants reported previously, wrongful conviction in sexual assaults included several other multiple false confession cases, such as the Norfolk Four and the Beatrice Six. The Dixmoor Five and Englewood Four cases received considerable regional and national media attention largely as a result of *Chicago Tribune* coverage (Mills & Lighty, 2016a; b) and the CBS *60 Minutes*, "Chicago: False Confession Capital," segment (Rosen & Schonder, 2012). However, the racially biased aspects of the investigation and prosecution have not been adequately presented.

The Dixmoor Five were African American juveniles (Robert Taylor, Jonathan Barr, James Harden, Robert Lee Veal, and Shainne Sharp) wrongly convicted in the stranger rape and murder of 14-year-old Cateresa Matthews (*Johnathan Barr—National Registry of Exonerations*, n.d.). Cateresa, an African American adolescent, went missing November 19, 1991. She was last seen leaving her grandmother's home in Dixmoor, a Cook County Chicago suburb. Her body was discovered 3 weeks later in the same community. She suffered a bullet wound to the head with a .25-caliber pistol. It was apparent she had been raped as well.

The case was cold for 10 months until the police reportedly received a tip from a juvenile (Keno Barnes) that Johnathan Barr said he had seen Cateresa getting in a car with Robert Veal and Robert Taylor. On October 29, 1992, the 15-year-old Robert Veal was brought in for questioning, and after 5 hours, without a parent or counsel, signed a statement incriminating himself as well as four other juveniles. Later that day, a written confession was obtained from Robert Taylor, and on October 31, 1992, an incriminating admission was obtained from Shainne Sharp. However, the three statements included contradictory accounts of the offenses.

Pretrial testing of crime scene DNA found none of the five suspects was a match. Sharp and Veal agreed to pled guilty and testify against Barr, Harden, and

Taylor in exchange for leniency in sentencing. Barr, Harden, and Taylor were subsequently convicted. Prior to 2009, multiple appeals were denied. In 2010, following judicial intervention, the crime scene DNA was submitted to the DNA databank. The semen sample was matched to a known serial sex offender (Willie Randolph) who was on parole at the time of the offense and resided in the area. In 2014, the five exonerees won the largest wrongful conviction settlement in state history (Mills, 2014). In 2016, Randolph was formally charged (Mills & Lighty, 2016a).

The prosecution of this case has elements of an organized conspiracy to manufacture evidence through coercing the first confession and using it to leverage the others (as described by Kassin and cited in Drizin & Leo, 2004). With the confessions secured, the threat of severe penalties was apparently used to extort false testimony and secure convictions. In circumstances other than a criminal prosecution, this would be considered organized criminal activity. However, police officers and prosecutors are, in effect, protected from criminal penalties associated with their conduct in the course of prosecution. Because the victim of the original offense (Cateresa Matthews) was African American, as were the defendants, it might appear that racial bias did not play a role. The formal legal record and the accounts in wrongful conviction sources such as the Innocence Project and National Registry of Exonerations websites do not highlight race bias in presenting the Dixmoor Five wrongful conviction and exoneration. However, the Chicago Police and Cook County prosecutors have a noteworthy, documented history of abusive interrogation targeting African American suspects (Goldston, 1990; Scully, 2008; Stainthorpe, 1998).

The Englewood Four

The Englewood Four were African American juveniles (Vincent Thames, Terrill Swift, Harold Richardson, and Michael Saunders) from the southside Chicago, Englewood community. They were wrongfully convicted in the rape and murder of Nina Glover (Mills & Lighty, 2016b). The case was prosecuted as an acquaintance assault under the erroneous theory the victim had ties to the juvenile defendants. However, postconviction investigation and DNA evidence indicated the offense was likely committed by serial sexual offender Johnny Douglass. Ms. Glover was a Black woman whose naked body was found in a dumpster on November 7, 1994. She had been strangled to death. She was known to have been involved in prostitution and illicit drug use (*Vincent Thames—National Registry of Exonerations*, n.d.). Though the police initially interviewed people, there were no arrests until March 1995, when 18-year-old Jerry Fincher approached the police with information in exchange for benefits for a friend who was being held for an unrelated offense. During the subsequent 2 days of interrogation, Fincher reportedly stated he was involved in the rape and murder of Glover along with Swift, Richardson, and Saunders at the home of Vincent Thames. Within a few days of Fincher's reported admissions, the four defendants (who ranged in age from 15 to 18 at the time) were arrested, and the police secured confessions. While there were some inconsistencies among the incriminating statements, they all included rape, an assault with an instrument, and carrying the body to the dumpster. Even though pretrial DNA testing of crime scene semen did not match any of the defendants, and there was no physical evidence linking the defendants or Thames' home to the crime, the prosecution proceeded to trial in 1998. The case against Fincher was dismissed after his confession was ruled inadmissible because of coercion. Swift, Richardson, and Saunders each had separate bench trials before the same judge. Each was convicted. Richardson and Saunders received 40-year sentences. Swift got 30 years. Thames then accepted a plea bargain for a 30-year sentence.

In 2010, Swift and Saunders filed a motion arguing for more advanced DNA testing that could potentially match the semen to an offender on the state DNA database. The prosecution initially opposed the motion, but agreed when Richardson joined the request. In 2011, the Illinois State Police reported the crime scene semen matched to Johnny Douglass, 1 of the 4 people initially questioned about the offense. Douglass had a history of multiple arrests for sexual and other criminal offenses. Reportedly he was linked to two rapes and murders that occurred after the attack on Ms. Glover. At the time of the DNA match, Douglass was deceased as a result of a fatal shot from a woman who claimed self-defense and was acquitted. The Englewood Four were formally exonerated in 2012. Civil claims alleging physical abuse and other methods of coercion were filed (Mills & Lighty, 2016b). The case was settled in January 2019, awarding $24 million to three of the four (Saunders, Thames, Richardson); this followed a July 2017 award of $5.6 million to Swift.

Similar to the Dixmoor Five case, the prosecution of the Englewood Four proceeded under the erroneous formulation the juvenile defendants had ties with the victim. Without a capable victim/witness to identify or describe assailants, the investigation relied on black box methods and produced unreliable confession evidence, sufficient for conviction, though false. Several of the Dixmoor Five and Englewood Four defendants were featured on the CBS *60 Minutes* broadcast segment, "Chicago: False Confession Capital" (Rosen & Schonder, 2012), noting the concentration of confirmed false confessions in the Chicago, Cook County, area. Most of the coverage was focused on why the defendants had given false confessions. The officers who took the confessions, and obviously scripted the content (Drizin, 2013), did not appear. Even though each of the defendants was Black, as well as the *60 Minutes* interviewer, the issue of race bias was not presented in the broadcast segment.

Drizin's (2013) commentary informed by the actual transcripts of confessions signed by the juvenile suspects in the Dixmoor Five, Englewood Four, and other cases illustrates how race bias and discrimination can enter legal processing in the post–civil rights era. The Northwestern University Law School, Center on Wrongful Conviction of Youth, documented 18 false confessions by youth from 1986 to 1999. Each false confessor was African American. In the Englewood Four and Dixmoor Five cases, police interrogators coerced juvenile suspects to sign confession statements with fabricated references to well-known Black street gangs, drug trafficking, and gangster rap terminology. The content and language of the false confession narratives corresponded to common negative stereotypes of Black inner-city lawlessness and thus achieved the intended impact on attorneys, judges, and jurors: conviction.

While these dramatic examples of black box manufactured evidence may not be representative, it is a clear illustration of post–civil rights era racial discrimination against Black defendants. So, without lynch mobs, overt due process deprivations, or racially discriminatory legal presumptions, the wrongful conviction of innocent Black defendants charged with rape and other high crimes was the result. As noted by K. K. Russell (2001) and consistent with Leo's (2008) observations, race bias enters via informal, covert processing where law enforcement officials have discretion, and it is hidden from view and the official record (as in custodial interrogation). Therefore, racially coded messages and insinuations inserted in the confession narratives appeal to explicit and implicit racial biases (of jurors as well as judges), color the perception of evidence, and effectively seal convictions.

Only with the benefit of vigorous postconviction representation, coupled with exculpatory DNA, and aided by the fact that one legal center was involved with the representation of multiple cases, were these patterns across cases able to become apparent. The officers were not only scripting confession statements, but also there is evidence police officers were sharing and recycling elements of the false confession narratives and using them in several different cases (Drizin, 2013). Drizin noted the State of Illinois has now adopted a requirement that the entire interrogation in homicide and other serious felonies be electronically recorded. This reform should provide transparency and a record of where the incriminating elements in a confession originate and thus move the interrogation process out of the black box.

PATH DIVERGENCE

As noted in Chapter 2, two common and distinguishable paths in wrongful conviction in stranger rape are apparent: the capable victim, misidentification path as well as the incapacitated victim, false confession path. These two paths are observable regardless of the race/ethnicity of the defendants and victims. However, there are wrongful rape convictions that diverge from the two common paths. Two noteworthy cases illustrating the divergence are described here. Darryl Hunt was wrongfully convicted in the stranger rape and murder of a young white woman in North Carolina. The Byron Halsey case from New Jersey involved an intra-familial rape prosecution with incapacitated victims and false confession. While these cases diverged from the two common paths, they illustrate other types of erroneous formulations that mislead investigations and result in wrongful conviction.

Darryl Hunt: Incapacitated Victim, Misidentification by Witnesses Other Than the Victim

Debra Sykes, a white journalist, was murdered and raped in 1984 in the Winston-Salem area of North Carolina. She was found with 16 stab wounds, naked from the waist down, and with semen on her body. Reward money was offered for information about the offense (Stern & Sundberg, 2006; *Darryl Hunt—National Registry of Exonerations*, n.d.). Johnny Gray called the police and reported the attack though he identified himself as Sammy Mitchell. The next day, the police went to question Mitchell and also met Mitchell's friend, Darryl Hunt. A local man reported observing Sykes with an African American man on the morning of the crime. The description he provided was consistent with Hunt. Gray first identified another man as being with Sykes, but later, after Hunt became a suspect, Gray said it was Hunt. Hunt's girlfriend was arrested on an outstanding warrant and initially provided an alibi for Hunt. She later stated Hunt admitted committing the offense and then later recanted and refused to testify for the state.

Hunt was formally charged with murder, though not rape. Hunt was first convicted, and sentenced to life, in 1985 based on the state's witnesses that he was seen with Sykes on the morning of the offense and also seen leaving bloody towels in a local hotel bathroom. The first conviction was reversed by the North Carolina Supreme Court because the trial judge had allowed the state to present Hunt's girlfriend's incriminating statements although she had recanted the statements. At this point, Hunt rejected a plea offer to admit guilt and be released for time served. He proceeded to his second trial, with a change of venue resulting in a rural location with an all-white jury. The state's main two witnesses testified again as well as two jailhouse informants who testified Hunt admitted guilt while incarcerated. He was again sentenced to life in 1990. In 1994, DNA testing excluded him as the donor of the crime scene semen, but the state argued it did not prove innocence, and Hunt remained in prison. In 2004, the DNA was matched to Willard E. Brown, a local man who was serving time for another murder. Brown pled guilty to the offense. Hunt was exonerated and released in 2005.

In the investigation of the rape and murder of Deborah Sykes, the police were faced with a high-profile, white victim/Black defendant, stranger rape with a murdered (incapacitated) victim. Obviously, racial dynamics contributed to the investigation and prosecution of such an offense. The press and public reaction to this crime was dramatic, particularly since the victim was herself a journalist. The prosecution included black box manufactured evidence associated with Hunt's conviction at both trials. The black box nature of the investigation meant the circumstances that produced the incriminating statement and subsequent recantation from Hunt's girlfriend at the first trial are not known, as well as the two apparently erroneous witness identifications provided at each trial. The production of the two jailhouse informants at the second trial is a clear demonstration of black box, manufactured evidence. When Hunt was DNA excluded from the crime scene semen in 1994, the state used its authority to keep him imprisoned another 10 years under the theory he could have committed the rape and murder even though he had not deposited the semen. This specious formulation was asserted even though at trial the prosecutor relied on a thinly veiled appeal to overt and implicit racial bias (S.L. Johnson, 2001; S. L. Johnson, 1993) when he noted, "He [Hunt] spread those legs, right there, apart and he crawled down inside her and he raped and ravaged her, and deposited some thick yellow sickening fluid in her body" (Stern & Sundberg, 2006).

Byron Halsey: Incapacitated Victims, Coerced False Confession, Capital Prosecution

In 1985, Byron Halsey became the suspect in the rape and murder of his girlfriend's son and daughter, aged 8 and 7, respectively. Halsey was African American, as were the two children (Tyrone and Tina Urquhart). Without surviving victims to make identifications, the investigation was heavily reliant on obtaining confessions (M. B. Johnson & Drucker, 2009). As a cohabiting stepparent, Halsey was a likely suspect. His formal education was limited to the sixth grade, he was subjected to prolonged interrogation, and he was informed he had failed a polygraph. He subsequently made incriminating admissions that were clearly contrary to the physical evidence in the case. Two officers then sat with Halsey more than 5 hours preparing a written incriminating statement, which Halsey signed, consistent with available evidence.

The Halsey case was prosecuted as a double, intra-familial, sex murder. As is typical during the post–civil rights era, racial bias was not part of the official record. However, a photo of the dark, burly, and handcuffed Halsey was featured on the front page of the regional newspaper reporting the "depraved" rape and torture of the young children (Messick, 1985). The prosecutor announced he would seek the death penalty at a press conference where graphic x-rays displayed the nails that were driven in the male child's head. At trial, a state's witness who resided in the same boarding house as Halsey, the children, and the mother, testified he had driven Halsey across town on the night the children went missing. Also, one of the interrogating officers testified Halsey intentionally included erroneous content in his admissions to divert the investigation (consistent with the Inbau, Reid, Buckley, & Jayne, 2005 formulation).

In 1988, Halsey was found guilty of the lesser charges and thus spared a death sentence. His initial appeals were denied, but in 2006 with the assistance of the Innocence Project at the Cardoza Law School, DNA testing was conducted that cleared Halsey and matched Cliff Hall, the state's witness who testified at Halsey's trial (M. B. Johnson & Drucker, 2009). At that time, Hall was serving time for three separate sex crimes he committed after the death of Tyrone and Tina Urquhart.

This crime involved the double murder and rape of child victims. The moral violation associated with the offense was pronounced. Without a capable victim, the investigation relied on black box methods to produce a coerced false confession from a vulnerable suspect under the erroneous formulation it was an intra-familial offense. The premature commitment to the intra-familial theory of the crime, coupled with the aggressive capital prosecution, blinded the investigators from the actual perpetrator, who was in plain view. The Halsey prosecution also was characteristic of wrongful convictions in murder where the perpetrator frames an innocent (as described in Gross et al., 2005).

SUMMARY

Throughout US history, the legal definition and societal response to rape (and rape allegations) have been influenced by considerations of race. These considerations were consistently made to the detriment of Black defendants charged with rape. During the period of "legal" race-based enslavement, the definitions and penalties for rape varied based on the race of the perpetrator and victim. Following the Civil War (despite the equal protection embodied in Fourteenth Amendment), the notion of the "dangerous Black rapist" was created and promoted to undermine support for African American political and economic rights. Political violence in the form of mob lynching was commonly tolerated, if not abetted, by legal authorities. Black defendants were also vulnerable in sham trials, legal lynchings, where they were systemically deprived of basic due process protections and subjected to more severe penalties than similarly situated white defendants.

During the current post–civil rights period, racial discrimination against African American defendants charged with rape has been prohibited. However, Black defendants continue to endure an increased risk of wrongful conviction, related to the legacy of the dangerous Black rapist. This increased risk of wrongful conviction is most pronounced in Black defendant/white victim cases, where the prevailing sense of moral violation is commonly heightened among the largely white public. In addition, adverse bias against Black defendants is apparent in a variety of factors that are not part of the formal legal record. These include structural/systemic risks and disadvantage; explicit and implicit, adverse racial bias affecting investigators, prosecutors, judges, jurors, the press, and the public; and a lack of protection from cross-racial misidentification and all-white juries. These adverse effects operate through processes described as petit apartheid, where law enforcement authorities have relative discretion, the biases are largely hidden from public view (as in black box investigations), and decisions reinforce racially biased conceptions of deviance.

NOTES

1. In many cases, enslaved Black women were not protected from rape by Black men as well. Wriggins (1983) cited an 1859 ruling by the Mississippi Supreme Court that dismissed the rape charge facing a slave for the rape of a slave girl, noting there was no statute that applied to the rape of a female slave; see *George, a slave, v. State*, 37 *Miss. 306* (1859).
2. According to Sommerville, often it was consistent with the interest of well-to-do owners of enslaved Blacks to hire capable attorneys to defend them. Also, when

the complainants were white women of lower social class, support for a Black defendant might be increased in some quarters.

3. Except through penal consequences as noted in the Thirteenth Amendment, which abolished slavery and involuntary servitude "except as punishment for crime"; see Blackmon (2010), *Slavery by Another Name.*

4. *The New York Times* (1893) headline, "Another Negro Burned," is indicative of the popular acceptance of lynching violence. The article includes the insinuation of rape, and that was sufficient to prevent any protest about the mob torture and execution without trial.

5. The Sam Hose lynching was by no means the most cruel or brutal of the lynchings described by J. Allen et al. (2000).

6. Duster (1970) provided Wells's account of an African American rifle club that stood guard for three nights to prevent the lynching of three Memphis Black men charged with assaults on whites. When it was learned the detained men were safe, the rifle club stood down, and that night the arrested Black men were taken from the jail and lynched (also see Kinshasha, 2006).

7. The Without Sanctuary lynching photography can be viewed at http://withoutsanctuary.org.

8. In the film *Birth of a Nation*, a white woman fleeing a dishonorable attack by a Black man throws herself off a cliff.

9. In 1922, Mary Burnett Talbert organized the Anti-Lynching Crusaders at the request of the NAACP (blackpast.org, n.d.). In 1930, Jessie Ames Daniels organized the Association of Southern Women for the Prevention of Lynching (J. Allen et al., 2000).

10. See https://www.congress.gov/bill/109th-congress/senate-resolution/39.

11. Equally brutal, but less well known, was the 1944 lynching of Willie James Howard in Florida. Willie was a 15-year-old Black youth who sent a Christmas card and flirtatious letter a white girl. The girl's father and two other white men abducted Willie from his home at gunpoint. They then picked up Willie's father from his job. Willie and his father were taken to the Suwannee River. Willie was bound and given the option of being shot or thrown in the river. Crying, Willie fell off the river bank and drowned. The perpetrators presented an affidavit to the County Sheriff that they intended to have the father give Willie a whipping for the violation but Willie committed suicide. The father signed the affidavit. Three days later, Willie's family sold their home, moved to Orlando, and the father recanted the affidavit. Despite legal assistance from the NAACP, the perpetrators were not indicted (G. King, 2012; Green, 1999).

12. The Mann Act; see http://law2.umkc.edu/faculty/projects/ftrials/scottsboro/SB_BBates.html.

13. A similar overtly racist legal presumption characteristic of legal lynching indicated where attempted rape of a white woman was charged, a Black defendant's race could be considered an indication of criminal intent (see Wriggins, 1983, as well as Duru, 2004, citing the Alabama Supreme Court 1908 *Pumphrey v. State* ruling as derived from 1893 Georgia case law).

14. In Louisiana, while this "legal" framework for rape prosecution was in place, records indicate 335 African Americans suffered extralegal mob lynching between 1882 and 1948 (Patterson, 1951).

15. For instance, Willie McGhee and the Martinsville 7 defendants were eventually executed. Also, only one of the two adult Groveland defendants who were sentenced to death saw freedom again in his lifetime.

16. This undermining of democracy, a legacy of the 3/5s clause of the US Constitution, led Malcolm X to comment in 1964, "Of the 16 senatorial committees that run the Senate, 10 of them are in the hands of the southern segregationists. Of the 20 congressional committees that run the government, 12 of them are in the hands of southern segregationists and they going to tell you and me that the south lost the war" (X, 1964).

17. For instance, William Bernard Jackson, Calvin Johnson Jr., Bernard Webster, James Waller, Herman Atkins, and Kurt Bloodsworth were all misidentified by multiple eyewitnesses.

18. Note the distinction between suggestive police-directed eyewitness identification procedures referred to as "system" sources of misidentification versus event-related, "estimator," contributors to misidentification such as stress, distance and lighting, weapons focus, cross-racial identification challenge, and others.

19. Ironically, both these attacks resulted in the wrongful conviction of innocent Black defendants, Ronald Cotton and Darryl Hunt.

Serial Rapists and Wrongful Conviction

> . . . a system in which preventable errors are continually made and re-
> peated should not be tolerated.
> —ROBERT J. RAMSEY (2020, p. 144)

The Norfolk Four defendants (Danial Williams; Joe Dick, Jr.; Eric Wilson; and
Derek Tice [all naval sailors]) were officially exonerated by Governor's pardon
in 2017 (Reuters, 2017). The wrongful convictions followed the familiar incapacitated victim, false confession path even though it was an acquaintance rather
than a stranger rape. Death penalty threats were also a contributing factor in the
coerced false confessions. The prosecution of the Norfolk Four illustrates the
not uncommon outcome where a serial sex offender's crime results in wrongful
convictions of innocent defendants. The Norfolk Four case is especially noteworthy because the serial rapist's responsibility for the crime was well known at
the time of the trials, yet the erroneous outcome was ratified and sealed (Leo &
Davis, 2010; T. Wells & Leo, 2008). Governor Terry McAuliffe's pardon followed
substantial postconviction advocacy on behalf of the defendants and an October
2016 ruling by US District Judge John Gibney that vacated two of the convictions.
Due to procedural obstacles, the Governor's full pardon was the only way to clear
all four defendants (Reuters, 2017). Further details of the investigation and prosecution are provided in this chapter.

The chapter examines the phenomenon of innocent defendants convicted
of sexual assaults committed by serial rapists. These cases account for a significant portion not only of the wrongful convictions in sexual assaults, but also
of all confirmed wrongful convictions. These cases are principally concentrated
among "stranger rapes" and highlight the challenges faced by law enforcement in
investigating stranger rapes (the stranger rape thesis) as presented in Chapter 2.

"ERRORS" LEADING TO WRONGFUL CONVICTION IN SEXUAL ASSAULT

The primary focus of research on wrongful conviction has been on trial features and evidence (Leo, 2005). Psychologists and other researchers have made substantial contributions to understanding, preventing, and correcting wrongful convictions, principally in the areas of eyewitness misidentification (Lampien et al., 2012; G. L. Wells, 2006; Loftus, 2005; Cutler & Kovera, 2010); child suggestibility (Bruck & Ceci, 1995); and false confessions (Kassin, 2015; Kassin et al., 2010; Leo, 2008; Gudjonsson, 2003). Also, as noted in the Introduction, the advent of DNA applications to crime investigation has led to increased research demonstrating multiple forms of unreliable evidence, such as various types of "scientific" and "expert" testimony (Garrett & Neufeld, 2009; Dror & Bucht, 2012; Hsu, 2012); incentivized informant testimony (Neuschatz et al., 2012); and the process of discounting alibi evidence (Burke & Marion, 2012). These data indicate that in wrongful conviction, cases are developed against innocent defendants based on faulty and/or unreliable evidence. In this sense, the conviction of the innocent can be viewed as reflecting two groups of errors. Errors of omission (i.e., failure to identify and apprehend the actual offender) coupled with prosecuting an innocent defendant (an error of commission). Each of these two errors has various contributing sources, and arguably the first only becomes an error when associated with the second.

Confirmed wrongful convictions are concentrated in sexual assaults, and further disaggregation indicates they are primarily concentrated in stranger rapes. Recent literature on rape investigation highlighted several issues relevant to wrongful conviction in sexual assaults. In addition to detailing the severe, adverse consequences of rape and sexual assault (Basile & Smith, 2011), the rape investigation literature has devoted considerable attention to the consistent finding that most rapes are not reported to law enforcement authorities (Belknap, 2010). Also, among those reported, most are not prosecuted fully (Shaw, Campbell, & Cain, 2016; Alderden & Ullman, 2012; Lonsway & Archambault, 2012).

These findings have contributed to a substantial research focus on "rape attrition," that is why such a small proportion of rapes are prosecuted as felonies. Much of this research has examined the law enforcement decision-making process during rape investigation, that is how sexual assault reports are assessed and why cases fail to proceed to full prosecution. In many ways, this research focus is contrary to the focus of wrongful conviction research on factors that contribute to the prosecution of innocent defendants. As noted in Chapter 2, the criminal investigation literature focused on "crime control" is, by and large, a separate literature from the wrongful conviction literature focused on "due process," and the research in these two areas has had limited influence on each other.

RAPE ATTRITION

Menaker, Campbell, and Wells (2017) examined police decision-making and rape attrition, with a particular focus on the use of forensic science evidence (from sexual assault kits). Barrett and Hamilton-Giachritsis (2013) focused on decision-making by detectives in rape cases to identify factors associated with attrition as well as how victims are treated and regarded. Shaw et al. (2016) investigated police decision-making and rape case attrition using Social Dominance Theory (SDT) to highlight how police justify decisions not to pursue prosecution. Alderden and Ullman (2012) examined both police and prosecutorial decision-making at various stages in sexual assault investigation and resulting rape attrition. The consideration of wrongful conviction is absent from this literature. These researchers (Menaker et al., 2017; Barrett & Hamilton-Giachritsis, 2013; Shaw et al., 2016; Alderden & Ullman, 2012) referred to challenges associated with unreliable or false reports by rape complainants; however, false rape charges are not substantial contributors to wrongful conviction in sexual assault. Rather, wrongful conviction in sexual assault is related to faulty evidence (witness misidentifications, false confessions, and various types of associated secondary evidence) in cases where victims were clearly assaulted.

So, a major premise of the rape investigation literature has been the lack of full prosecution without consideration of the problem of prosecution of innocents. This likely stems from the fact that the number of confirmed wrongful convictions is minor in the context of the dramatically larger number of rape cases lost to attrition. However, since the conviction of innocents facilitates the actual perpetrators' continued attacks, the matter of wrongful conviction in sexual assault warrants attention in the rape investigation research literature and the broader crime control literature. Additionally, the rape attrition literature has focused principally on "capable" (surviving) rape victims, while a substantial number of wrongful convictions in sexual assault occur where the victim has been killed or is otherwise incapacitated, as noted in the Chapter 2 presentation of the stranger rape thesis and illustrated in material that follows.

Psychological research has demonstrated that stranger rapes present special difficulties in investigation (Slater et al., 2015; Santtila et al., 2005). When the victim had no prior relationship with the perpetrator, generating prospective suspects is a challenge, and reliable identification of the perpetrator is also an obstacle (M. B. Johnson et al., 2013; Castelle & Loftus, 2008; Innocence Project, 2009). It is well established that apprehended serial rape offenders are typically prosecuted for only a limited number of their offenses (Hazelwood & Warren, 1999). Thus, an additional contribution in this area is that many innocent defendants have been convicted of crimes committed by serial rape offenders.

In this context, 67 innocent defendants wrongly convicted of rapes committed by serial sex offenders are presented. Review of these cases reveals common obstacles and challenges faced by law enforcement in the investigation of rape, particularly stranger rape. The wrongful conviction of innocents produces substantial harm to defendants and their families (Wildeman, Costelloe, & Schehr,

2011; Grounds, 2004). Also, postconviction exoneration, which is the recognition and correcting of the wrongful convictions, often retraumatizes victims of the initial crime (Williamson, Stricker, Irazola, & Niedzwiecki, 2016; Irazola, Williamson, Stricker, & Niedzwiecki, 2013).

APPROACH

In identifying innocent defendants convicted of sexual offenses committed by serial sex offenders, the following approach was used: Only major sex offenses where force or threat of force was used are considered (that is excluding offenses such as voyeurism, frotteurism, exhibitionism, and harassment). Only cases where defendants were determined guilty by trial conviction or plea and later exonerated based on evidence of innocence are considered. Only cases where the actual sexual offender (typically named) had a conviction of at least one other sexual offense in addition to the one that led to the wrongful conviction are considered. For instance, the Beatrice Six defendants were wrongly convicted of a rape later DNA matched to Bruce Allen Smith (Pilger, 2016). While it is likely this was not Smith's lone sexual offense, because his official criminal history record does not include other sexual assault convictions, the Beatrice Six defendants are not included in the series. In defining stranger rape, the LeBeau (1987) classification approach (as presented in Chapter 2) is used, and *stranger rape* is defined as those instances where the victim had no prior contact with the perpetrator or where the perpetrator only became known to the victim just before the assault.

Using these criteria, 67 innocent defendants convicted of sexual offenses committed by 43 serial sexual offenders were identified. Several serial rapists (10) committed offenses that resulted in the wrongful conviction of multiple innocent defendants, in some instances related to one prosecution and in others connected to multiple prosecutions. Among the 67 innocent defendants convicted of sexual assaults committed by serial sex offenders, 63 of the cases are reported on both the Innocence Project (IP) and the National Registry of Exonerations (NRE) databases. Three cases (Edward Carter, Claude McCollum, and Randall Lynn Ayers) involved non–DNA-reliant exonerations and are reported on the NRE but not on the IP database. One case (William Bernard Jackson) is not identified in either of the two major wrongful conviction data sites but is well reported in other sources (*The New York Times*, 1982; Associated Press, 1983).

A primary shared characteristic of these crimes is that they were predominantly stranger assaults, despite data indicating the large majority of rape victims are attacked by assailants they know (Planty et al., 2013). That is, 50 of the 67 cases were prosecuted as stranger rapes, 10 were prosecuted as "acquaintance rapes," 4 were prosecuted as "intra-familial sexual assaults," and in 3 cases the prosecution formulation could not be determined. Some of these prosecutions reflected erroneous formulation of the relational aspect of the offense as elaborated in the following material. The large proportion of stranger assaults among innocents convicted of serious sexual crimes committed by serial rapists is consistent with the stranger rape thesis (Chapter 2), which describes obstacles inherent in the investigation of stranger rape. Thirty-one of the offenses were sexual assaults without homicide, and 36 were rape/murders. Appendix C presents the 67 innocents convicted of sexual assaults committed by serial rape offenders along with associated findings.

Examination of the 17 wrongful convictions that were other than stranger rape prosecutions suggests some particular challenges in investigation. All four cases that were prosecuted as intra-familial assaults shared incorrect formulation of the relational aspect. In the Kennedy Brewer, Levon Brooks, Byron Halsey, and Clarence Elkins prosecutions, innocent family members of the crime victims were convicted of offenses committed by serial rapists who were not family members. Thus, suggesting an early erroneous formulation of the relational aspect (i.e., an "anchoring effect"; Rossmo, 2006) became an obstacle to apprehending the actual perpetrator. Erroneous formulation of the relational aspect also contributed to the wrongful conviction of Jeffrey Deskovic, where the investigation and prosecution proceeded under the mistaken theory it was an acquaintance rape although it was actually a stranger rape. In the Ray Krone acquaintance assault prosecution, the actual perpetrator's relationship to the victim is not known. The acquaintance rape formulation in the Norfolk Four prosecutions was actually correct, though four innocents were nonetheless convicted (as described further in this chapter).

VICTIM STATUS PATHS

As reported in Chapter 2, review of wrongful convictions in sexual assault (excluding cases with child victims) reveals two common paths to the erroneous outcome. Cases with capable victims are associated with misidentification by the victim, while cases with incapacitated victims are associated with false confessions. While these two paths predominate among wrongful convictions in sexual assault, there are cases that diverge from these two common paths. This observation is readily apparent among the series of 67 defendants wrongly convicted of crimes committed by serial sexual offenders. As presented in Table 4.1, 41 defendants were

Table 4.1 VICTIM STATUS AND PRIMARY CONVICTION EVIDENCE AMONG (67) INNOCENTS CONVICTED OF SEXUAL ASSAULTS COMMITTED BY SERIAL SEXUAL OFFENDERS

Victim Status	Total	False Confessions	Eyewitness Misidentification	Circumstantial Evidence
Incapacitated victim cases	41[a]	34	6[b]	1
Capable victim cases	26	0	26[c]	0
N	67	34	32	1

[a] The 41 incapacitated victim cases are 36 convictions with murder and 5 convictions from an incapacitated victim (CPJ); [b] by other than victim; [c] by victim.

wrongly convicted of crimes with incapacitated victims, of which 34 resulted in wrongful convictions reliant on false confession evidence. The convictions of six defendants from incapacitated victim crimes were the result of misidentifications by witnesses other than the victim. In one incapacitated victim case (Robert Dewey), the primary conviction evidence was circumstantial. Twenty-six defendants were convicted of crimes with capable victims, and in each of these cases the wrongful conviction was associated with misidentification by the crime victim.

CASE ILLUSTRATIONS

Several cases presented in previous chapters illustrate sexual assaults committed by serial rape offenders that resulted in convictions of innocent defendants. Some of the cases are revisited here to underline the particular investigation challenges associated with serial rape perpetration that contributed to the erroneous outcome. This is followed by the introduction of additional wrongful convictions in sexual assaults associated with serial rape perpetration that were not presented in prior chapters. Combined, these cases illustrate wrongful conviction risk factors ("black box" investigation, manufactured evidence, erroneous formulation of the relational aspect) described in previous chapters as well as a distinct omission in investigation, the failure to investigate evidence of other sexual offending in the vicinity. These cases also illustrate the wrongful sexual assault conviction risks associated with the two distinct "victim status" paths. That is, where victims were killed or otherwise incapacitated, the primary evidence is false confessions, and where the sexual assault victim is capable of assisting with the investigation, the primary evidence is misidentification by the victim/witness.

PREVIOUSLY PRESENTED CASES

The Edward Carter wrongful conviction was presented in the Introduction. Carter was misidentified by the capable rape victim and imprisoned for 35 years prior to exoneration. As reported by Gross and Shaffer (2012), in addition to his verifiable alibi, Carter's exoneration was based on fingerprint evidence linking the crime to a serial rapist who committed other assaults in the vicinity. Gross and Shaffer (2012) did not report whether the serial rapist's other offenses occurred before or after the offense that led to Carter's wrongful conviction, but there is ample evidence to indicate early investigation of sexual offending in the vicinity could have led to Carter's acquittal or more timely exoneration.

As presented in Chapter 2, Steve Avery was wrongfully convicted of a 1985 sexual assault stemming from his misidentification by capable rape victim Penny Beerntsen. DNA testing in 2002 linked the attack on Beerntsen to Gregory Allen, who had committed a rape at the same location in 1983 (Chandler, 2006). Avery was misidentified via black box investigation methods involving a composite sketch, repeat presentation of Avery in mug shots, and a live lineup

(Lautenschlager, 2003), combined with the discounting of his substantial alibi evidence. Adequate investigation of prior sexual assaults in the vicinity could have prevented Avery's wrongful conviction or lengthy period of confinement.

The wrongful conviction of the Central Park Five defendants involved serial rape perpetration by a single offender that resulted in five wrongful convictions. In this case, with the incapacitated victim, the reliance on black box interrogation methods derailed investigation into rape offending in the immediate vicinity even though the "Eastside Rapist" had been the subject of considerable journalistic attention in the preceding months (Burns, 2011). Burns (2011, p. 125) commented, "While the investigation into the Central Park Jogger was ongoing, Matias Reyes (the 'Eastside Rapist') attacked at least five other women, all clustered on the East Side and within a mile of the location of the [Central Park Jogger's] rape." Burns and others (Ryan, 2002) noted the similarities in the manner of attack as well as the locale. However, rushed black box interrogation produced "confessions" within 36 hours of the discovery of the victimized jogger. No doubt the competition between investigative units, the Sex Crimes Unit versus the Homicide Unit, only contributed to compromising the efficiency of the investigation (Sullivan, 1992).

The William Bernard Jackson wrongful rape conviction illustrated Black defendant vulnerability to cross-racial misidentification, including multiple-eyewitness misidentification (MEM) by capable rape victims. In this case, the erroneous identification was ratified by an all-white jury. Interestingly, an investigator did correctly link an instant sexual assault with an earlier rape in the vicinity. As reported by Jackson (1983), while investigating a home invasion rape in Columbus, Ohio, the detective realized marked similarities with an assault 2 weeks earlier, only a mile away. After the first victim's description produced a composite sketch, she picked William Bernard Jackson's photo from a group of mug shots. The same detective then presented the photos to the second victim, and she reportedly also picked William Bernard Jackson. The detective had correctly connected the two offenses, but the prosecution mistakenly proceeded against an innocent defendant rather than the actual perpetrator.

Similarly, the cross-racial misidentification by a capable rape victim led to African American defendant Timothy Cole's wrongful conviction by an all-white jury. As noted, the defense sought to present evidence of rapes continuing in the vicinity after Cole's arrest, as well as the fingerprints from earlier rapes that did not match Cole. However, the trial judge ruled this evidence was inadmissible ("Timothy Cole—Innocence Project," n.d.). Examination of the pattern of sexual assault offending in the vicinity was relevant evidence with the potential to prevent Cole's wrongful conviction or support his postconviction appeals. The failure to recognize the relevance of this evidence contributed to the Cole's misery (and death), as well as the suffering of his family members. Also, the rape victim, who suffered for years with the trauma of the original assault, was retraumatized when she learned she had identified an innocent man (Kix, 2016; Williamson et al., 2016).

ADDITIONAL ILLUSTRATIONS

The Norfolk Four case introduced this chapter. The crime victim, Michelle Moore-Bosko, was raped, and murdered with multiple stab wounds, in her garden apartment home on July 7, 1997. The following day, Mrs. Bosko's husband, Billy, returned from a week at sea and discovered his wife's body. Billy went to his neighbor Danial Williams who called the police (Leo & Davis, 2010; Wells & Leo, 2008). There were no signs of forced entry, and the investigation proceeded under the assumption it was an acquaintance assault. Tamika Taylor, a friend of Michelle's who resided in the same apartment complex, suggested Williams was a suspect because he was attracted to Michelle.

Williams was subjected to an all-night interrogation, principally by Detective Robert Ford, and Williams "confessed" to murdering Michelle. Later, on July 9, Williams signed a revised confession statement to correspond to the autopsy report. In December, DNA results indicated Williams was excluded as the contributor of crime scene semen. This information was withheld from the defense ("The Confessions: Case Timeline," n.d.).

In January 1998, Williams' roommate, Joe Dick, Jr., was interrogated by Detective Ford. Dick confessed he and Williams committed the rape and murder. However, in March, Dick was also DNA excluded from the crime scene evidence. Interrogation by Ford continued, and Dick implicated Eric Wilson, who confessed, but Wilson was also DNA excluded. With further interrogation by Detective Ford, Dick named Derek Tice, who confessed to Ford and named two other assailants (Richard Palley and Geoff Farris), but Tice, Palley, and Farris were DNA excluded in August. Interrogation by Ford continued, and Tice identified another assailant, John Danser. Danser had a solid alibi, and under interrogation by Ford, Danser did not confess. On February 18, all seven men identified as assailants during interrogations were DNA excluded by more advanced DNA analysis.

The prosecution continued pretrial investigations and negotiations. On February 22, 1999, the police were given a copy of a threatening letter addressed to a young woman in the community. The letter was ostensibly written by Omar Ballard, and within the letter Ballard admitted he killed Michelle Bosko (Wells & Leo, 2008; Public Broadcasting System, n.d.). At the time, Ballard was serving a prison sentence for two offenses: an attack on a young woman (Melissa Morse) with a baseball bat on June 24, 1997, and the rape and beating of a 14-year-old teen on July 17, 1997. The first assault occurred at the apartment complex where Michelle Bosko resided, and the attack on the 14-year-old teen occurred within a mile of the residence. The rape and murder of Michelle Bosko occurred on July 7, 1997, which is within the 3-week interval of the two offenses. Ballard was thereafter DNA matched to the crime scene semen, and under interrogation by Ford reportedly admitted he murdered Michelle Bosko and acted alone.

On April 14, 1999, Danial Williams sought to withdraw his guilty plea but the motion was denied. Williams was subsequently sentenced to two life terms without parole. In May, the state withdrew the charges against Palley, Farris, and Danser due to lack of evidence.

On June 16, Eric Wilson proceeded to trial. Joe Dick testified he committed the crime along with Wilson, Williams, Tice, Palley, Farris, Danser, and Ballard, though according to Dick's testimony, Wilson did not stab Bosko. When called as a witness, Ballard exercised his right to silence. Wilson was found guilty of rape, acquitted of murder, and sentenced to 8.5 years. On September 8, 1999, Dick entered a guilty plea and was sentenced to two life terms.

On February 8, 2000, Derek Tice's trial began. Dick gave the same testimony he provided in Wilson's trial. The judge ruled the defense could not question Ballard about the confession letter. Ballard's earlier confession and evidence of Ballard's other assaults on women were ruled inadmissible, and the defense motion to call an expert on false confessions was denied. Tice was convicted of rape and murder and sentenced to two life terms. On March 22, Ballard pled to rape and capital murder and was sentenced to two life terms.

A few features warrant mention prior to presenting the matter of sexual assault offending in the vicinity. The wrongful convictions of the Norfolk Four were characteristic of the reliance on coerced confessions (black box methods) in sexual assaults with incapacitated victims as described in Chapter 2. The multiple false confessions were enabled by the unrecorded, secret interrogation procedure and further facilitated by coercive death penalty threats in a state with frequent executions. In addition, the primary interrogator, Detective Robert Ford, was noted to be especially aggressive (Leo & Davis, 2010; Wells & Leo, 2008). Another noteworthy element was the apparent "internalized false confession" of Norfolk Four defendant Joe Dick, Jr., which facilitated his presentation of (false) incriminating testimony for the state at both the Eric Wilson and the Derek Tice trials. Reliable accounts indicate Dick did exhibit the rare "internalized false confession" (Wells & Leo, 2008; "The Confessions: The Timeline," n.d.), meaning, as described by Kassin (2007), for a considerable period of time he came to believe he committed the crime though he initially had no memory of the act. However, Dick's delivery of evidence for the prosecution can reasonably be explained as merely self-interest given his predicament. That is, even if his confession had been compliant, rather than internalized, the prosecution could have coerced the same trial testimony from him with the threat of death penalty exposure for failure to cooperate.

Postconviction review clearly demonstrates Ballard was the sole perpetrator. This was consistent with Ballard's pretrial secondary confession letter, the DNA evidence, Ballard's admissions prior to trial and was supported by his offense history. Ballard's role in the incrimination of the Norfolk Four defendants was orchestrated by the prosecution to support and preserve the prior erroneous investigation and secured by the state's threat of execution. The outstanding omission in the investigation of the July 7, 1997, rape and murder of Michelle Bosko was the record of sex offending in the vicinity. This evidence points toward Ballard as the sole offender and points away from the coerced confession admissions by the Norfolk Four, which were also undermined by the DNA evidence. Investigation of the record of recent sexual offending in the vicinity would reveal Ballard had a prior friendly relationship with Michelle Bosko, which would account for the lack of forced entry to her apartment. Michelle Bosko, and her husband Billy, had actually sheltered Ballard in their apartment when he was being threatened with a retributive attack following his June 24 assault on Melissa Morse. According to the *Frontline* documentary ("The Confessions: The Timeline," n.d.), during pretrial investigation, Danial Williams' attorney was granted $1,000.00 to investigate crimes in the community, but the money was never used.

Further, Ballard was an African American from New Jersey, a high school dropout with a lengthy history of criminal offending. He was raised in a series of foster care placements following separation from his mother, who was drug involved and allegedly a prostitute (Wells & Leo, 2008). The idea that Ballard committed the offense along with the four white naval sailors, who had no history of criminal offending, is highly remote at best. Whether Joseph Dick's internalized false confession was sufficient to cause police and prosecutors to actually believe their theory of multiple offenders in the attack on Michelle Bosko remains an unanswered question.

Commenting on the Norfolk Four wrongful convictions, former FBI Special Agent Gregg McCrary noted,

> Sexual homicides are very rare. In that year, 1997, in the United States, based on FBI statistics, there were 67 rape-murders. . . . That's out of over 15,000 murders. . . . So, someone who is sexually violent is a very unusual sort of crime. So, you need to look for any prior similar crimes at all. And here we had this brutal rape and murder. And then three weeks later, another brutal rape, but not a murder, a beating. But then we had the beating of a woman just before this, 100 feet from Michelle Bosko's apartment. They [the police investigators] ignored that. ("The Confessions: The Timeline," n.d.)

Julius Ruffin, a Black defendant, was misidentified by the white victim of a December 1981 knifepoint home invasion, stranger rape in Norfolk, Virginia. In this case, the misidentification was not linked to black box investigation measures. It was actually spontaneous: The white victim (Ann Meng) encountered Ruffin on an elevator at her job, 6 weeks after the December 12, 1981, assault (Newsome, 2007). Meng was positive Ruffin was the attacker. Reportedly, Meng then contacted the police and subsequently selected Ruffin via a voice identification procedure. Despite inconsistencies between Meng's initial description of the attacker and Ruffin's appearance, as well as Ruffin's several alibi witnesses, the prosecution proceeded to trial. After two trials with deadlocked, racially divided juries, the prosecution used peremptory challenges to seat an all-white jury and obtained a conviction (Acker, 2013). Ruffin was imprisoned for 21 years before he was DNA excluded by crime scene evidence that was matched to Aaron Doxie III. Two months before Meng's assault, Doxie was given a suspended sentence for the attempted rape of an 11-year-old girl in Norfolk. In March 1983, Doxie was charged with burglary and rape with a knife and subsequently convicted.

DNA testing in 2002 not only identified Doxie as the perpetrator of the assault on Meng, but also DNA matched Doxie to two August 1981 Norfolk rapes that resulted in the wrongful conviction of Arthur Lee Whitfield (Acker, 2013).

Ricardo Rachell was wrongly convicted of the stranger rape of a 10-year-old boy in Houston, Texas. The offense occurred on October 20, 2002. The child victim was approached by a man on a bike, who offered $10 for help with cleaning trash. The child was taken to an abandoned house and anally raped by the perpetrator. The child ran crying and reported to his mother a man tried to kill him (Acker, 2013). When interviewed by police, the child and a 6-year-old friend described the man on the bike only as a Black man about 30 years old.

The following day, the child's mother observed Rachell near their home and suspected he might be the assailant. Rachell had a marked facial deformity secondary to a shotgun injury and was known as "Scary Man" (Acker, 2013, p. 1662) in the neighborhood. The mother returned with the child and the child identified Rachell as the offender. The police were notified, and Rachell was apprehended. The child then identified Rachell as he was seated in a patrol car. At this time, the child reported the sexual nature of the assault, and a rape kit was taken. Later, the child victim and the 6-year-old friend identified Rachell from a photo spread ("Ricardo Rachell—Innocence Project," n.d.).

Rachell was arrested October 24, 2002. He asserted his innocence and voluntarily offered DNA samples. In the course of the next year while Rachell was in jail, there were three sexual assaults on preadolescent boys by a man riding a bicycle in the community. Rachell was convicted at trial in June 2003 based on the identifications of the two witnesses (MEM).

In November 2003, Andrew Hawthorne was arrested for a sexual attack against a boy. Hawthorne lived 2 miles from Rachell. Hawthorne was subsequently charged with three separate offenses against boys where he rode a bicycle and offered money for help with jobs. According to Acker (2013), officers involved in Hawthorne's arrest had also investigated the case against Rachell. While the police did not make the connection, Rachell asserted Hawthorne was the offender in his case and sought DNA testing. Though the process was delayed, in 2008 Rachell was excluded as the perpetrator, and the offense DNA was matched to Hawthorne. As Acker (2013) pointed out, had the DNA testing occurred in 2002, it would have been readily matched to Hawthorne, a registered sex offender whose DNA profile was on record at the time. This would have prevented Hawthorne's subsequent attacks on children.

David Vasquez was wrongly convicted of a 1984 rape/murder in Virginia. The prosecution followed the incapacitated victim, false confession path, and Vasquez was vulnerable secondary to intellectual limitations. Also, erroneous eyewitness testimony was provided by witnesses other than the victim ("David Vasquez—National Registry of Exonerations," n.d.; Acker, 2013). Death penalty threats contributed to a false guilty plea (M. B. Johnson & Cunningham, 2015).

The victim, a 32-year-old Arlington, Virginia, lawyer, suffered a home invasion rape and murder sometime after 10:00 p.m. on January 23, 1984. Her naked body was discovered 2 days later, in the basement with her hands tied behind her back.

The police received two calls suggesting Vasquez was a suspect. On January 29, it was reported the "creepy" Vasquez was seen in the neighborhood on the evening of January 23 ("David Vasquez—National Registry of Exonerations," n.d.). The next day, a caller reported Vasquez was seen in the neighborhood after the body was discovered, and he seemed unusually disinterested in the crime.

Vasquez was interrogated by two officers on February 4 without *Miranda* warnings. Vasquez denied involvement, but when presented with false incriminating evidence made incriminating statements. Two days later, Vasquez was questioned further following oral *Miranda* warnings. Vasquez maintained his innocence but provided dream content that was considered to be incriminating. The following day, questioning resumed after written *Miranda* warnings. Vasquez provided the incriminating dream content again. The judge ruled that given the written *Miranda* warnings, the incriminating aspects of the third interrogation were admissible.

Even though Vasquez was serologically excluded from the crime scene semen, the prosecution proceeded to trial under the theory Vasquez had an accomplice. A day before trial, on advice from defense counsel, Vasquez entered an Alford plea to avert a death sentence if found guilty.

Three years later, a 44-year-old woman was raped and strangled in the same Arlington neighborhood. One of the detectives who had questioned Vasquez was assigned the case. Investigators initially believed this offense was committed by Vasquez's accomplice. However, they learned of more than a dozen similar unsolved rapes (and rape/murders) in that area of Virginia dating back to 1983. Survivors of assaults described a slim, African American assailant who used a knife and cord to subdue victims. One investigator noted there were no offenses from January 1984 to September 1987. Proceeding from this observation, the investigator determined the perpetrator was likely Timothy Spencer, who was incarcerated during the period when there were no offenses. DNA samples were secured from Spencer and matched to crime scene semen in the series of rapes. He was convicted in four cases, sentenced to death, and executed in 1994. Suggesting that after committing the rape/murder that resulted in Vasquez's wrongful conviction, Spencer committed at least rape/murders and several rapes with surviving victims before his apprehension via examination of a rape offending pattern in the vicinity. There was insufficient DNA to link Spencer to the semen from the rape that resulted in Vasquez's conviction but due to the remarkable similarity in the crimes, Vasquez was pardoned by Virginia Governor Baliles in 1989.

SUMMARY

This chapter examined the phenomenon of innocent defendants convicted of sexual assaults committed by serial rapists. Sixty-six cases were identified from the IP and the NREs web listings, and one additional case came from other published sources. The 67 cases were predominantly stranger rape assault prosecutions (50). There were 10 cases prosecuted as acquaintance assaults, 4 cases prosecuted as intra-familial assaults and 3 cases where the prosecution formulation was un-clear. Among the other than stranger rape prosecutions, a common error in in-vestigation was incorrect assessment of the relational aspect of the offense, such as proceeding under an assumption the offense was committed by an acquaint-ance or a family member and failing to consider evidence of a stranger assault. Two common paths in wrongful conviction in sexual assaults were also apparent. Cases with incapacitated victims were likely dependent on false confessions, and cases with capable victims were the product of misidentifications by the offense victims. Only 7 of the 67 cases did not follow one of the two paths.

The primary focus of wrongful conviction research has been on trial features (misidentifications, false confessions, other unreliable evidence, and official mis-conduct). This chapter focused on offense type rather than trial evidence. In examining sexual assaults as an offense type, available data revealed wrongful convictions were disproportionally associated with stranger rape rather than ac-quaintance or intra-familial assaults. Each wrongful conviction reflected a failure to identify and apprehend the actual offender, coupled with prosecution of inno-cent defendants. While the record of wrongful conviction in sexual assault has been growing, as reflected on the IP and NRE web sites, the issue of offense type (the increased risk of wrongful conviction in stranger rape) has been largely ab-sent in the wrongful conviction, as well as the rape investigation, literatures. In fact, a primary focus of rape investigation literature has been on rape attrition, why more cases are not prosecuted fully rather than the virtual opposite question, why rape cases are prosecuted against innocent defendants.

The concentration of stranger rapes among the 67 innocent defendants convicted of sexual assaults committed by serial sex offenders is consistent with the four-part stranger rape thesis, introduced in Chapter 2. The prevailing re-sponse to stranger rape is a pronounced "moral outrage," experienced by law en-forcement officers as well as the community at large. There is thus an associated pressure on law enforcement for swift apprehension. Also, the circumstances of stranger rape, where the victim had no prior relationship with the offender, means it is difficult to formulate a motive and generate potential suspects. A third ele-ment in the stranger rape thesis is the obstacles to reliable identification when the victim was either incapacitated or had no prior relationship with the offender. The fourth part is moral correction, precipitated by the sense of moral violation inherent in the crime. The cognitive and emotional reaction to the offense is to restore justice through apprehension and adjudication of the offender. The pursuit of moral correction can lower the threshold in the evaluation of evidence of guilt.

The characteristics of stranger rape, that is the moral outrage response and associated features, precipitate and magnify the operation of various processes described by researchers as "tunnel vision," "confirmation bias," "misinforma-tion" effects, "evidence corruption," and "anchoring effects," which have been used in the literature to account for the erroneous decision-making observed in wrongful conviction. The data and analysis presented here suggest these factors or processes are more pronounced given the circumstances of certain types of crimes (i.e., sexual assaults in general and stranger rapes in particular), but certainly not exclusive to sexual assaults or stranger rapes. The focus on sexual assault, and stranger rape in particular, merely provides a means to illustrate that offense characteristics likely contribute to increased risk of wrongful conviction.

These findings suggest further examination of wrongful conviction, focused on the differential challenges presented in the investigation of different crimes (and subtypes of crime), can enhance the available knowledge in the field and contribute to remedies or recommendations. Findings and concepts from this research can provide guidance for both criminal investigation and prosecution as well as criminal defense effectiveness. The phenomena of moral outrage and moral correction are elaborated further in the Chapter 6, presentation of Concepts, Processes, and Models in Wrongful Conviction.

The review of innocent defendants convicted of crimes committed by serial sex offenders highlights several sources of error in the investigation of these offenses. A substantial literature has addressed misidentifications (Lampien et al., 2012; Loftus, 2005; Cutler & Kovera, 2010) and false confessions (Kassin, 2015; Kassin et al., 2010; Leo 2008; Gudjonsson, 2003) as primary sources of unreliable evidence in wrongful conviction. This literature also includes various proposed remedies designed to reduce and prevent wrongful conviction. The findings reported here link false confessions and misidentifications to victim status in sexual assault cases. The connection to victim status suggests how criminal investigation is influenced by these sources of evidence. It is critical to examine the pretrial investigative process because lessons from wrongful conviction cases indicate erroneous formulations and assumptions in investigation can produce unreliable evidence that is accepted uncritically by jurors (as well as by courts as a basis for false guilty pleas). In this regard, the term *black box investigation* was introduced to highlight the lack of transparency, the lack of objective recording of the processes that result in witness identifications, as well as incriminating statements from interrogation. This black box characteristic applies as well to the production of "analyst" and "expert" evidence (Dror & Bucht, 2012; Garrett & Neufeld, 2009), incentivized informant testimony (Neuschatz et al., 2012), and other types of prosecution evidence in many cases.

Further, specifically regarding misidentifications, among the 67 innocent defendants wrongfully convicted of crimes committed by serial rapists, 26 were misidentified by the rape victim. The prominent role of eyewitness misidentification in wrongful conviction is well established, and as noted here research-informed recommendations to reduce this form of error have been generated. The available literature indicates there are two (general) sources of misidentification: actual victims who are unable to reliably identify the assailant (the larger source) and complainants who make false rape allegations (a smaller source). Among the cases reported in this chapter, none of the wrongful convictions was related to false rape charges, while 26 of the 67 cases were associated with misidentification by the rape victim.

The rape investigation literature suggests law enforcement investigators focus attention on identifying false reports but are less effective in identifying the larger source of error, misidentifications by victims who were actually assaulted. In the investigation of rape, especially the interviewing and assessment of victims/complainants, it is critical that a supportive environment is provided to encourage victims to come forward and report assaults. It is also important for such reports to be evaluated to rule out (intentionally) false reports, as well as to determine if reliable identifications of assailants can be made where there is an actual assault. The difficult challenge for investigators is to be supportive of complainants while also rigorously evaluating complaints. This points to a need for research-informed recommendations to improve the interviewing and assessment of sexual assault complaints.

Two additional factors contributing to the 67 wrongful convictions warrant attention. The first is the erroneous assessment of the relational aspect of the offense, that is, the relationship of the offender to the rape victim. As illustrated, an inaccurate formulation regarding this aspect of a crime can mislead an investigation. However, especially when the rape victim is incapacitated, it can be very difficult to know with certainty the relationship the victim had with the offender. It is critical for investigators to maintain an open mind and recognize that assessment of the relational aspect is merely hypothetical and may warrant revisiting as contrary evidence emerges.

The second source is an error of omission, which is failure to investigate the pattern of sexual offending in the vicinity. As described, this omission contributed to many wrongful convictions in sexual assaults as well delays in the exoneration process in several cases. This observation is offered with recognition that reliably linking serial rape, or even the rarer serial rape/murder, offenses can be quite challenging. This is demonstrated in the sexual assault investigation literature where efforts to empirically establish consistency and distinctiveness in serial sex offending are proceeding (Slater et al., 2015; Harbers et al., 2012).

Rossmo (2009) also illustrated the challenge when he described two child sexual assault/murders where the victims were strangled and the bodies were transported and concealed. While these offenses might appear to be linked, closer examination would reveal a 3-year-old male victim versus a 14-year-old female victim, anal versus vaginal assault, manual versus ligature strangulation, short transport on foot versus longer transport by car, and concealment in a dumpster versus a river. These features suggest no linkage. However, ongoing investigation of patterns of sex offending in the vicinity can prevent wrongful conviction in some cases, as well as the associated harms to the innocent defendant's family and loved ones; it can prevent further crimes by the actual offenders; and it can protect crime victims from misidentifying innocents with the associated distress and trauma that will occur at exoneration. Research findings (Williamson et al., 2016) and personal accounts from capable victims who misidentified innocents as their rapists (Kix, 2016; Newsome, 2009; Thompson-Cannino, Cotton, & Torneo, 2009; Green, 2014) demonstrate the trauma associated with learning the misidentification contributed to wrongful imprisonment can be substantial.

Child Sexual Abuse Hysteria

In the Kern County community of Bakersfield, California, 41-year-old carpenter John Stoll was convicted in 1985 on 17 counts of child molestation and sentenced to 40 years in prison. The alleged victims were Stoll's 6-year-old son and other young boys who frequently played at Stoll's home (Jones, 2004; Nachman & Hardy, 2009).

In August 1985, Ileana Fuster, 18 years old, pled guilty to multiple counts of child sexual abuse in Dade County, Florida (Nathan & Snedeker, 1995). Ileana operated an in-home child care service in a Miami suburb. Prosecutors had elicited reports from more than 20 children implicating Ileana and her husband in rape and related charges. Ileana was sentenced to 10 years.

In a New Jersey bedroom community, 25-year-old Margaret Kelly Michaels was convicted in 1988 of 115 of 163 counts of sexual abuse of 19 preschool children. Michaels had been employed less than a year as a teacher in a church-based child care center in the New York City suburb. Michaels was given a 47-year sentence (Rosenthal, 1995; Bruck & Ceci, 1995).

In 1991, Robert Kelly, owner with his wife of the Little Rascals Day Care Center in Edenton, North Carolina, went on trial for 100 counts of child sexual abuse. Twelve children testified for the prosecution as well as several parents and expert witnesses, who found evidence consistent with abuse. Kelly was convicted on 99 counts and sentenced to consecutive life terms ("Robert Kelly—National Registry of Exonerations," n.d.).

Beginning in the early 1980s and continuing into the 1990s, there was a series of wrongful convictions associated with what has come to be called a "child sexual abuse hysteria" (Gross et al., 2005) that emerged in the United States (de Young, 2004; Nathan & Snedeker, 1995; Nachman & Hardy, 2009). In their 2012 review of US exonerations, Gross and Shaffer (2012) pointed out more than 150 adults were charged in these cases, with more than 70 convictions. Gross and Shaffer noted while some very small proportion may have been guilty of some offense, the great majority were completely innocent but deprived of a fair trial due to the hysteria that infected portions of the public and many professionals. As noted in the Introduction, there is good reason to expect there are many other defendants from these prosecutions who unfortunately have been unable to establish their innocence. The National Registry of Exonerations (n.d.) lists 59 defendants convicted during this prosecution hysteria who have since been exonerated. The exonerated defendants and features of the prosecutions are listed in Appendix D. The allegations in many of these cases emerged from day care centers, and several involved accusations of vaguely defined satanic abuse (G. S. Goodman, Qin, Bottoms, & Shaver, 1994).

In this chapter, the phenomenon of child sexual abuse hysteria and the prosecutions associated with these cases are examined. The prosecutions warrant attention and close analysis. While these cases are different in certain respects from the wrongful convictions in sexual assaults presented in previous chapters, they clearly are additional examples of wrongful conviction in sexual assault. The child sexual abuse hysteria cases were, by and large, "false rape charge"—"no-crime"—cases. Thus, they differ from the prosecutions covered in previous chapters in which victims were indeed sexually assaulted but innocent defendants, rather than the actual perpetrators, were convicted. In these no-crime cases, the convictions were typically dependent on testimony from purported child victims as well as unreliable opinions from child abuse experts. The convictions were largely absent biologically testable or other physical evidence, which were common routes to establishing innocence in many of the other wrongful convictions reported in other chapters. Thus, convincing evidence of innocence may be lacking in one or another of these cases. However, when viewed as a series, the pattern and processes in the prosecutions illustrate the vulnerability of defendants when sexual assault allegations are raised. The child sex abuse hysteria cases share with the wrongful convictions described in prior chapters a heavy reliance on "black box" methods to manufacture evidence, but the evidence is false accusations from presumed child victims and supporting testimony from "experts" rather than the misidentifications, false confessions, and associated secondary evidence that are apparent in the cases reported in Chapters 2, 3, and 4.

The notion of "social hysteria" and "moral panic" refers to "religious and political witch hunts, temperance movements and drug panics, anti-pornography and censorship campaigns, law and order crusades and public health battles," which seek to define moral boundaries, authority, and regulations (de Young, 2004, p. 3). Gardner (1991) referred to a "sexual abuse hysteria" that emerged in the 1980s commonly associated with claims in contested divorce. Nathan and Snedeker (1995) suggested that a more accurate and less gendered description of the phenomenon is "mass sociogenic illness," and they described a localized episode from Georgia in 1988 when the children of parents who mistakenly believed there was a gas leak in an elementary school developed associated symptoms (Philen et al., 1989).

It is difficult to identify all the elements that contributed to the child sexual abuse hysteria, but certain factors clearly played a role. Reactions to the social liberalism of the 1960s coupled with both the ascendancy and doubts about feminism and gender roles contributed to social anxieties that were often disruptive to marriages. Day care centers became both actual and symbolic institutional representations of these anxieties. Public day care provided an avenue for women to pursue equal workforce participation, yet many women struggled with doubt about leaving their tender age children with strangers. These anxieties were increased where these women had husbands who opposed their wives' workforce participation or mothers (and/or mothers-in-law) who frowned on public day care. Many women harbored their own guilt feelings about leaving their children with others, particularly among middle-class and professional families where public child care was an option rather than a necessity. Thus, in many ways public day care was threatening to the common (patriarchal) aspects of middle-class social life.

These anxieties were further aggravated by contributions from literature and the media. Several authors cited the contribution of *Michelle Remembers* (M. Smith & Padzer, 1980), an ostensibly true account published by a young woman and her psychiatrist of recovered childhood memories of satanic abuse at the hands of the author's mother. By the end of the decade, *Michelle Remembers* was recognized as completely fictionalized (Nathan & Snedeker, 1995; D. Allen & Midwinter, 1990), but the story's penetration and influence within the culture had already occurred. *Michelle Remembers* was only one of several similar contributors to the hysteria. *Kiss Daddy Goodnight* (L. Armstrong, 1978), *Father's Days* (Brady, 1979), *Daddy's Girl* (C. V. Allen, 1980), and *I Never Told Anyone* (Bass & Thornton, 1983) were others. In January 1984, ABC-TV reached an audience of 60 million with its broadcast presentation *Something About Amelia*. This dramatization presented an affluent family where the father sexually abused the teenage daughter (Nathan & Snedeker, 1995). The following month, the Manhattan Beach, California, McMartin preschool sex abuse case became national headline news (Gross & Shaffer, 2012; Nathan, 2005; Nathan & Snedeker, 1995). Originally, seven defendants faced 321 counts of sexual abuse against children. After 20 months of pretrial hearings, a 3-year trial began that became one of the most costly and lengthy criminal trials in US history. Ultimately, there were no convictions, but the substantial media coverage demonstrated and contributed to the prevailing anxiety about hidden child sexual abuse.

The backlash reaction to 1960s social liberalism was pronounced in law enforcement circles. Among elements in law enforcement there developed a belief that widespread and organized groups or "rings" of child sex abusers and/or pornographers were operating in the United States. Some believed this was tied to satanic beliefs and practices. Both the US Justice Department and the FBI sponsored conferences and seminars that disseminated alerts of this type to law enforcement and child protective agency personnel (Nathan & Snedeker, 1995). In this way, law enforcement concern also became both a contributor and a product of child sexual abuse hysteria.

A review of these cases revealed a recurring pattern in the prosecutions. A complaint/report from a young child emerged, often via a parent. For instance, in the Margaret Kelly Michaels case, a 4-year-old child from the Wee Care Center reportedly remarked, "That's what my teacher does to me at nap time . . . " (Rabinowitz, 1990, p. 54). Similarly, in the Ileana Fuster prosecution, a 3-year-old child from Country Walk Child Care reportedly said, "Ileana kisses all the baby's bodies"

(Nathan & Snedeker, 1995). Parents of other children at the day care center were informed an investigation was initiated. Often in these cases, there are reports in the press. Moreover, the parents are "educated" about child sexual abuse, asked to question their children about abuse, and also directed to observe their children for signs of abuse (though actually there are no reliable behavioral signs of sexual abuse). In some cases, parents were law enforcement officials or had close personal ties to law enforcement. As noted, during this period law enforcement authorities in many communities received training and related alerts about child sex abuse rings, child pornography, and satanic ritual abuse.

Parents who believed their children were abused, as well as those who were doubtful but concerned, sent the children to therapists for evaluation or treatment. In some cases, these therapists harbored preconceived notions abuse had occurred and/or were selected and being paid by state authorities. These therapists then "discover," elicit, or manufacture via suggestive interviewing (see Bruck & Ceci, 1995, as discussed in the material that follows) additional reports of abuse, often naming other children as victims, who would then be questioned by parents, child protection authority (CPA) specialists, and police. As a result of the continual and repeated questioning by authorities (parents, police, CPA specialists, and therapists) and the ambiguity of the indicators of sexual abuse, the number and bizarre nature of complaints expanded. Also, as a result of the questioning by officials and parents, as well as the parents' understandable anxiety, children who were never abused began to exhibit symptoms.

Much of the questioning by police, CPA specialists, therapists, and (to the extent that they conveyed their presumptions to) parents, was guided by "child sexual abuse discovery theories" organized around the "believe the children"[1] premise. A critical look at the premise, and resultant evaluation approach, indicates it meant in effect believe child reports that provide incriminating evidence but disbelieve child reports that are contrary the prosecution case. So, evaluators were trained to believe the children when the children make accusations suggesting sexual abuse because children do not lie or do not fabricate detailed sexual abuse allegations. However, if the children denied abuse or recanted abuse, they were probably doing so because they had been threatened or otherwise feared retaliation from their abusers. In these situations, the children should not be believed. Further, due to the fears harbored by abused children, they often will not openly report sexual abuse and have to be questioned repeatedly over a period of time, with direct leading questions because if they are not asked directly, they will not tell. That is, the children needed to be assured the examiner was willing to discuss sexual content before the children will tell. Therefore, the interviewer has to introduce sexual material into the interview, such as through the use of anatomically detailed dolls or drawings.

This orientation results in (intentional and inadvertent) suggestive and biased interviews and often coercive investigative interviews (described in material that follows). According to child sexual abuse discovery theories, this perspective and approach are necessary to protect the children from sexual abusers. However, the reliability of the resultant accusations will be questionable, particularly when there is no objective recording of the interviews that illicit the accusations (Bruck & Ceci, 1995).

By the mid-1990s, the psychosocial processes that converged to create false accusations of sexual assaults by young children were well researched and documented (Bruck & Ceci, 1995). Dissemination of this material to the courts was critical to the exoneration of many defendants convicted during the child sexual abuse hysteria prosecutions. An amicus brief citing controlled research (Bruck & Ceci, 1995; Rosenthal, 1995) submitted to the New Jersey Supreme Court in the review of the Margaret Kelly Michaels conviction clarified what had been difficult to conceptualize for many. When approached by interviewers with preconceived bias, many young children will provide information to confirm the bias. By injecting a certain emotional tone into the interview, by asking certain questions repeatedly, by inadvertently supplying (mis)information, and by selectively rewarding some while ignoring other responses, the adult's actions could shape responses from children. Further, the research demonstrated that once children incorporated the misleading suggestions and information, adults (even those experienced in interviewing children) could not distinguish genuine memories from those that were a product of suggestion and misinformation (Bruck & Ceci, 1995). Unfortunately, research findings indicate such false beliefs and "memories" may persist indefinitely. The resultant harm to the wrongfully convicted is apparent. The resultant harm to the integrity of the legal system is also a matter of concern (where it can harm legitimate prosecutions). There is also harm to children who grow up with an internalized (false) belief that they were sexually abused (Rabinowitz, 1990; Jones, 2004; Chammah, 2017).

It was not just lay jurors who were misled by false accusations elicited from young children. It was also the professionals closest to the case whose evaluation of the evidence became so distorted. The threshold for acceptance and evaluation of evidence was lowered by the sexual assault allegations, illustrating the moral outrage—moral correction process—described in Chapter 2. The pervasive, though hidden, child sexual abuse menace, coupled with anxieties and fears associated with public day care, contributed to the adverse outcomes. Neither the advanced training of psychologists and therapists nor the procedural training of lawyers and judges helped them recognize the manufactured and unreliable nature of the evidence.

ILLUSTRATIVE CASES

John Stoll

John Stoll's was merely one of several child sexual abuse hysteria prosecutions from Kern County, California, in the 1980s. The allegations against John Stoll did not emerge in the context of a day care center but rather child custody related to divorce. It is well documented in journalistic sources (Jones, 2004) that Kern County became an epicenter for these prosecutions (Nathan & Snedeker, 1995;

Nachman & Hardy, 2009). Stoll and his ex-wife Ann Karlan had joint custody of their 6-year-old son, Jed. On June 10, 1984, Stoll's ex-wife reported she believed her son had been molested by Grant Self,[2] a tenant who rented Stoll's pool house. Police began an investigation into whether the child had been abused by his father or any adult (Jones, 2004; Nathan & Snedeker, 1995). In a series of interviews, Jed reported sexual abuse by Marjorie Grafton, her boyfriend Tim Palomo, Grant Self, and eventually his father, John Stoll. Five of Jed's friends (aged 6–8) who spent time at the Stoll's home were also interviewed. With the use of suggestive and coercive methods, allegations against the four defendants were elicited.

Despite inconsistencies among the allegations, the four defendants were arrested. Prior to trial, the judge denied a defense request to have the children medically examined for evidence of abuse, and also ruled the defense could not present evidence by a psychologist that Grafton and Palomo were not likely predators. In September 1985, a jury convicted all four defendants based on the testimony of the six children.

In 1989, an appeals court reversed the convictions of Grafton and Palomo based on the exclusion of the psychological evidence and limitations of other state evidence. The Northern California Innocence Project began investigating Stoll's case ("John Stoll—Northern California Innocence Project," n.d.). Four of the six child witnesses recanted their incriminating trial testimony (Jones, 2004). Another former accuser reported he did not recall being abused. Jed, however, in adulthood, maintained he had been sexually abused by his father but indicated he had no recall of the details (Jones, 2004; Nachman & Hardy, 2009). In 2004, the Kern County Superior Court vacated Stoll's conviction based on unreliable testimony; Stoll was released, and the charges were dismissed. The state attorney general recognized Stoll's innocence, and Stoll was awarded compensation (McGagin, 2007) and later awarded 5 million dollars for wrongful prosecution and imprisonment. John Stoll's conviction and exoneration are the principal focus of the Nachman and Hardy (2009) documentary, *Witch Hunt*.

In 2004, a *New York Times* journalist (Jones, 2004) interviewed Eddie Sampley, one of the 6 children who testified against Stoll and others at the 1985 trial. At the time of the interview, Sampley was 28 years old and a father himself. Sampley recalled that his testimony against Stoll was false, and he knew it to be when he gave it. He described how, as an 8-year-old child, he complied at the insistence of the CPA investigators over the course of several interviews and provided sexual abuse allegations against Stoll. Sampley also described the long-term adverse effects he suffered in terms of guilt and impairment in his interaction with his own children. Also reported by Jones (2004), another of the child accusers (Victor Monge) was vulnerable because his mother was an undocumented Mexican immigrant. The former accuser explained that as an 8-year-old he gave in to investigators' demands and provided incriminating testimony against Stoll believing this would protect his mother from deportation.

In this case, the allegations against Stoll emerged in the context of child placement disputes secondary to divorce proceedings (Gardner, 1991). Prior to Stoll's ex-wife reporting her suspicion Jed had been sexually molested, Stoll had reported his concern Jed was being emotionally abused by his ex-wife and the stepfather ("John Stoll—Northern California Innocence Project," n.d.). The postexoneration child sexual abuse conviction against Grant Self ("Grant Self—National Registry of Exonerations," n.d.) suggested the likelihood Jed was abused by Self even though the prosecution of Stoll was based entirely on erroneous manufactured evidence (suggestive and coercive interviews with young children). While Stoll's wrongful conviction illustrates child sex abuse hysteria, it also can be categorized as a wrongful conviction where intra-familial child sex assault was alleged, as presented in Chapter 2.

Margaret Kelly Michaels

In September 1984, Margaret Kelly Michaels, a 23-year-old aspiring actress, was hired as a teacher's aide at the Wee Care Child Care Center in Maplewood, New Jersey. Michaels had no experience in education. Within a month, she was promoted to pre-K teacher. She remained at Wee Care until April 1985, when she obtained a teaching position closer to her home in East Orange, New Jersey.

Four days after Michaels left Wee Care, one of her former preschoolers had a pediatric visit. According to the testimony of the pediatrician's assistant, the male child, in his mother's presence, while the assistant was taking his temperature rectally and rubbing his back commented, "That's what my teacher does to me at nap time at school" (Rosenthal, 1995, p. 248). Neither the mother nor the pediatrician's assistant mentioned the comment to the pediatrician. However, the child was questioned further at home and reportedly named two other children whose temperatures were taken by Michaels. After a phone consultation with the pediatrician, the mother called the CPA and the day care center director. The director thereafter informed the mother of one of the named children, "There were complaints of sex abuse at Wee Care and [your child] had been named" (Rosenthal, 1995 p. 248). The official reporting led to investigations by the CPA, the county prosecutor's office, and the local police. As a result, multiple children, parents, teachers, and other Wee Care staff were interviewed as well as Michaels.

Two weeks after the investigations began, the Wee Care parents were invited to a meeting to discuss the allegations. At this meeting, the parents were informed, by a sexual abuse consultant and a psychologist, that three children had been abused in the nap room.[3] The local weekly published the story the following day. Over the next 6 weeks, there were two additional meetings where parents were "educated" about sexual abuse (Rabinowitz, 1990). Simultaneously, the CPA was conducting an investigation that resulted in 82 child interviews and 19 parent interviews.

None of the initial child interviews were recorded. It was revealed at trial the CPA chief investigator's approach to questioning the children was based on an assumption the children had been abused and they would benefit therapeutically from disclosing the details of their abuse (Rosenthal, 1995). He described the church where the day care center was housed as a "pedophile's paradise" (Rabinowitz, 1990, p. 57); thus, he approached the investigation with the presumption the children had in fact been abused. With the continuing child and parent interviews, group and individual therapy sessions, consultation provided to parents by sex abuse "experts," and the resultant anxieties throughout the community, the amount and severity of the allegations against Michaels expanded (Rabinowitz, 1990; Rosenthal, 1995).[4]

At trial, Michaels faced 163 counts of sexual abuse against 19 children. Children testified they were sexually violated with forks, sticks, knives, and spoons. These offenses were alleged to have occurred during the 7-month period Michaels was employed at Wee Care. However, the church minister, sexton, custodians, and secretaries testified they never observed indications of abuse during their trips through the building. Also, there were no injuries or other evidence identified from physical examinations to support the testimony. The prosecution did produce a jailhouse informant who testified Michaels made incriminating admissions while housed in the county jail; however, it was revealed this testimony was provided in exchange for benefits related to the informant's legal charges (Nathan & Snedeker, 1995). In August 1988, Michaels was convicted of 115 counts and given a 47-year sentence.

In 1993, the appellate court reversed Michaels' conviction, citing the improper use of expert testimony; the appearance of judicial partiality (the judge exhibited support for the child witnesses during in-camera proceedings, which was adverse to the defense); the role of leading and suggestive interviews in gathering evidence against Michaels (children were encouraged to help the police and threatened that their failure to make reports would be communicated to their peers); and the introduction of sexual content amounted to methods that would cause children to diverge from the truth. The reversal was upheld in a state supreme court ruling (*State v. Michaels*, 1994; also see Schreiber et al., 2006) that determined the state would have to prove the reliability of the evidence against Michaels before she could be retried. In this ruling the New Jersey Supreme Court determined, "to ensure defendant's right to a fair trial, a pretrial taint hearing is essential to demonstrate the reliability of the resultant evidence" (*State v. Michaels*, 1994). With this ruling, the state decided against further prosecution of Michaels and dismissed the charges.

The Bruck and Ceci (1995) amicus brief, supported by 45 academic psychologist cosigners, was instrumental in clarifying the erroneous basis of the incriminating evidence that had been used to convict Michaels, as well as other defendants, in many child sexual abuse prosecutions around the country. It also provided direction to improve the practice of assessing and interviewing children when sexual abuse was suspected (London et al., 2005). The pretrial taint hearing was established as a legal remedy to a particular type of black box manufactured evidence. That is, where children are subjected to repeated, suggestive, and leading questioning and there is no objective record of the tone or content of the interviews, pretrial admissibility review of the resulting evidence is indicated. It is relevant to note, as presented in Chapter 3, the New Jersey Supreme Court more recently adopted a pretrial procedure for evaluating the reliability of eyewitness identifications by adults (*State v. Henderson*, 2011), indicating recognition that children are not alone in their vulnerability to suggestive processes in the preparation of evidence.

Ileana Fuster

The prosecution of (Honduran immigrant) Ileana Fuster stemmed from a 3-year-old child's report that "Ileana kisses all the babies' bodies" (Nathan & Snedeker, 1995, p. 169). The case became more urgent when it was learned Ileana's husband (Frank) had a criminal record and was recently charged with fondling a 9-year-old relative. Within weeks, more than 20 children had reported accusations against Ileana and Frank. However, the prosecution faced a problem with proceeding to a conviction because the investigators who interviewed the children had used deceptive and coercive assessment methods (Nathan & Snedeker, 1995). In August 1984, Dade County prosecutor Janet Reno had 17-year-old Ileana Fuster arrested and placed in solitary confinement. Ileana remained in a small cell, lit 24 hours a day, for 6 months. She was then offered a reduced sentence if she would testify against her husband. Even though Ileana was suffering from insomnia and weight loss, she refused the offer.

In subsequent months, her defense was severed from her husband's, which meant they now had different lawyers. Ileana's attorney began to formulate a battered wife or child victim defense, that is, Ileana committed offenses under the duress of her husband. Ileana was provided some relief in March 1985 when she was released from solitary and housed with other women in a dormitory-type setting. But, after a few weeks she was returned to solitary confinement.

According to testimony by a prison chaplain (Nathan & Snedeker, 1995), by the summer Ileana began to report that Frank had in fact assaulted her, but she maintained there had been no sexual abuse at the child care service. At this point, her attorney, in collaboration with the prosecution, engaged a well-known Miami psychiatrist, Charles Mutter, MD, to further examine Ileana. Dr. Mutter conducted 14 sessions with Ileana, but she never admitted she or Frank had abused any children. In July, a defense investigator who had been periodically visiting Ileana became increasingly concerned about her physical and mental condition. Ileana's attorney directed the investigator to discontinue contact with her.

With a trial date approaching, the defense attorney engaged psychologists Rapaport and Haber to prepare Ileana for trial. Over a period of 3 to 4 weeks, Rapaport and Haber had at least 35 (day and evening) sessions with Ileana. The psychologists used guided imagery and visualization exercises, coupled with providing Ileana details of allegations contained in transcripts from leading and suggestive interviews with children, to induce Ileana's "recall" of sexual abuse incidents consistent with the state's case. Following the psychologists' intervention, Ileana pled guilty to multiple counts of sexual abuse.[5] The psychologists also met with Ileana again to prepare for her trial testimony against her husband. Frank was convicted and sentenced to multiple life terms. Ileana was sentenced to a juvenile facility, paroled, and deported to Honduras after serving 3½ years.

Ileana Fuster's apparent wrongful conviction of day care child sexual abuse was reliant on suggestive questioning of children as seen in other child sexual abuse hysteria prosecutions. In this prosecution, the state supplemented the reports of abuse with clearly coercive interrogation methods: the punitive solitary confinement of a youthful defendant coupled with psychologist-induced guided imagery and visualization exercises to manufacture evidence supportive of the prosecution's case.

Robert Kelly

The prosecution of Robert Kelly, his wife, Betsy, and five other defendants from the Little Rascals Day Care Center in Edenton, North Carolina, was covered extensively by *Frontline* producer Ofra Bikel in the *Innocence Lost* documentary trilogy (*Frontline*, n.d.). Robert Kelly and Katherine Dawn Wilson were convicted at trials (though later exonerated). After the trial convictions, Betsy Kelly and another defendant accepted plea bargains, and charges were dropped against the other defendants.

Similar to other child sexual abuse hysteria cases, the investigation began when the parent of a 3-year-old reported to a police officer (Brenda Toppin) that her child made the remark, "Stick your finger in my butt, Mommy." The child indicated he had been playing doctor with an older child. The child attended Little Rascals and was reportedly unhappy there. On further questioning by the parent, it was reported the child said he played doctor with Mr. Bob at day care. This led to the 3-year-old, and other children, being questioned by the CPA and police and an investigation of Kelly's day care center. As reported in the *Frontline* summary ("Innocence Lost," *Frontline*, n.d.), both Officer Toppin and the prosecutor (H. P. Williams) had recently attended a seminar on child sexual abuse. In January 1989, when Kelly learned about the investigation, he personally met parents as they came to the center and informed them.

According to the *Frontline* investigation, Robert and Betsey Kelly initially enjoyed widespread support in the community; however, as the investigation proceeded, support began to erode. Some parents, concerned their children may have been abused, sent their children to therapists recommended by the police or prosecutors. One of these therapists had a group meeting with four sets of parents.[6] Kelly was represented by a respected local attorney (Chris Bean), who had a child attending Little Rascals. Bean was informed by the prosecutor that some children named his son as a victim of Kelly. When Bean subsequently withdrew as Kelly's lawyer, it had an adverse effect on how Kelly was regarded in the small community of 6,000. The large majority of the 90 Little Rascals children who saw therapists went to four therapists recommended and paid by the state. In interviews with therapists, children named children, who named more children as well as Little Rascals staff, involved in sexual activities.

Robert Kelly was arrested in April 1989; his wife, Betsy, was arrested in September; and five other defendants were subsequently arrested. Twelve children testified against Kelly at trial, and there was conflicting testimony from medical experts. Also, the lead police investigator (Officer Toppin), who had conducted the first interview with most of the children, testified she did not keep her original handwritten notes and had lost the audiotapes. The prosecution's case relied on the testimony from the children. Even though they had attended "court school" to prepare, their testimony included outlandish allegations (e.g., infants having been killed at the day care center or taken to outer space in hot air balloons).

In 1992, Kelly was convicted of 99 of 100 counts and given several life sentences ("Robert Kelly—National Registry of Exonerations," n.d.). Kathryn Dawn Wilson's trial followed. She turned down a last-minute plea offer that would have exposed her to only months in prison. She was then convicted and sentenced to life. Following these verdicts, Kelly's wife, Betsy, accepted a plea offer. She had already been in jail 2 years and wanted to be reunited with her daughter. With a no-contest plea, Betsy was released in a year. Within 6 months of Betsy's release, Robert Kelly's and Kathryn Dawn Wilson's convictions were overturned (by the appellate court) based on prosecutorial errors ("Robert Kelly—National Registry of Exonerations," n.d.). One other defendant accepted a no-contest plea, and the charges were dropped against the three other defendants. The charges against Kelly were dismissed in 1996.

The prosecution of Robert Kelly and others affiliated with the Little Rascals Day Care in Edenton, North Carolina, shares features with other cases reported in this chapter. That is, the shared features were an ambiguous initial report from a toddler, consultation with a law enforcement officer recently exposed to alerts about child sexual abuse, a reported more incriminating statement from the child, widespread questioning of young children who attend the day care center without objective recording of the contents of the interviews, referral of children to therapists who were aligned with the prosecution, and increasing numbers of child victims, adult perpetrators, and offenses identified. The secretive black box character of the questioning of the children is central to the manufacture (intentional or inadvertent) of evidence.

SUMMARY

The four case illustrations reported highlight common features among many child sexual abuse hysteria prosecutions. The National Registry of Exonerations reported 59 defendants who were convicted in these prosecutions have been subsequently exonerated. There is little doubt that others were wrongly convicted who lack the resources, or willingness, to pursue official exoneration. As noted in previous chapters, it appears that when sexual assault allegations are leveled, the moral violation inherent in the (alleged) offense precipitates a search for a moral correction, and there is a lowered threshold in the evaluation of evidence.

When these cases from divergent communities across the country are considered together, the manufactured and sociogenic nature of the prosecution's evidence is apparent. That is, it was not only the suggestiveness of child witnesses, but also the broader sociogenic process that influenced parents, elements in law enforcement, judges, lawyers, jurors, and therapists that they were protecting children from a hidden sexual menace that produced the child sexual abuse hysteria prosecutions. Also, the notion that many children who were never sexually abused were harmed in the process was generally not appreciated. Fortunately, the research informed Bruck and Ceci's (1995) amicus brief, and subsequent contributions (London et al., 2005; Ceci, Crossman, Scullin, Gilstrap & Huffman, 2001), along with legal protections (e.g., the taint hearing described previously) began to inform and redirect the preparation and training of professionals (in law enforcement, CPA, psychologists, and social workers) in more reliable investigative methods where child sexual abuse is suspected. Since the latter part of the 1990s, child sexual abuse hysteria prosecutions have been reduced substantially. However, the possibility remains that suggestive questioning of children by parents, professionals, and other parties will still occur in certain circumstances.

NOTES

1. The believe the children presumption is problematic because, like any presumption to believe (or disbelieve) a particular class of persons, children, police, doctors, or criminal defendants, it invites the abuse of that presumption and undermines thorough evaluation of reliability. If we always believe the children or the doctors or the police this opens the door for false testimony from these groups.
2. According to the National Registry of Exonerations summary (Grant Self—National Registry of Exonerations, n.d.), prior to the allegations in connection with Stoll, Grant Self had two earlier sex abuse convictions. In the case where Self and Stoll were codefendants, Self was convicted, exonerated, released, and in 2013 pled guilty to other child sexual assaults.
3. This occurred even though the professionals had been advised by the prosecutor's office against encouraging rumors of sexual abuse (Rosenthal, 1995).
4. One child testified she observed Michaels lick peanut butter from another child's penis and rectum. Other children testified they were forced to consume feces and urine and observed blood on Michaels' vagina. Children testified that knives, sticks, and wooden spoons were inserted in their orifices. One child said Michaels put a light bulb in her vagina (Rosenthal, 1995), though there was no physical evidence to support these allegations. The prosecutor acknowledged in his opening statement that the children had said and would say things during the trial that were not true.
5. It is relevant to note Ileana Furster's in-court plea statement as reported by *Frontline*, "I am pleading guilty not because I feel guilty, but because I think it's the best interest . . . for the children and for the court and for the people that are working on the case. I am innocent of all the charges. I wouldn't have done anything to harm any children".
6. This therapist (social worker Judith Abbott) published an account supportive of the prosecution prior to Kelly's conviction reversal and subsequent exoneration (Abbott, 1994).

Concepts, Processes, and Models in Wrongful Conviction

Where does forensic bias come from, and how can we minimize it?
—Itiel E. Dror (2018, p. 243)

The fate of the "Central Park Five" defendants was determined in two separate criminal trials in 1990 (Burns, 2011; Sullivan, 1992). An essential prosecution witness in each trial was the victim herself, the jogger, who suffered the near-fatal assault (Meili, 2003). While she was unable to describe the assault, or connect the assault to the defendants, her physical presence, and especially her residual injuries, vividly demonstrated the severity of the moral violation in the crime. She testified she had no recall of what occurred on the night of the attack, and she described her remaining impairment, difficulty with walking, balance, and coordination; loss of the sense of smell; and troubling double vision (Burns, 2011; Sullivan, 1992). While the jogger's testimony did address a legally relevant issue regarding her past consensual sex partner, primarily and strategically the prosecutor knew the jogger's presence gave the jury "a victim to avenge" (Sullivan, 1992 p. 150).[1]

As noted in previous chapters, wrongful conviction research and scholarship has expanded dramatically in the past 30 years (Gould & Leo, 2010). The literature has been largely problem focused and pragmatic, rather than centered on concepts or theory. The predominant focus has been on discernible features found in confirmed wrongful convictions, such as witness misidentifications (G. L. Wells, 2006; Cutler & Kovera, 2010; Loftus, 2005); false confessions (Kassin, 2015; Leo, 2008; Gudjonsson, 2003); unreliable evidence from "scientific" and other "experts" (Garrett & Neufeld, 2009); racial bias (Parker et al., 2008; E. Smith & Hattery, 2011; M. B. Johnson et al., 2013); suggestibility among child witnesses (Bruck & Ceci, 1995); unreliable testimony from incentivized witnesses (Neuschatz et al., 2012); pressure on law enforcement and resulting error (S.

R. Gross, 1996); prosecutorial zeal and misconduct; supported by an adversarial, "win-at-any-cost" approach (Medwed, 2013), and related legal features. Much of the research has focused on establishing the occurrence of wrongful conviction, demonstrating wrongful convictions are not rare anomalies, and linking wrongful conviction to common investigation practices (e.g., witness identifications, police interrogations, informant, and expert testimony). Research has also elaborated the effects and consequences for defendants and their families (Wildeman et al., 2011); the original crime victim (Williamson et al., 2016); victims of offenses committed by the unapprehended actual offender (Norris, Weintraub, Acker, Redlich, & Bonventre, 2019; Acker, 2013); and having wrongful conviction regarded as a central concern that demands attention and policy reform.

Several researchers have advanced concepts to describe the psychological and cognitive processes contributing to wrongful criminal conviction. One of the most widely cited processes is "tunnel vision" (Findley & Scott, 2006) where there is a premature, erroneous focus on a suspect, increased attention to evidence supporting guilt, and inattention to contrary evidence. Related processes have also been described, such as "misinformation effects" (Castelle & Loftus, 2008) where acceptance of one faulty piece of evidence can divert and derail an investigation. Kassin et al. (2012) described a process of "forensic confirmation bias" where a false confession, or witness misidentification, "corrupt" the assessment of other evidence (expert analyst or informant testimony) and produce multiple sources of erroneous incriminating evidence. Dror and Bucht (2012) noted there are several well-researched psychological/cognitive processes (such as "self-fulling prophecy," "belief perseverance," "confirmation bias," "cognitive dissonance," "escalation of commitment") that characterize cognitive components of decision-making processes that contribute to wrongful conviction. In this chapter, the "moral outrage–moral correction" process, introduced in the Chapter 2 presentation of the stranger rape thesis, is elaborated further as a model that links wrongful conviction processes to their social context and explains the increased risk on wrongful conviction given certain case characteristics.

MODELS OF WRONGFUL CONVICTION

Leo (2005) provided an overview of wrongful conviction research and called for more sophisticated thinking and conceptualizing in the field. He noted the lack of adequate theoretical formulations and called for social scientists to advance concepts and theory (also see Leo & Gould, 2009). Leo pointed out that Huff et al. (1996) advanced Packer's (1968) crime control versus due process distinction as a potential model for understanding the occurrence of wrongful conviction. According to this distinction, criminal justice focus on crime control will produce more wrongful conviction, while focus on due process will produce less. Leo suggested the crime control versus due process dichotomy provides a relevant description of two competing orientations in criminal justice policy, but the distinction alone is less than a theoretical formulation.

According to Leo (2005), Lofquist (2008) presented a promising theoretical model focused on alternative perspectives regarding intentionality and agency in wrongful conviction. As presented by Leo, a valuable feature in Lofquist's model is the recognition of the social/organizational context of wrongful conviction. Lofquist described the rational choice or agency perspective on wrongful conviction, which seeks to identify intentional (malicious) activity on the part of key actors (police, prosecutors, legal/judicial personnel, and/or the press); individual and organization planning; police and prosecutorial decisions; along with greed or career ambitions. This perspective is reflected in Moran's (2007) remark that more than half of the wrongful convictions (he studied) were "willful, malicious prosecutions by criminal justice personnel" (para. 3). Alternately, the organizational process or structure perspective views wrongful conviction as a convergence of common forces that lead to the premature identification of a suspect, inattention to alternative scenarios, escalating commitment, with typical procedure prosecution, absent malicious intent. This perspective is consistent with the Gross et al. (2005, p. 542) characterization of wrongful convictions as "accidents . . . caused by a mix of carelessness, misconduct, and bad luck."

THE DISTRIBUTION OF WRONGFUL CONVICTION

The differentiation identified by Packer (crime control vs. due process) and the distinction by Lofquist (agency vs. structural process) are valuable models that focus attention on processes that influence the occurrence of wrongful conviction. However, these two models consider wrongful conviction as a general process in criminal adjudication; that is, they do not consider the evidence wrongful conviction is distributed differentially based on factors such as offense type, offense severity, subtypes of offenses, defendant and victim race/ethnicity, or victim status. For instance, Gross (1996), drawing from Bedau and Radelet (1987) and other sources, developed and elaborated the role of offense type in wrongful conviction in the influential article, "The Risks of Death: Why Erroneous Convictions Are Common in Capital Cases." This work (as well as Gross et al., 2005) demonstrated the increased risk of wrongful conviction in murder and capital murder prosecutions, thus illustrating variable risk of wrongful conviction based on offense.[2] Gross (1996) suggested this risk results from features inherent to the offense (i.e., the lack of a capable victim/witness) as well as the response to the offense, which Gross refers to as "public outrage" (p. 494).

Similarly, Drizin and Leo (2004) observed false confessions as contributors to wrongful convictions, "tend to be concentrated in the most serious and high-profile cases" (p. 944). Likewise, Dror and Fraser-Mackenzie (2009), discussing faulty fingerprint identifications, suggested, "Such failures may be more likely in serious, high profile cases than in high-volume, day-to-day crimes" (p. 61) due to "motivational biases" associated with solving a high-profile crime. Further, Dror and Fraser-Mackenzie (2009, p.64) stated, "The emotional context of an investigation could potentially influence the processing of evidence and investigative decision making," supporting the observation that wrongful conviction risk is not distributed randomly among offenses.

Further demonstrating differential distribution of risk, data on race and rape, presented in previous chapters (E. Smith & Hattery, 2011; Olney & Bonn, 2014; Free & Ruesink, 2012; Garrett, 2011; Gross et al., 2005; Gross, 2008), indicate Black defendants face increased risk for wrongful conviction, especially where the offense involves a white victim. Thus, an element in a viable theory of wrongful conviction would address the observation of variable risk distribution based on characteristics of offenses.

Leo (2005) asserted the commonly cited "causes" of wrongful conviction (eyewitness misidentifications, false confessions, unreliable testimony from "experts" and informants) that have consumed the attention of researchers and scholars are actually not causes but merely legal categories associated with wrongful conviction. According to Leo, if misidentifications, false confessions, and associated unreliable evidence are considered causes of wrongful conviction, this only raises the question, What causes these features? Leo (2005, p. 210–211) proposed that, "One must go beyond the study of individual sources of error to understand how social forces, institutional logics, and erroneous human judgments and decisions come together to produce wrongful convictions."

Following Leo's (2005) formulation, the current work identified the social context of wrongful conviction as criminal investigation and adjudication. That is, the risk of wrongful conviction emerges in the aftermath of crime (or the belief crime has occurred), when a process of criminal investigation and adjudication is initiated. Certainly, criminal investigation and adjudication occur in social and organizational contexts. As presented in the Chapter 2 discussion of stranger rape, certain crimes produce more profound reactions not only among law enforcement but also among the public and the media, which contribute to the social context. The stranger rape thesis refers to the moral outrage perceived in certain crimes. The moral outrage response to criminal offenses has both emotional and cognitive components. According to the stranger rape thesis, once the moral outrage has been precipitated, the social group, law enforcement, and the community seek resolution via a moral correction. The search for moral correction is driven by the moral outrage, the complex emotional reactions (anger, fear, shame, retribution, anxiety) to the crime.

CONCEPTS INFORMING MORAL CORRECTION

The elaboration of moral correction draws from several recognized scientific observations. The concept of homeostasis emerged from physiological research and refers to self-regulatory processes in the human body (Cooper, 2008). That is, the body spontaneously adapts to changes in the environment (e.g., temperature), the introduction of contaminants (e.g., viruses), or the perception of danger (with adrenaline-supported "fight or flight"). These spontaneous adaptations occur to maintain equilibrium and effective functioning. Moral correction posits a similar process where a perceived moral violation or outrage is psychologically disruptive, produces complex distress (fear, anger, shame, retribution, anxiety), and a spontaneous/automatic drive to restore equilibrium via a remedy or correction. In crime, the remedy, the moral correction, is the apprehension, adjudication, and punishment of the offender(s). This process of moral correction is operative for individuals, such as family members of crime victims, law enforcement officials, as well as the broader social community.

For instance, in some circumstances, prosecutors will counsel murder victim family members that the conviction and execution of the defendant will provide relief and closure. The priming by the moral violation precipitates a drive for moral correction where the threshold for sufficient evidence of guilt is reduced. Stated differently, a cognitive component of the drive for moral correction is the less critical evaluation of evidence of guilt.

Clearly, the degree of moral outrage, and how broadly it is shared within the community, does not solely determine the outcome. Other factors such as practical difficulties posed by the investigation, police and prosecutorial discretion, social/political contingencies, available resources, chance, and luck factors all contribute to outcomes as well.

ZEIGARNIK EFFECT

Moral correction also draws from the Zeigarnik effect, an observation regarding cognition that is rooted in Gestalt psychology. The Zeigarnik effect refers to the finding that people remember an incomplete or interrupted task better than a complete task (Baumeister & Bushman, 2010). Psychologist Bluma Zeigarnik first published research describing the effect in 1927 (Zeigarnik, 1927; 1938). While some subsequent researchers failed to find support for the effect, Farley and Mealia (1973) found the Zeigarnik effect was operative under conditions of high need for achievement. Baumeister and Bushman (2010) noted intrusive thoughts emerge when a task once pursued remains incomplete. The formulation of moral correction draws on the Zeigarnik effect where the moral outrage response to the criminal offense has the effect of an incomplete task. The moral violation precipitates distress, which can be relieved by a moral correction in the form of the apprehension and adjudication of an offender. In this way, moral correction is inherently rewarding. Where the moral violation/outrage is pronounced, the potential reward is likewise enlarged. This intrinsic reward becomes a "motivational bias," as described by Charlton, Dror, and Fraser-MacKenzie (2008).

SIGNAL DETECTION THEORY

An additional contributor to the formulation of moral correction is *signal detection theory* (SD Theory). SD Theory emerged to address certain inadequacies in classical psychophysics and perception research (D. C. Anderson & Borkowski,

1978). Prior to SD Theory, the research paradigm regarding human perception of stimuli was focused on the intensity of the stimulus, such as how much brighter must a light be or louder must a sound be, for the human subject to detect a difference. SD Theory illustrated the provision of reward for correct perception, or penalty for missed perception, could improve subjects' performance. Thus, the ability to detect stimuli was influenced by not only the strength of the stimulus but also the reinforcement, or payoff, matrix. In the context of moral correction, SD Theory suggests that those burdened with the anguish from perceived moral violation will accept less substantial evidence (of guilt) in order to receive the reward (closure).

MORAL CORRECTION AND TUNNEL VISION AS MODELS OF WRONGFUL CONVICTION

The Findley and Scott (2006) law review is one of the most widely cited sources on tunnel vision in criminal adjudication. As noted, in tunnel vision there is premature, erroneous focus on a suspect, increased attention to evidence supporting guilt, and inattention to contrary evidence. An important element in the Findley and Scott (2006) elaboration of tunnel vision is recognition that tunnel vision is an extension of common human cognitive processes that are reinforced and amplified by institutional and system factors (e.g., the adversarial character of criminal proceedings, particular rules of evidence, and limitations in appellate review) in criminal investigation and legal processing. These common cognitive processes, known as *heuristics*, or cognitive shortcuts, are used to organize and filter information. As a result of these processes, people do not fully evaluate every piece of information encountered. Instead, judgments are made based on prior experience and expectancy. These heuristics (expectancy bias, confirmation bias, belief perseverance, hindsight, and outcome bias) typically improve efficiency in decision-making, though sometimes at the expense of accuracy.

In their review, Findley and Scott (2006) used four cases to illustrate tunnel vision in criminal investigation and prosecution. It is relevant to note, in the context of the differential distribution of wrongful conviction risk, that each of the four case illustrations are "stranger rape" wrongful convictions. Marvin Anderson became a suspect in a sexual attack on a young white woman by an African American assailant because the victim stated the attacker claimed he had a white girlfriend (Findley and Scott, 2006). Anderson was the only Black man local police knew who lived with a white woman. Even though Anderson's appearance diverged from the victim's initial description of her attacker, the victim selected Anderson's photo from a biased array, where Anderson's was the only color photo and only photo presented with a social security number. Thirty minutes later (in the familiar repeat presentation of the suspect), the victim again chose Anderson from a live lineup that did not include any of the fillers whose photos she had just seen. Despite Anderson's four alibi witnesses and a lack of physical evidence linking him to the rape, Anderson was convicted in a 5-hour trial. As Findley and

Scott pointed out, there was substantial pretrial evidence pointing to the actual perpetrator (Otis Lincoln), but after the victim's identification of Anderson, the police failed to pursue further leads.

Findley and Scott pointed out Steve Avery was wrongly convicted of rape in Wisconsin when evidence pointing to the actual perpetrator was also readily available to investigators. The rape victim was attacked in broad daylight, and while receiving medical care, she provided a description of the rapist. The local authorities believed the resultant sketch resembled Avery, who had prior run-ins with the law. The victim believed the perpetrator was in the array of nine photos she was shown, and she picked Avery. Three days later, the victim chose Avery from a live lineup that did not include any of the other men whose photos she had seen and where Avery was distinctive. At trial, Avery presented 16 alibi witnesses, and documentary evidence, which should have demonstrated the state's theory of the crime was implausible. According to Findley and Scott (2006), the prevailing tunnel vision allowed the sheriff's officers, prosecutors, and jurors to accept the implausible. The prosecutor had actually convicted the true offender (Gregory Allen) just 2 years earlier for an attempted sexual assault at the same location. Allen remained under surveillance by the local police, who urged the prosecutors to investigate him in connection with the case against Avery. The persistent belief in Avery's guilt continued as he sought postconviction relief until advanced DNA analysis confirmed his innocence after 18 years of imprisonment.

Commenting on the Central Park Jogger case, Findley and Scott (2006) stated that tunnel vision does not mean the police investigation was unwarranted or improper. Rather, awareness of tunnel vision should be caution to consider other possibilities even when evidence against a suspect appears to be strong. However, despite the DNA evidence that confirmed Matias Reyes's 2002 admission he was the sole perpetrator of the attack on the jogger, the DNA determination the hair recovered from one defendant was not the jogger's, and Reyes's history of rape offending in the vicinity of the Central Park jogger attack, the NYPD issued a report in 2003 (M. F. Armstrong, Hammerman, & Martin, 2003) challenging Reyes' confession and advancing theories suggesting the five juvenile defendants had in fact committed the assault on the jogger, thus illustrating how resistant tunnel vision can be to strong alternate evidence.

According to Findley and Scott (2006), tunnel vision can also distort the view of defense attorneys who learn most defendants are guilty and there are benefits for cooperation with the prosecution. Christopher Ochoa was subjected to a lengthy coercive interrogation, with death penalty threats, in connection to an Austin, Texas, rape and murder. After signing a confession written by the interrogator, he sought support from his defense counsel, who refused to investigate his innocence claim and advised him to further cooperate with the state to avoid execution. Ochoa pled guilty, testified (falsely) against a codefendant, and received a life sentence along with the codefendant. Findley and Scott reported the defense counsel was so convinced of the defendant's guilt that he urged the postconviction counsel there was no chance Ochoa was innocent prior to the DNA exoneration of Ochoa and the codefendant.

While Findley and Scott (2006) provided compelling descriptions of the pervasive influence of tunnel vision in investigation, prosecution, guilt determination, and postconviction appellate review, a relevant critique of the Findley and Scott perspective has emerged. Snook and Cullen (2009) cautioned that tunnel vision is an ambiguous concept. Tunnel vision should not be indicted retrospectively when it is associated with criminal investigative failures yet embraced (as diligence and determined focus) when it contributes to a sound conviction. As elaborated by Snook and Cullen (2009), the criticisms of tunnel vision (Cory, 2001; Kennedy, 2004; MacFarlane, 2004; Canadian Federal-Provincial-Territorial Heads of Prosecutions—FPT Heads Committee, 2004; Synder et al., 2007) are based on an unrealistic standard that suggests criminal investigations have unlimited time, mental, and human resources. In the real world of criminal investigations (i.e., considering ecological validity), decisions are made based on the best available information, and each and every possible lead and suspect cannot realistically be evaluated. Snook and Cullen suggested there are instances where wrongful conviction is the result of official misconduct (including "noble cause" corruption) where law enforcement failure is apparent. However, they clarified that tunnel vision is not misconduct and suggested the recommendations that law enforcement should not use tunnel vision are not justified in the absence of systematic evaluation of the role of tunnel vision in successful investigations. The Snook and Cullen rebuttal, to the critiques of tunnel vision, warrants attention and research to clarify ambiguity surrounding the concept of tunnel vision as well as the role of tunnel vision in sound convictions.

While the conclusion tunnel vision, per se, is the primary culprit in wrongful conviction is premature, the elaboration of tunnel vision by Findley and Scott (2006) and others is valuable in describing processes and the various cognitive elements (expectancy bias, confirmation biases, self-fulling prophecy, belief perseverance, escalation of commitment) operating in confirmed wrongful convictions. It provides direction for further social science and legal research, as well as review and evaluation of investigative practices.

Tunnel vision, as described in the material presented here, and moral correction are both models that describe processes that lead to the conviction of the innocent. The moral conviction model is advanced here as a complement to tunnel vision rather than as an alternate model. As presently formulated, moral correction is a framework within which tunnel vision and the associated cognitive elements—heuristics (expectancy bias, misinformation effect, confirmation bias, self-fulfilling prophecy)—operate. Moral correction is presented as the motivating force or tendency, while tunnel vision describes the operative cognitive mechanisms.

The literature on tunnel vision, while recognizing it stems from common human cognitive processes, has focused on its influence among law enforcement and prosecutors. Findley and Scott (2006), however, have noted tunnel vision operates among jurors and defense counsel as well. However, moral correction as articulated here addresses the broader human narrative of injury and redemption, loss and restoration, crime and justice. The notion of moral correction recognizes the social, as well as the individual, psychology where law enforcement and prosecutors not only are responding to community, and often political, pressures to make arrests and win convictions as well as career incentives but also have a personal investment (desire) in "correcting" what they perceive to be moral violations and outrages. Likewise, moral correction corresponds to the outlook of victims and their family members, concerned community members, the press, and media sources.

Moral correction suggests that tunnel vision is the product of the emotional and cognitive reactions to crime, which are magnified in line with the degree of moral violation perceived in particular criminal offending. That is, the concept of moral correction as a process suggests the complex distress reactions to severe crime (anger, fear, shame, anxiety, sadness, loss, retribution) are adverse, disruptive, and debilitating. These emotions propel a search for repair and restoration via apprehension and adjudication of the perpetrator(s). In major crime, the distress that drives this search is substantial; thus, the relief or reward associated with various steps in the process (obtaining evidence, an arrest, an indictment, a conviction) is likewise considerable. Moral correction posits that the inherent reinforcement in achieving moral correction will influence the process such that the threshold for acceptable or adequate evidence of guilt will be lowered: Operating under the burden of moral violation, the standard for judging evidence of guilt is reduced. This is the increased risk of wrongful conviction observed in high-profile crime (capital murders, serial and stranger rape, Black defendant/white victim offenses).

Several terms and concepts introduced in previous chapters illustrate aspects of the moral correction process. Responding to the moral violation in crime, police investigators search for evidence, witnesses, and suspects. While the prevailing view is that evidence is discovered, in some instances the evidence is actually "manufactured" by the investigation. In wrongful conviction in sexual assault, the two primary forms of prosecution evidence are witness misidentifications and false confessions. Where a rape victim has limited visual recall of a stranger assailant and she is guided through a composite sketch process, viewing mug shots, photos arrays, and then a live lineup, with repeat presentation of a particular suspect, the resulting identification has been manufactured. Where a suspect is subjected to custodial interrogation and provided false incriminating information and details of the offense prior to making a "confession" that incorporates those details, that statement has been manufactured. Moral correction suggests that absent the perception that an actual crime has occurred, these sources of evidence will be assessed more critically, while priming by an actual offense will make these sources of evidence seem more persuasive and indicative of guilt.

As suggested by the "Continuum of Intentionality," the degree of intentionality in the manufacture of evidence varies from minimal (where there is a spontaneous misidentification and secondary supporting testimony from a hair/fiber expert is manufactured), to substantial (where youthful defendants are coerced to adopt incriminating confession narratives). Regardless of the degree of intentionality, the plausibility of the manufactured evidence is supported by the moral correction process.

The term *black box* investigation was introduced and elaborated to underline the lack of transparency in the manufacture of evidence. Black box witness identification procedures mean there is no record of the witness' initial reports or level of confidence in the identification or record of the exchanges between the witness, other witnesses, and the investigators or the number of times the suspect was presented prior to the identification. Black box interrogation means there is no objective record of where the incriminating or corroborating elements of the confession statement originated. Black box production of laboratory evidence means it is not known what contextual and potentially biasing information was provided to forensic analysts or scientists prior to their analysis. Black box procedure in the acquisition of informant and incentivized testimony means there is no record of the information, incentives, and inducements provided to witnesses in the arrangement of their testimony.

RESEARCH DIRECTIONS

Elaborating viable models, or theories, of wrongful conviction that can advance research and guide policy proposals presents several challenges. As Leo (2005) suggested, wrongful conviction research will be enhanced by moving beyond the notion that the apparent individual legal features in confirmed wrongful convictions are actual causes. And further, as Leo noted, the social character of wrongful conviction needs to be recognized as the errors occur in a specific social context. In this regard, Kassin's (2015) remarks about false confessions apply equally to mistaken identifications. False confessions pose a problem because they are not recognized as such by police, lawyers, judges, and jurors, illustrating the social context of the error as noted by Leo (2005). The moral violation–moral correction model described in this chapter identifies the social context of wrongful conviction as criminal apprehension and adjudication. It is the reaction to crime that initiates the risks of wrongful conviction. That is, the reaction is the complex emotional responses that precipitate and magnify tunnel vision and the associated cognitive features that have been described by legal scholars and social scientists. Where criminal offenses are especially reprehensible to the community and/or threatening, the emotional reactions are proportional, and the quest for moral correction adversely affects the investigation and adjudication process. Thus, the risk of wrongful conviction will vary based on the reactions to the offense.

Many of the processes identified in the presentation of the moral violation–moral correction model are illustrated in the empirical research on graphic gruesome evidence influencing mock jurors' verdicts and related determinations. Bright and Goodman-Delahunty (2006) reported gruesome photographic and verbal evidence affect juror emotional states and conviction ratings, as in anger toward the defendant and increased ratings of the inculpatory significance of prosecution evidence. In recognition of these processes, US, and other, courts allow judges to limit the admissibility of certain forms of evidence that are considered to be "more prejudicial than probative." Bright and Goodman-Delahunty (2006) remarked, "Jurors exposed to gruesome evidence may employ a lower threshold in applying the legal standard, 'beyond reasonable doubt'" (p. 185). Similarly, Gross (1996, p. 495) commented, "In a close criminal case the jury is supposed to release a defendant who is in their opinion, probably guilty. This is a distasteful task under any circumstances, but it becomes increasingly unpalatable—and unlikely—as we move up the scale from non-violent crime, to violent crime, to homicide, to aggravated grisly murder." This observation by Gross is consistent with the concept/process of moral correction, but moral correction involves more than consideration of potential harm presented by a defendant who is "probably" guilty. Moral correction also involves the "priming" by the offense, the propensity to undo or correct the initial violation, to restore the equilibrium that was disrupted by the initial outrage. As illustrated by the Central Park Jogger trial, the presentation of the jogger to the jurors provided a "victim to avenge," an injury to correct.

Alicke (2000) introduced a model (the "culpable control model") to assess culpability judgments in the context of civil and criminal disputes. The model recognizes that, despite "reasonable person" guidance in the law, judgments may be other than rational, particularly where there are "spontaneous emotional reactions to the evidence" (Bright & Goodman–Delahunty, 2006, p. 188). Further, Bright and Goodman-Delahunty (2006) pointed out Alicke's model suggests relevant variables that can be assessed empirically, such as altered evidentiary standards, altered evaluations of evidence, and biased search for evidence. Bright and Goodman-Delahunty (2006, p. 188) remarked, "The culpable control model asserts that the need to restore or preserve justice results in . . . spontaneous emotional reactions to a victim's suffering, and a consequential lowering of the evidential threshold." These findings are consistent with moral correction and suggest that empirical investigations guided by comprehensive observations and informed formulations can advance viable models and theories of wrongful conviction.

NOTES

1. Because the crime scene semen had not been matched to any of the defendants, the jogger's testimony was necessary to establish the semen was not the result of some prior consensual sexual activity.
2. Two points are worthy of note here. While the Gross focus on murder and capital murder was an eye-opener in demonstrating the increased risk of wrongful conviction in certain offenses, his method of classifying offenses by the highest charge masked the role of sexual assault in wrongful conviction. Also, in his later work, Gross (2008) moved away from the notion that wrongful conviction was more common in murder and suggested it was only more likely to be discovered.

Prospective and Future Directions

The field of wrongful convictions has a lengthy and extensive history of scholarship that has expanded substantially in the past 30 years. Investigators have focused on identifying various mechanisms of error that facilitate wrongful conviction and recommended safeguards and protections for defendants. A robust and varied set of reforms have been identified by major research groups and organizations. This chapter includes reference to this important and extensive literature. However, rather than providing a detailed presentation of this literature, which has been done aptly by others in various wrongful conviction subfields, this chapter focuses on identifying common concerns and obstacles to reform that have been identified in the literature. In addition, this chapter considers how the investigation of wrongful conviction in sexual assault, presented in this volume, contributes to the literature on reducing and preventing the conviction of innocents.

Wrongful conviction in sexual assault shares wrongful conviction risks with other types of offenses even though there are also risks unique to sexual offenses. A host of major researchers and scholars have addressed the shared risks and proposed various remedies. Major contributions have been provided regarding eyewitness identification (Cutler, 2013; G. A. Wells & Quigley-McBride, 2016; G. L. Wells, 2006; G. L. Wells et al., 1998; Loftus, 2005), interrogation and confession (Smalarz, Scherr, & Kassin, 2016; Kassin, 2015; Kassin et al., 2010; Leo, 2008, 2009; Gudjonsson, 2003), forensic "sciences" and analysts (Garrett & Neufeld, 2009; National Academy of Sciences, 2009), child suggestibility (London et al., 2005; Bruck & Ceci, 1995), official misconduct and suppression of exculpatory evidence (Medwed, 2013), and incentivized informant testimony (Neuschatz et al., 2012; Warden, 2004).

Eyewitness misidentification is recognized as the single largest contributor to wrongful conviction across offenses. Systematic research in this area began with G. L. Wells' (1978) early work. A scientifically informed body of recommendations was published by the American Psychology–Law Society (APLS) in 1998 (G. L. Wells et al., 1998). The APLS recommendations were incorporated in the subsequent body of research-informed reforms issued by the Department of Justice (DOJ; US Department of Justice, Office of Justice Programs,

National Institute of Justice, 1999). As noted in several reviews (Smith & Cutler, 2013; Wells & Quigley-McBride, 2016), these reforms have been highly influential; many have been adopted by state and local law enforcement agencies and professional groups. The DOJ reforms, and continued ongoing research, have also informed and guided state court rulings concerning eyewitness testimony (*State v. Henderson*, 2011; *State v. Lawson*, 2012). As noted by A. M. Smith and Cutler (2013), certain reforms have been embraced more than others. The most commonly adopted reform has been the use of unbiased lineup instructions, that is, informing the witness "the perpetrator may or may not be in the lineup." In some cases, the adoption of reforms has been in the form of mandates on practice. In other situations, reforms were adopted as recommendations and thus were not binding. As a result, it is not clear to what degree the reforms have actually been incorporated in law enforcement practice.

Costanzo and Krauss (2018) identified several challenges and obstacles in advancing research-derived reforms to law enforcement practice. One such challenge is how to determine when there is sufficient reliable research to support a particular change in policy or practice. Costanzo and Krauss, citing Steblay and Loftus (2008), pointed out resistance to reform often takes the form of arguments such as the following: The system is not broken and does not need to be fixed; the costs of reforms will be burdensome; reforms will stall investigations; reforms are soft on crime; reforms favor the defense; and reforms create a training burden. Further, Costanzo and Krauss (2018) explained the benefits of certain research-informed reforms are realized with a cost. For example, accumulated research indicates the sequential lineup presentation procedure reduces false identifications while jeopardizing some correct identifications. These various challenges and obstacles illustrate that reform is proceeding, but the pace of reform is variable. A well-established research foundation is necessary, but competing values and priorities are also considerations. Active collaboration and exchange among researchers, law enforcement practitioners, and policymakers (Smith & Cutler, 2013) are required to realize meaningful reform.

Reform in the area of criminal interrogation involves not only the problem of false confession and wrongful conviction but also more broadly what police actions are permissible during interrogation. Leo (2008) provided a retrospective on interrogation reform in the United States that views reform as a protracted process with meaningful reform emerging. Leo identified four general periods in US interrogation practice. The first was the period of third-degree interrogation, where police use of physical abuse during interrogation was not uncommon, as documented in the "Wickersham Report" (National Commission on Law Observance and Enforcement, 1931). According to Leo, this period continued until the US Supreme Court *Brown v. Mississippi* (1936) decision that prohibited the use of physical abuse in interrogation.

Leo referred to the subsequent phase as the period of professional reform and psychological interrogation, noting the *Miranda v. Arizona* (1966) ruling that psychological interrogation methods can also be coercive. Leo indicated that beginning in the 1990s, a third period emerged, which he described as the "era of innocence" with the expanding number of exonerations. This third period has coexisted with the second period and has been characterized by adoption of electronic recording mandates in a growing number of states and police departments (Innocence Project, 2017). Leo projected that as recording mandates are adopted more widely (black box interrogation methods are eradicated), a fourth period will emerge. This will entail a reevaluation of the legal support for deceptive and coercive interrogation practices, and fundamental reform will result.

Smalarz et al. (2016) concluded that the past 50 years have demonstrated the Miranda warning procedure does not provide adequate protection even for suspects without disabilities. Mandated videorecording of criminal interrogations (some version of which is in effect in 20 states) is a more efficient procedure. Such a mandate does not require suspect activation, will deter police coercive practices, and will provide the trial and appellate courts with an objective record of what occurred. Clearly, mandated electronic recording of custodial interrogation is an essential reform (Kassin, 2015), but "moral correction" pressures on police investigators will remain and likely result in extralegal efforts to circumvent the mandate via "off-the-record" coercive measures (Costanzo & Krauss, 2018) that will require continued vigilance to maintain due process and the integrity of criminal investigation.

Reform in the area of the forensic sciences has also faced considerable challenges. The forensic sciences enjoy an aura of certainty, but research scrutiny (Dror & Bucht, 2012; National Academy of Sciences, 2009; Garrett & Neufeld, 2009) has exposed substantial error associated with certain forms of forensic science evidence. Faulty forensic science testimony has been identified as the second leading contributor to DNA-confirmed wrongful convictions, apparent in half of the cases (Mnookin, 2018). This finding, coupled with the limited reliability associated with certain forms of forensic science, has resulted in the National Academy of Sciences (NAS; 2009) recommendation that crime laboratories be severed from law enforcement and prosecution control. Many leading forms of forensic science (fingerprint analysis, ballistics, bite marks, blood spatter, arson, hair and fiber analysis) were developed in crime laboratories without connection to rigorous scientific and statistical methods (Mnookin, 2018; Hsu, 2012).[1] With the exception of fingerprint and standard DNA analysis,[2] foundational research studies to clarify error rates have not been conducted in many forensic science fields (Mnookin, 2018).

The 2009 NAS report also called for establishment of an administrative agency to review forensic science standards and practices. In 2013, the National Commission of Forensic Science (NCFS) emerged as a joint project of the DOJ and National Institute of Standards and Technology (NIST). The NCFS comprised research scientists, forensic practitioners, judges, and law enforcement stakeholders "to promote scientific validity, reduce fragmentation, and improve federal coordination of forensic science" (NIST, n.d.).

In early 2015, controversy emerged when Federal District Court Judge Rakoff resigned from the NCFS in protest of the DOJ's (prosecution-friendly) decision to remove pretrial discovery of forensic evidence from the scope of the commission's work. Following media exposure, the DOJ reversed itself, and Rakoff rejoined the commission. The commission subsequently issued advisory recommendations regarding critical issues in forensic science, such as forensic examiners should be appropriately accredited; forensic laboratories should have written policies regarding documentation, reporting, and interpretation; and there should be improved procedures to enhance pretrial discovery. The recommendations were clearly in a positive direction and actually quite modest. However, there were no legally binding mandates issued or any resulting legislation.

In 2017, the DOJ disbanded the NCFS (Costakes, 2017). The attorney general indicated some internal review, informed by forensic practitioners, would continue but without independent academic scientists. With this decision, substantial forensic science reform was effectively curtailed, further demonstrating the formidable obstacles and challenges to reform. Reforms require not only technical and scientific considerations but also recognition there is a need for change and better outcomes are achievable. As noted in the Introduction, there are concerns in some quarters that the focus on wrongful conviction is detrimental to the US legal system, will result in unfavorable oversight and regulation of law enforcement, and detracts from the heralded esteem of US legal institutions. These are some of the very real challenges and obstacles to meaningful reform. Yet, the growing record of confirmed wrongful criminal convictions demands attention and reform.

CONCEPTS DERIVED FROM EXAMINING WRONGFUL CONVICTION IN SEXUAL ASSAULT

Another set of obstacles to reform is the assortment of emotional and cognitive factors (tunnel vision, confirmation bias, misinformation effects, expectancy bias, belief perseverance) operative in the moral correction process. A perspective that influenced the examination of wrongful conviction in sexual assault in this book was Leo's (2005, p. 213) proposition that wrongful conviction is the result of "human error in social and organizational contexts." As presented in previous chapters, it is valuable to point out that wrongful criminal conviction is not about random error but rather increased risk of error in certain circumstances. The social context of the error is the aftermath of crime, or perceived crime. As presented in Chapter 6, the "moral outrage" that follows high-profile crime initiates complex emotions and cognitive sets that limit the evaluation of evidence in the search for moral correction. The risk of wrongful conviction resides in the pressures for evidence and a conviction, where the rewards are immediate and gratifying, and the prospect of a wrongful conviction is distant. Moral correction pressures enable wrongful convictions, and the various manifestations of moral correction need to be identified and studied systematically.

In the current research, relying largely on available archival data sources such as the Innocence Project and National Registry of Exonerations, noteworthy relationships and processes in wrongful conviction are apparent. The resulting observations and findings provide clarity and invite hypotheses for further research with a variety of methods. For instance, is there evidence the rate of wrongful convictions, or the character of wrongful convictions, in the past decade is different from it was 20 or 30 years ago? Many exonerations reported in this volume stemmed from convictions that occurred prior to widespread use of DNA in criminal investigation (the 1980s and early 1990s). The average length of time from conviction to exoneration is 11.9 years (Gross & Shaffer, 2012). Given the increased availability of DNA testing, especially pretrial, it is expected that the frequency of wrongful conviction would decrease. Obviously, there are challenges to measuring this because the rate of wrongful conviction remains less than clear. Also, concurrent with increased availability of DNA, the past 30 years have also witnessed increased innocence advocacy, which reasonably would lead to less wrongful conviction. Another way to frame the question is to ask, what has been the impact of wrongful conviction research and innocence advocacy on criminal investigation and prosecution practice so far.

The acquired knowledge from confirmed wrongful convictions can be applied to reduce future wrongful convictions. Reducing wrongful convictions can be accomplished without jeopardizing sound convictions. It can be achieved through improved investigation, enhanced defense representation, reform and oversight of forensic science practice, and educating judges and jurors (the public) about known risks (Findley, 2009; Norris et al., 2019).

The focus on wrongful conviction in sexual assault throughout this volume has demonstrated that sexual offenses predominate among confirmed wrongful convictions. This opened the door to other important distinctions and findings. There is a pronounced concentration of confirmed wrongful convictions among stranger rapes even though acquaintance rapes are more common. This knowledge, and associated concepts describing processes in wrongful conviction, can inform research and practical efforts to reduce and prevent future wrongful conviction. The continued work will be challenging because moral correction pressures will persist and resist many reform efforts. But, recognition of the magnitude and severity of wrongful criminal conviction will produce innovative research and practical approaches to diminish risks and reduce wrongful conviction.

NOTES

1. Unreliable bite mark and hair analyses have been presented as evidence in sexual assault prosecutions leading to the wrongful rape convictions (i.e., Levon Brooks, Kennedy Brewer, the Central Park Five, Tim Cole, Gary Dotson, Steve Avery, Ralph Armstrong, John Kogut, John Restivo, Dennis Halstead).
2. For instance, "complex DNA mixture" analyses (Mnookin, 2018) lack reliable substantiation.

Alford plea—A "no-contest" plea entered by a criminal defendant asserting they are not guilty but cannot present an adequate defense to the charges. It differs from a guilty plea where the defendant is admitting guilt. Not recognized in all states.

"Black box" investigation—Investigation methods that lack transparency and are unrecorded, such as unrecorded criminal interrogation or eyewitness identification procedures. Likewise, it refers to the lack of an objective record of communications between prosecutors and expert witnesses as well as informants.

Blind (and nonblind) administrator—Refers to whether the administrator during witness identification procedures is aware which person or photo is the suspect. When the administrator is aware (nonblind), they can inadvertently or intentionally convey that information to the witness.

Capable victim—A victim of a sexual assault (or other crime) who can assist in the investigation of the crime. See "victim status."

"Continuum of intentionality"—Refers to the degree of intentionality on the part of investigators in the creation of prosecution evidence, which ranges from inadvertent (positive reinforcement following a witness' identification) to deliberate (providing fabricated testimony).

Cross-racial identification—Refers to the challenge for a witness of one racial/ethnic group in reliably identifying a perpetrator of another racial/ethnic group due to the increased risk of error in the cross-race context. This is also referred to as "cross-race" or "own-race" bias.

False confession—A confession, or incriminating statement, by a criminal suspect that is determined to be untrue.

False incriminating evidence—Refers to exaggerated or fabricated evidence indicating a suspect is guilty, that is conveyed to the suspect during interrogation to suggest the defendant will be found guilty at trial.

Forensic confirmation bias—A tendency among forensic examiners to find and/or interpret evidence to confirm a preexisting theory of the crime. Refers to the tendency to search for and find evidence that is supportive of guilt while overlooking and/or dismissing evidence suggesting innocence.

Heuristics—Methods commonly used to organize information efficiently though sometimes at the expense of accuracy. The absence of heuristics would require each single bit of information to be evaluated independently.

Incapacitated victim—A victim of a sexual assault (or other crime) who cannot assist in the investigation of the crime due to death or pronounced disability. As distinguished from a "capable" crime victim, who can describe the attack, the assailant, and otherwise assist in the investigation. See "victim status."

Incentivized testimony—Refers to testimony from a witness who is receiving some benefits from the prosecution for the testimony, such as money or reduction in criminal penalties. This includes informants and also defendants who cooperate with the prosecution for benefits. It does not include fees paid to expert witnesses.

Multiple eyewitness misidentification (MEM)—This refers to instances where several witnesses make the same misidentification of a culprit.

Multiple false confession (MFC)—When several criminal suspects provide confessions or provide incrimination statements regarding an offense that are determined to be untrue.

Relational aspect of the offense—In sexual assault (and other interpersonal crime), the relationship of the victim to the perpetrator (i.e., a stranger, an acquaintance, or a family member).

Spontaneous misidentification—This refers to a sexual assault (or any crime) victim making an incorrect identification of a perpetrator without any prompting by law enforcement officers, as opposed to misidentifications that stem from biased photo spreads, lineups, or show up identifications.

Tunnel vision—A narrow focus in an investigation on a particular suspect or offense formulation. There is attention to evidence that supports the focus and inattention or dismissal of contrary evidence.

Victim status (victim status path)—Refers to the observed relationship in wrongful conviction in sexual assault where prosecution of capable victim cases is largely based on misidentifications and in incapacitated victim cases is based on false confessions.

Abbott, J. S. (1994). The Little Rascals Day Care Center case: The bitter lesson, a healthy reminder. *Journal of Child Sexual Abuse, 3*(2), 125–130.

Acker, J. R. (2007). *Scottsboro and its legacy: The cases that challenged American legal and social justice.* New York, NY: Praeger.

Acker, J. R. (2013). The flipside injustice of wrongful convictions: When the guilty go free. *Albany Law Review, 76,* 1629–1712.

Agopian, M. W., Chappell, D., & Geis, G. (1977). Black offender and white victim: A study of forcible rape in Oakland, California. In D. Chappell, R. Geis, & G. Geis (Eds.), *Forcible rape—The crime, the victim, and the offender.* Columbia University Press; New York, NY.

Aiken, M. M., Burgess, A. W., & Hazelwood, R. R. (1999). False rape allegations. In R. R. Hazelwood & A. W. Burgess (Eds.), *Practical aspects of rape investigation: A multidisciplinary approach* (pp. 219–240). Boca Raton, FL: CRC Press.

Alderden, M. A., & Ullman, S. E. (2012). Creating a more complete picture: Examining police and prosecutor decision-making when processing sexual assault cases. *Violence Against Women, 18*(5), 525–551.

Alexander, M. (2010). *The new Jim Crow: Mass incarceration in the age of colorblindness.* New York, NY: New Press.

Alicke, M. D. (2000). Culpable control and the psychology of blame. *Psychological Bulletin, 126*(4), 556–574.

Allen, C. V. (1980). *Daddy's girl.* New York, NY: Wyndham Books.

Allen, D., & Midwinter, J. (1990, September 30). Michelle remembers: The debunking of a myth. *Mail on Sunday,* p. 41.

Allen, J., Als, H., Lewis, J., & Litwack, L. F. (2000). *Without sanctuary: Lynching photography in America.* Santa Fe, NM: Twin Palms.

Almukhtar, S., Gold, M., & Buchanan, L. (2018a, January 11). After Weinstein: 51 men accused of sexual misconduct and their fall from power. *The New York Times.* Retrieved from https://www.nytimes.com/interactive/2017/11/10/us/men-accused-sexual-misconduct-weinstein.html

Almukhtar, S., Gold, M., & Buchanan, L. (2018b, February 8). After Weinstein: 51 Men accused of sexual misconduct and their fall from power. *The New York Times.* Retrieved from https://www.nytimes.com/interactive/2017/11/10/us/men-accused-sexual-misconduct-weinstein.html

America's experiment with capital punishment (2nd ed.). Durham, NC: Carolina Academic Press.

Amine Baba-Ali—National Registry of Exonerations. (n.d.). Retrieved from https://www. law.umich.edu/special/exoneration/Pages/casedetail.aspx?caseid=3790

Anderson, D. C., & Borkowski, J. G. (1978). *Experimental psychology*. Glenview, IL: Scott, Foresman.

Anderson, E. (2017, August 16). Two former inmates win judgments against state in wrongful imprisonment suits. *Detroit Free Press*. Retrieved from http://www.freep. com/story/news/local/michigan/2017/08/16/judgments-against-state-wrongful-imprisonment/573425001/

Anderson, R. (2013, May 7). Washington State's wrongfully convicted. *Seattle Weekly News*. Retrieved from https://web.archive.org/web/20160405015909/http:// www.seattleweekly.com:80/home/946785-129/spencer-henderson-prison-titus-case-says

Aretha, D. (2008). *The trial of the Scottsboro boys: The civil rights movement*. Greensboro, NC: Morgan Reynolds.

Arizona v. Fulminante, 499 US 279–1991.

Armstrong, L. (1978). *Kiss Daddy goodnight, a speakout on incest*. New York, NY: Pocket Books.

Armstrong, M. F., Hammerman, S. L., & Martin, J. (2003). *Executive summary—Central Park Jogger case panel report*. Retrieved from www.nyc.gov/htlm...d/html/dcpi/ executivesumm_cpjc.html

Associated Press. (1983, August 24). Ohio rape defendant as esteemed as physician. *The New York Times*. Retrieved from http://www.nytimes.com/1983/08/24/us/ohio-rape-defendant-was-esteemed-as-physican.html?pagewanted=print

Associated Press. (2002, November 8). DNA evidence frees Baltimore man jailed 20 years. *Los Angeles Times*.

Associated Press. (2005, December 8). DNA tests clear Georgia inmate of rape. *FOX News*. Retrieved from http://www.foxnews.com/story/2005/12/08/dna-tests-clear-georgia-inmate-rape.html

Associated Press. (2006, July 20). Innocent man free after 23 years. *Sydney Morning Herald*. Retrieved from http://www.smh.com.au/articles/2006/07/20/1153166494221.html

Associated Press. (2010, September 17). DNA used to set two free after 30 years. *The Hamilton Spectator*, p. A10.

Aviv, R. (2017, June 19). Remembering the murder you didn't commit. *The New Yorker*. Retrieved from https://www.newyorker.com/magazine/2017/06/19/ remembering-the-murder-you-didnt-commit

Bachman, R., & Paternoster, R. (1993). A contemporary look at rape law reform: How Far have we really come? *Journal of Criminal Law and Criminology, 84*(3), 554–574.

Baldus, D. C., & Woodworth, G. (2003). Race discrimination and the death penalty: An empirical and legal overview. In James R. Acker, Robert M. Bohm, & Charles S. Lanier (Eds.). *America's experiment with capital punishment* (2nd ed.). Durham, NC: Carolina Academic Press.

Ballou, B. R. (2011, July 29). Wrongly convicted sees rapist sentenced. *The Boston Globe*. Retrieved from http://archive.boston.com/news/local/massachusetts/articles/2011/ 07/29/wrongly_convicted_sees_rapist_sentenced/

Barber, B. (1997, March 2). Closing the door on the past. *Tulsa World*. Retrieved from http://www.tulsaworld.com/archives/closing-the-door-on-the-past/article_36b67152-2082-59bb-bba7-1c289074fd5e.html

Barrett, E. C., & Hamilton-Giachritsis, C. (2013). The victim as a means to an end: Detective decision making in a simulated investigation of attempted rape. *Journal of Investigative Psychology and Offender Profiling, 10*, 200–218.

Basile, K. C., & Smith S. G. (2011). Sexual violence victimization of women: Prevalence, characteristics, and the role of public health and prevention. *American Journal of Lifestyle Medicine, 5*, 407–417.

Bass, E., & Thornton, L. (1983). *I never told anyone*. New York, NY: Harper and Row.

Baumeister, R. F., & Bushman, B. J. (2010). *Social psychology and human nature*. Stamford, CT: Wadsworth.

BBC News. (2017, December 20). *Harvey Weinstein timeline: How the scandal unfolded*. Retrieved from http://www.bbc.com/news/entertainment-arts-41594672

Bedau, H. A., & Radelet, M. L. (1987). Miscarriages of justice in potentially capital cases. *Stanford Law Review, 40*(1), 21–179.

Belknap, J. (2001). *The invisible woman* (2nd ed.). Boulder, CO: Wadsworth.

Belknap, J. (2010). Rape: Too hard to report and too easy to discredit victims. *Violence Against Women, 16*(12), 1335–1344.

Berliner, L. (2011). Child sexual abuse: Definitions, prevalence, and consequences. In J. E. B. Myers (Ed.), *The APSAC handbook on child maltreatment* (3rd ed.). Thousand Oaks, CA: Sage.

Bernard Webster—Innocence Project. (n.d.). Retrieved from https://www.innocenceproject.org/cases/bernard-webster/

Bernard Webster—Northwestern School of Law. (n.d.). Retrieved from https://www.law.umich.edu/special/exoneration/Pages/casedetail.aspx?caseid=3729

Bever, L. (2014, December 18). It took 10 minutes to convict 14-year-old George Stinney Jr. It took 70 years after his execution to exonerate him. *The Washington Post*. Retrieved from https://www.washingtonpost.com/news/morning-mix/wp/2014/12/18/the-rush-job-conviction-of-14-year-old-george-stinney-exonerated-70-years-after-execution/

Blackmon, D. A. (2010). *Slavery by another name*. New York, NY: Anchor Books.

Blackpast.org. (n.d.). *Mary B. Talbert, 1866–1923*. Retrieved from http://www.blackpast.org/aah/talbert-mary-b-1866-1923

Blalock, H. M. (1967). Status inconsistency, social mobility, status integration, and structural effects. *American Sociological Review, 32*, 790–801.

Blinder, A. (2013, November 21). Alabama pardons 3 "Scottsboro boys" after 80 years. *The New York Times*. Retrieved from http://www.nytimes.com/2013/11/22/us/with-last-3-pardons-alabama-hopes-to-put-infamous-scottsboro-boys-case-to-rest.html

Blinder, A. (2018, July 12). US reopens Emmett Till investigation, almost 63 years after his murder. *The New York Times*. https://www.nytimes.com/2018/07/12/us/emmett-till-death-investigation.html

Bookbinder, S. H., & Brainerd, C. J. (2016). Emotion and false memory: The context–content paradox. *Psychological Bulletin, 142*(12), 1315–1351. doi:10.1037/bul0000077

Borchard, E. M. (1932). *Convicting the innocent: Sixty-five actual errors of criminal justice*. Garden City, NY: Doubleday.

Brady, K. (1979). *Father's days: A true story of incest*. New York, NY: Seaview Books.

Braun, B. (2005, November 24). Giving thanks and finding peace amid injustice and tragedy. *The Star-Ledger*, pp. 39, 43.

Braun, L. S., & Thom, M. (2007). *Bella Abzug: How one tough broad from the Bronx fought Jim Crow and Joe McCarthy, pissed off Jimmy Carter, battled for the rights of women and workers, rallied against war and for the planet, and shook up politics along the way*. New York, NY: Farrar, Straus and Giroux.

Brian Banks—National Registry of Exonerations. (n.d.). Retrieved from https://www.law.umich.edu/special/exoneration/Pages/casedetail.aspx?caseid=3901

Brigham, J. C., Bennett, L. B., Meissner, C. A., & Mitchell, T. L. (2006). The influence of race on eyewitness memory. In R. C. L. Lindsay, M. P. Toglia, D. F. Ross, & J. D. Read (Eds.), *Handbook of eyewitness psychology* (pp. 257–281). Mahwah, NJ: Erlbaum.

Bright, D. A., & Goodman-Delahunty, J. (2006). Gruesome evidence and emotion: Anger, blame, and jury decision making. *Law and Human Behavior, 30*, 183–202.

Brown v. Mississippi. (1936). 297 U. S. 278.

Brownmiller, S. (1975). *Against our will: Men, women, & rape*. New York, NY: Simon & Schuster.

Bruck, M., & Ceci, S. J. (1995). Amicus brief for the case of *State of New Jersey v. Michaels* presented by Committee of Concerned Social Scientists. *Psychology, Public Policy, and Law, 1*(2), 272–322.

Bryden, D. P., & Lengnick, S. (1997). Rape in the criminal justice system. *Journal of Criminal Law & Criminology, 87*(4), 1194–1384.

Bunkley, N. (2007). Parolee linked to killing of 5 women in michigan capital. *The New York Times*. Retrieved from https://www.nytimes.com/2007/09/01/us/01arrest.html

Bureau of Prisons. (1969, August). *Capital punishment 1930–1968* (National Prisoner's Statistics, Bulletin No. 45). Washington, DC: Author.

Burke, T. M., & Marion, S. B. (2012). Alibi witnesses. In B. Cutler (Ed.), *Convicting the innocent: Lessons from psychological research*. Washington, DC: American Psychological Association.

Burns, S. (2011). *The Central Park five: The untold story behind one of New York City's most infamous crimes*. New York, NY: Vintage Books.

Calvin Wayne Cunningham—Innocence Project. (n.d.). Retrieved from https://www.innocenceproject.org/cases/calvin-wayne-cunningham/

Castelle, G., & Loftus, E. F. (2008). Misinformation and wrongful conviction. In S. D. Westervelt & J. A. Humphrey (Eds.), *Wrongly convicted: Perspectives on failed justice*. New Brunswick, NJ: Rutgers University Press.

Ceci, S. J., Crossman, A., L., Scullin, M., Gilstrap, L., & Huffman, M. (2001). Children's suggestibility research: Implications for the courtroom and the forensic interview. In H. L. Westcott, G. M. Davies, & R. Bull (Eds.), Children's testimony: *A handbook of psychological research and forensic practice*. Chichester, UK: Wiley.

Centurion Ministries. (n.d.). *John Kogut, 20 years served*. Retrieved from http://centurion.org/cases/kogut-john/

Chad Heins—Innocence Project. (n.d.). Retrieved from https://www.innocenceproject.org/cases/chad-heins/

Chammah, M. (2017, May 22). Ray spencer didn't molest his kids. So why did he spend 20 years in prison for it? *Esquire*. Retrieved from http://www.esquire.com/news-politics/a54715/ray-spencer-false-sexual-abuse-accusation/

Chandler, K. (2006, May 1). Blood Simple. *Milwaukee Magazine*. Retrieved from https://www.milwaukeemag.com/blood-simple/

Charles Dabbs—Innocence Project. (n.d.). Retrieved from https://www.innocenceproject.org/cases/charles-dabbs/

Charlton, D., Dror, I. E., & Fraser-MacKenzie, P. A. F. (2008). *A qualitative study investigating the emotional rewards and motivating factors associated with forensic fingerprint analysis* (Technical Report). Southampton, UK: University of Southampton, School of Psychology.

Christopher Burrowes—National Registry of Exonerations. (n.d.). Retrieved from https://www.law.umich.edu/special/exoneration/Pages/casedetail.aspx?caseid=4045

Claude McCollum—National Registry of Exonerations. (n.d). Retrieved from https://www.law.umich.edu/special/exoneration/Pages/casedetail.aspx?caseid=3421

Cleaver, E. (1968). *Soul on ice.* New York, NY: Ramparts Books/McGraw Hill Books.

Cohn, E. S., Bucolo, D., & Sommers, S. (2012). Race and racism. In B. L. Cutler (Ed.), *Conviction of the innocent: Lessons from psychological research.* Washington, DC: American Psychological Association.

Coker v. Georgia, 433 U. S. 584 (1977).

Costakes, A. (2017). Department of Justice to end National Commission on Forensic Science, 4/11/17. Retrieved from https://www.innocenceproject.org/department-justice-ends-national-commission-forensic-science/

The Columbus Dispatch. (2008, August 12). Hello freedom: Robert McClendon joins his family as a free man. Retrieved from http://www.dispatch.com/content/stories/local/2008/08/12/DNAfreeRT_ART_08-12-08_A1_I7B0I8G.html

The Confessions: Case Timeline. (n.d.). Retrieved from https://www.pbs.org/wgbh/pages/frontline/the-confessions/timeline-of-the-case/

Connelly, L. (2015). Cross-racial identifications: Solutions to the "they all look alike" effect. *Michigan Journal of Race & Law, 21*(1), *125*(2015)

Connors, E., Lundregan, T., Miller, N., & McEwen, T. (1996). *Convicted by juries, exonerated by science: Case studies in the use of DNA evidence to establish innocence after trial.* Alexandria, VA: National Institute of Justice, US Department of Justice.

Cooper, S. J. (2008). From Claude Bernard to Walter Cannon. Emergence of the concept of homeostasis. *Appetite, 51*, 419–427. doi:10.1016/j.appet.2008.06.005

Cory, P. (2001). Commission of Inquiry regarding Thomas Sophonow. Manitoba. mb.ca/justice/sophonow/index.html

Costanzo, M., & Krause, D. (2018). Forensic & legal psychology: Psychological science applied to law (3rd ed.). New York, NY: Worth.

Crocker, P. L. (2001). Feminism and the criminal law: Is the death penalty good for women? *Buffalo Criminal Law Review, 4*(2), 917–965.

Curtis, L. A. (1974). *Criminal violence: National patterns and behavior.* Lexington, MA: Lexington Books.

Cutler, B. L. (Ed.). (2012). *Convicting the innocent: Lessons from psychological research.* Washington, DC: American Psychological Association.

Cutler, B. L. (2013). *Reform of eyewitness identification procedures.* Washington, DC: American Psychological Association.

Cutler, B. L., & Kovera, M. B. (2010). *Evaluating eyewitness identification.* New York, NY: Oxford University Press.

Darryl Hunt—National Registry of Exonerations. (n.d.). Retrieved from https://www.law. umich.edu/special/exoneration/Pages/casedetail.aspx?caseid=3314

Davenport, P. (2006, August 18). Phoenix man gets prison in slaying previously pinned on wrong man. *Tucson Citizen.* Retrieved from http://tucsoncitizen.com/morgue/ 2006/08/18/23213-phoenix-man-gets-prison-in-slaying-previously-pinned-on-wrong-man/

David Vasquez—National Registry of Exonerations. (n.d.). Retrieved from https://www. law.umich.edu/special/exoneration/Pages/casedetail.aspx?caseid=3705

Davidson, A. (2012, August 19). What does Todd Akin think "legitimate rape" is? *The New Yorker.* Retrieved from http://www.newyorker.com/online/blogs/closeread/ 2012/08/what-does-todd-akin-think-legitimate-rape-is.html

Davis, A. (1983). *Women, race, & class.* New York, NY: Vintage Books.

Deblinger, E., Mannarino, A. P., & Cohen, J. A. (2015). Child sexual abuse (2nd ed.). New York, NY: Oxford University Press.

Debra Shelden—National Registry of Exonerations. (n.d.). Retrieved from https://www. law.umich.edu/special/exoneration/Pages/casedetail.aspx?caseid=3629

Deffenbacher, K. A., Bornstein, B. H., Penrod, S. D. (2006). Mugshot exposure effects: Retroactive interference, mugshot commitment, source confusion, and unconscious transference. *Law and Human Behavior, 30*(3), 287–307.

Deffenbacher, K. A., Bornstein, B. H., Penrod, S. D., & McGorty, E. K. (2004). A meta-analytic review of the effects of high stress on eyewitness memory. *Law and Human Behavior, 28*(6), 687–706.

DeGue, S., Simon, T. R., Basile, K. C., Yee, S. L., Lang, K., & Spivak, H. (2012). Moving forward by looking back: Reflecting on a decade of CDC's work in sexual violence prevention, 2000–2010. *Journal of Women's Health, 21*(12), 1211–1218.

Demaris, O. (1970). *America the violent.* New York, NY: Cowles.

DePanfilis, D. (2011). Child protection system. In J. E. B. Myers (Ed.), The APSAC handbook on child maltreatment (3rd ed.). Thousand Oaks, CA: Sage.

Dewan, S. (2005, December 8). After 24 years in prison, man has a reason to smile. *The New York Times.* Retrieved from http://www.nytimes.com/2005/12/08/us/after-24-years-in-prison-man-has-a-reason-to-smile.html

de Young, M. (2004). *The day care ritual abuse panic.* Jefferson, NC: McFarland.

Dixon, T. (1902). *The Leopard's Spots: A Romance of the White Man's Burden – 1865–1900.* New York, NY: Doubleday, Page, & Company.

Dixon, T. (1905). *The Clansman: An Historical Romance of the Ku Klux Klan.* New York, NY: A Wessels & Company.

Dovidio, J. F., & Gaertner, S. L. (2004). Aversive racism. In M. P. Zanna (Ed.), *Advances in experimental social psychology* (Vol. 36, pp. 1–51).

Dovidio, J. F., & Gaertner, S. L. (2008). New directions in aversive racism research: Persistence and pervasiveness. In C. Willis-Esqueda (Ed.), *Motivational aspects of prejudice and racism* (pp. 43–67). New York, NY: Springer Science and Business Media.

Dovidio, J. F., Kawakami, K., Johnson, C. Johnson, B., & Howard, A. (1997). On the nature of prejudice: Automatic and controlled processes. *Journal of Experimental Social Psychology, 33,* 510–540.

Dred Scott v. Sanford 60 U. S. 393 (1856).

Drizin, S. A. (2013, November 20). Confession contamination in Cook County: Demonizing youth in confession narratives. *The Huffington Post*. Retrieved from http://www.huffingtonpost.com/steve-drizin/confession-contamination-cook-county_b_4293092.html

Drizin, S. A., & Leo, R. A. (2004). The problem of false confessions in the post-DNA world. *North Carolina Law Review, 82*, 891–1007.

Dror, I. E. (2018). Biases in Forensic Experts. *Science, 360*(6386), 243.

Dror, I. E., & Bucht, R. (2012). Psychological perspectives on problems with forensic science evidence. In B. L. Cutler (Ed.), *Conviction of the innocent: Lessons from psychological research*. Washington, DC: American Psychological Association.

Dror, I. E., & Fraser-MacKenzie, P. A. F. (2009). Cognitive biases in human perception, judgment, and decision making: Bridging theory and the real world. In D. Kim Rossmo (Ed.), *Criminal investigative failures*. Boca Raton, FL: CRC Press.

Duggan, J. (2016, October 25). Beatrice 6 member says threat of death penalty persuaded her to confess to a slaying she didn't commit. *Omaha World-Herald*. Retrieved from http://www.omaha.com/news/crime/beatrice-member-says-threat-of-death-penalty-persuaded-her-to/article_51ebcf4f-7299-5d08-8dfa-ebae55f0f5c2.html

Dunker, C. (2017, January 18). Gage County seeks reversal on Beatrice 6 judgment. *Lincoln Journal Star*. Retrieved from http://journalstar.com/news/state-and-regional/nebraska/gage-county-seeks-reversal-on-beatrice-judgment/article_f89486d1-0141-5ecf-abc1-28640f86c0b1.html

Duru, N. J. (2004). The Central Park Five, The Scottsboro Boys, and The Myth of the Bestial Black Man. *Cardoza Law Review, 25*(4), 1315–1365.

Duster, A. M. (Ed.). (1970). *Crusade for justice: The autobiography of Ida B. Wells*. Chicago, IL: University of Chicago Press.

Engle, J., & O'Donohue, W. (2012). Pathways to false allegations of sexual assault. *Journal of Forensic Psychology Practice, 12*, 97–123.

Esposito, S. (2010, May 14). Having won freedom, he wants to help others; conviction tossed after 8 years, goal now is to become a lawyer. *Chicago Sun Times*, p. 11.

Estrich, S. (1987). *Real rape: How the legal system victimizes women who say no*. Cambridge, MA: Harvard University Press.

Fager, J. (Producer). (2008, May 4). 60 Minutes (CBS broadcast; (transcript on file with author).

Falkenberg, L. (2001, January 17). Man freed on DNA evidence. *Fort Worth Star-Telegram*, pp. 1, 13A.

Falssetti, J. (2016, October 10). Wrongfully convicted Oklahomans call for eyewitness identification reforms. *Fox 25 News*. Retrieved from http://okcfox.com/news/local/wrongfully-convicted-oklahomans-call-for-eyewitness-identification-reforms.

Farley, F. H, & Mealia, W. L. (1973). Motivation and the recall of completed and incomplete achievement items. *The Journal of Educational Research, 66*(7), 302–306.

Fedo, M. (2000). *The lynchings in Duluth*. St. Paul, MN: Minnesota Historical Society Press.

Findley, K. A. (2009). Toward a new paradigm of criminal justice: How the innocence movement merges crime control and due process. *Texas Tech Law Review, 41*, 1–41.

Findley, K. A., Barnes, P. D., Moran, D. A., & Squier, W. (2012). Shaken Baby Syndrome, abusive head trauma, and actual innocence: Getting it right. *Houston Journal of Health Law & Policy, 12*(2), 209–312.

Findley, K. A., & Scott, M. S. (2006, June). The multiple dimensions of tunnel vision in criminal cases. *Wisconsin Law Review,* 291–397.

Finkelstein, S. (Producer). (2009, March 6). Eyewitness: How accurate is visual memory? *60 Minutes.* CBS News. Retrieved from http://www.cbsnews.com/news/eyewitness-how-accurate-is-visual-memory/2/

Fontes, L. A. (2005). *Child abuse and culture.* New York, NY: Guildford Press.

Ford, T. (2017, December 7). The 19 women who accused president trump of sexual misconduct. *The Atlantic.* Retrieved from https://www.theatlantic.com/politics/archive/2017/12/what-about-the-19-women-who-accused-trump/547724/

Foster v. Chatman, 136 S. Ct. 1737 (2016), 219.

Foster v. Chatman. (2016b). Brief for petitioner Timothy Foster. Retrieved from https://www.schr.org/files/post/.../Brief%20of%20Petition%20Timothy%20Foster_.pdf

FPT Heads of Prosecution Committee Working Committee Group. (2004). *Report of the prevention of miscarriages of justice.* Ottawa, Canada: Department of Justice.

Free, M. D., & Ruesink, M. (2012). *Race and justice: Wrongful convictions of African American men.* Boulder, CO: Lynne Rienner.

Frontline. (n.d.). Innocence lost. Retrieved from https://www.pbs.org/wgbh/frontline/film/innocence-lost/

Galvin, J., & Polk, K. (1983). Attrition in rape case processing: Is rape unique? *Journal of Research in Crime and Delinquency, 20,* 126–153.

Gardner, R. (1991). *Sex abuse hysteria: Salem witch trials revisited.* Longwood, NJ: Creative Therapeutics.

Garland, T. (2009). An overview of sexual assault and sexual assault myths. In F. P. Reddington & B. W. Kreisel (Eds.), *Sexual assault: The victims, the perpetrators, and the criminal justice system* (2nd ed.). Durham, NC: Carolina Academic Press.

Garrett, B. L. (2010). The substance of false confessions. *Stanford Law Review, 62,* 1051–1119.

Garrett, B. L. (2011). *Convicting the innocent: Where criminal prosecutions go wrong.* Cambridge, MA: Harvard University Press.

Garrett, B. L., & Neufeld, P. (2009). Invalid forensic science testimony and wrongful conviction. *Virginia Law Review, 95*(1), 1–97.

Gary Dotson—Northwestern School of Law. (n.d.). Retrieved from http://www.law.northwestern.edu/legalclinic/wrongfulconvictions/exonerations/il/gary-dotson.html

Gaulkin, G. (2010). *Report of the special master in state of* New Jersey v. Larry D. Henderson. Supreme Court of New Jersey. Retrieved from http://www.judiciary.state.nj.us/pressrel/HENDERSON%20FINAL%20BRIEF%20.PDF%20%2800621142%29.PDF

Gialanella, D. (2016, August 15). Man exonerated by DNA tests moves forward with civil suit. *New Jersey Law Journal.*

Gibney, A. (2020). (Director) The Innocence Files, Episode 7 - The Prosecution: Wrong Place, Wrong Time. Los Gatos, CA: Netflix Production.

Gibson, R. A. (2010). *The Negro Holocaust: Lynching and Race Riots in the United States, 1880–1950.* New Haven: Yale-New Haven Teachers Institute.

Giddings, P. J. (2008). *Ida: A sword among lions.* New York, NY: Amistad.

Goff, P. A., Eberhardt, J. L., Williams, M. J., & Jackson, M. C. (2008). Not yet human: Implicit knowledge, historical de-humanization, and contemporary consequences. *Journal of Personality and Social Psychology, 94*(2), 292–306.

Goff, P. A., Jackson, M. C., Di Leone, B. A. L., Culotta, C. M., & DiTomasso, N. A. (2014). The essence of innocence: Consequences of dehumanizing Black children. *Journal of Personality and Social Psychology, 106*(4), 526–545.

Goldston, M. (1990). Special project conclusion report. Chicago, IL: Office of Professional Standards. On file with author.

Goodman, G. S., Qin, J., Bottoms, B. L., & Shaver, P. R. (1994). Characteristics and *sources of allegations of ritualistic child abuse*: Final report to the National Center on Child Abuse and Neglect (Grant No. 90CA1405). National Institute of Justice, Rockville, MD.

Goodman, J. (1994). *Stories of Scottsboro*. New York, NY: Pantheon.

Gootman, E. (2003, June 12). DNA evidence frees 3 men in 1984 murder of L.I. girl. *The New York Times*. Retrieved from http://www.nytimes.com/2003/06/12/nyregion/dna-evidence-frees-3-men-in-1984-murder-of-li-girl.html?mcubz=0

Gould, J. B. (2008). *The Innocence Commission: Preventing Wrongful Convictions and Restoring the Criminal Justice System*. New York, NY: New York University Press.

Gould, J. B., & Leo, R. A. (2010). One hundred years later: Wrongful convictions after a century of research. *Journal of Criminal Law & Criminology, 100*, 825–868.

Gowen, A. (2002, November 20). New '82 rape suspect is held without bond; DNA cleared 1 man, led police to another. *The Washington Post*, p. B04.

Graham-Bermann, S. A., & Howell, K. H. (2011). Child maltreatment in the context of intimate partner violence. In J. E. B. Myers (Ed.), *The APSAC handbook on child maltreatment* (3rd ed.). Thousand Oaks, CA: Sage.

Grant Self—National Registry of Exonerations. (n.d.). Retrieved from https://www.law.umich.edu/special/exoneration/Pages/casedetail.aspx?caseid=4163

Gray, E. (2015, June 18). The history of using white female sexuality to justify racist violence. *The Huffington Post*. Retrieved from http://www.huffingtonpost.com/2015/06/18/white-female-sexuality-and-racist-violence-a-history_n_7613048.html

Green, B. (1999). *Before His Time: The Untold Story of Harry T. Moore, America's First Civil Rights Martyr*. New York, NY: The Free Press.

Green, F. (2014). Acts of empathy, forgiveness help mistaken accuser find peace. Richmond Times-Dispatch, 7/26/14. Retrieved from https://richmond.com/news/virginia/acts-of-empathy-forgiveness-help-mistaken-accuser-find-peace/article_99d5ad20-79f2-5dd2-9713-b2bfbc6cb85a.html

Greenfield, L. A. (1997). Sex offenses and offenders, 1997. Washington, DC: US Department of Justice, Bureau of Justice Statistics.

Grissom, B. (2013, June 15). A freed man, an ex-wife and a lawsuit. *The New York Times*, p. 27A. Retrieved from http://www.nytimes.com/2013/06/16/us/a-freed-man-an-ex-wife-and-a-lawsuit.html?mcubz=0

Gross, S. R. (1996). The risks of death: Why erroneous convictions are common in capital cases. *Buffalo Law Review, 44*(2), 469–500.

Gross, S. R. (2008). Convicting the innocent. *Annual Review of Law and Social Science, 4*, 173–192.

Gross, S. R., Jacoby, K., Matheson, D. J., Montgomery, N., & Patil, S. (2005). Exonerations in the United States 1989 through 2003. *The Journal of Criminal Law & Criminology, 95*(2), 523–560.

Gross, S. R., & O'Brien, B. (2008). Frequency and predicators of false conviction: Why we know so little, and new data on capital. *Journal of Empirical Legal Studies, 5*(4), 927–962.

Gross, S. R., O'Brien, B., Hu, C., Kennedy, E. H. (2014). Rate of false conviction of criminal defendants who are sentenced to death. *Proceedings of the National Academy of Science of the United States of America, 111*(20), 7230–7235.

Gross, S. R., Possley, M., & Stephens, K. (2017). *Race and wrongful conviction in the United States.* Irvine, CA: National Registry of Exonerations, Newkirk Center for Science and Society, University of California-Irvine. Retrieved from http://www.law.umich.edu/special/exoneration/Documents/Race_and_Wrongful_Convictions.pdf

Gross, S. R., & Shaffer, M. (2012, June). *Exonerations in the United States, 1989–2012* (Public Law and Legal Theory Working Paper Series, Working Paper No 277). Ann Arbor, MI: University of Michigan Law School.

Grounds, A. (2004). Psychological consequences of wrongful conviction and imprisonment. *Canadian Journal of Criminology and Criminal Justice, 46*(2), 165–182.

Gruber, A. (2009). Rape, feminism, and the war on crime. *Washington Law Review, 84*, 581–658.

Gudjonsson, G. (2003). *The psychology of interrogations and confessions: A handbook.* Chichester, UK: Wiley.

Guilfoil, J. M. (2011, July 20). Guilty plea due in wrongful conviction. *The Boston Globe.* Retrieved from http://archive.boston.com/news/local/massachusetts/articles/2011/07/20/guilty_plea_due_in_wrongful_conviction/

Haines, R. (Director) (1984). *Something About Ameilia.* ABC-TV, January 9, 1984.

Hall, J. D. (1983). "The mind that burns in each body": Women, rape, and racial violence. In A. Snitow, C. Stannsel, & S. Thompson (Eds.), *Powers of desire: The politics of sexuality.* New York, NY: Monthly Review Press.

Hall, M. (2017, March). The trouble with innocence. *Texas Monthly.* Retrieved from https://features.texasmonthly.com/editorial/the-trouble-with-innocence/

Hanes, S. (2004, May 22). '84 investigation quick to overlook the culprit. *The Baltimore Sun.* Retrieved from http://articles.baltimoresun.com/2004-05-22/news/0405220166_1_ruffner-dawn-hamilton-bloodsworth

Harbers, E., Deslauriers-Varin, N., Beauregard, E., & Van Der Kemp, J. J. (2012). Testing the behavioural consistency of serial sex offenders: A signature approach. *Journal of Investigative Psychology and Offender Profiling, 9*, 259–273.

Harris, C. (1994). Whiteness as property. *Harvard Law Review, 106*(8), 1709–1791.

Haw, R. M., Dickinson, J. J., Meissner, C. A. (2007). The phenomenology of carryover effects between show-up and line-up identification. *Memory, 15*(1), 117–127.

Hazelwood, R. R., & Warren, J. I. (1999). The serial rapist. In R. R. Hazelwood & A. W. Burgess (Eds.), *Practical aspects of rape investigation: A multidisciplinary approach.* Boca Raton, FL: CRC Press.

Healy, J. (2013, March 13). Wrongfully convicted and seeking restitution. *The New York Times.* Retrieved from http://www.nytimes.com/2013/03/14/us/prisoners-seek-restitution-for-wrongful-convictions.html?mcubz=1

Healy, J. (2019, April 1). A rural county owes $28 million for wrongful convictions. It doesn't want to pay. *The New York Times*. Retrieved from https://www.nytimes.com/2019/04/01/us/beatrice-six-nebraska.html

Heard, A. (2011). *The eyes of Willie McGee: A tragedy of race, sex, and secrets in the Jim Crow south*. New York, NY: HarperCollins.

Heggie, V. (2012, August 20). Legitimate rape—A medieval medical concept. *The Guardian*. Retrieved from https://www.theguardian.com/science/the-h-word/2012/aug/20/legitimate-rape-medieval-medical-concept

Henderson, P. (1981, May 29). Guilt in rape case may hang on the tick, tick, tick of clock. *Seattle Times*. Retrieved from http://old.seattletimes.com/news/local/tituscase/clock.html

Herbert, B. (2008, January 22). The blight that is still with us. *The New York Times*. Retrieved from http://www.nytimes.com/2008/01/22/opinion/22herbert.html?_r=0

Herman Atkins—National Registry of Exonerations. (n.d.). Retrieved from https://www.law.umich.edu/special/exoneration/Pages/casedetail.aspx?caseid=3000).

Hinkel, D. (2017, December 18). City proposes $31 million settlement for Englewood Four's wrongful conviction. *The Chicago Tribune*. Retrieved from https://www.chicagotribune.com/news/local/breaking/ct-met-englewood-four-multimillion-settlement-20171208-story.html

Hirsch, J. S. (2002). *Riot and remembrance: The Tulsa race war and its legacy*. Boston, MA: Houghton Mifflin.

Holland, K. J., Rabelo, V. C., & Cortina, L. M. (2016). Collateral damage: Military sexual trauma and help-seeking barriers. *Psychology of Violence, 6*(2), 253–261.

Hsu, S. (2012, April 17.) Defendants left unaware of flaws found in cases. *The Washington Post*.

Huddle, C. (2009, May 6). Part four: Pointing fingers. *Lincoln Journal Star*. Retrieved from http://journalstar.com/special-section/presumed-guilty/part-four-pointing-fingers/article_671c164b-a9ab-514f-893f-244c454d7f01.html

Huff, R. C., Rattner, A., & Sagarin, E. (1996). *Convicted but innocent: Wrongful conviction and public policy*. Thousand Oaks, CA: Sage.

Huie, W. B. (1956, January 25). The shocking story of approved killing in Mississippi. *Look* Retrieved from https://webzoom.freewebs.com/mbrowningla/PDF%20of%20The%20Shocking%20Story%20of%20Approved%20Killing%20in%20Mississippi.pdf

Inbau, F. E., Reid, J. E., Buckley, J. P., & Jayne, B. C. (2005). *Criminal interrogation and confessions* (4th ed.). Gaithersburg, MD: Aspen.

Inbau, F. E., Reid, J. E., Buckley, J. P., & Jayne, B. C. (2013). *Criminal interrogation and confessions* (5th ed.). Burlington, MA: Jones & Bartlett.

Innocence Project. (2009). *Re-evaluating line-ups: Why witnesses make mistakes and how to reduce the chance of a mis-identification*. Retrieved from https://www.innocenceproject.org/reevaluating-lineups-why-witnesses-make-mistakes-and-how-to-reduce-the-chance-of-a-misidentification/

Innocence Project. (2017). *Recording of custodial interrogations briefing book*. Retrieved from https://www.leg.state.nv.us/Session/79th2017/Exhibits/Assembly/JUD/AJUD776K.pdf

In the Matters of Gregory W. and Gerald S., 19 N. Y. 2d 55 (1966).

Irazola, S., Williamson, E., Stricker, J., & Niedzwiecki, E. (2013). *Study of victim experiences of wrongful conviction.* Fairfax, VA: ICF.

Jackson, J. (Producer). (1983, February 27). An open-and-shut case (CBS broadcast). *60 Minutes.*

Jepheth Barnes—National Registry of Exonerations. (n.d.). Retrieved from https://www. law.umich.edu/special/exoneration/Pages/casedetail.aspx?caseid=4958

Jerry Miller—Innocence Project. (n.d.). Retrieved from https://www.innocenceproject. org/cases/jerry-miller/

Johnathan Barr—National Registry of Exonerations. (n.d.). Retrieved from https://www. law.umich.edu/special/exoneration/Pages/casedetail.aspx?caseid=3840

John Grega—National Registry of Exonerations. (n.d.). Retrieved from https://www.law. umich.edu/special/exoneration/Pages/casedetail.aspx?caseid=4245

Johnson, M. B. (2001). The emergence and significance of the "Mallott rule": The legal history. *Journal of Psychiatry & Law, 29*(Summer), 121–146.

Johnson, M. B. (2005). The Central Park jogger case—Police coercion and secrecy in interrogation: The 14th Annual Frantz Fanon MD Memorial Lecture. *Journal of Ethnicity in Criminal Justice, 3*(1/2), 131–143.

Johnson, M. B. (2013, October 3). Sex, race, and wrongful conviction. *The Crime Report.* Retrieved from http://www.thecrimereport.org/news/articles/2013-10-sex-race-and-wrongful-conviction

Johnson, M. B., Citron-Lippman, K., Massey, C., Raghavan, C., & Kavanaugh, A. M. (2015). Interrogation expectations: Individual and race/ethnic group variation among an adult sample. *Journal of Ethnicity in Criminal Justice, 13*(1), 16–29. doi:10.1080/15377938.2014.936641

Johnson, M. B., & Cunningham, S. (2015, June 30). *Why innocent defendants plead guilty to rape charges.* The Crime Report. Retrieved from https://thecrimereport.org/2015/06/30/2015-06-why-innocent-defendants-plead-guilty-to-rape-charges/

Johnson, M. B., & Drucker, J. (2009). Two recently confirmed false confessions: Byron A. Halsey and Jeffrey M. Deskovic. *Journal of Psychiatry & Law, 37*(Spring), 51–72.

Johnson, M. B., Griffith, S., & Barnaby, C. Y. (2013). African-Americans wrongly convicted of sexual assaults against whites: Witness mis-identification and other case features. *Journal of Ethnicity in Criminal Justice, 11*, 277–294.

Johnson, M. B., & Melendez, S. (2019). Spontaneous Misidentification in Wrongful Rape Conviction. *American Journal of Forensic Psychology, 37*(2), 5–20.

Johnson, S. L. (1984). Cross racial identification errors in criminal cases. *Cornell Law Review, 69*, 934–987.

Johnson, S. L. (1993). Racial imagery in criminal cases. *Tulane Law Review, 67*, 1739–1805.

Johnson, S. L. (2001). Racial derogation in prosecutor's closing arguments. In D. Milovanovic & K. K. Russell (Eds.), *Petit apartheid in the US criminal justice system.* Durham, NC: Carolina Academic Press.

John Stoll—Northern California Innocence Project. (n.d.). Retrieved from http://law.scu. edu/ncip/exonerations/john-stoll/

Jones, M. (2004, September 19). Who was abused? *The New York Times.* Retrieved from http://www.nytimes.com/2004/09/19/magazine/19KIDSL.html?pagewanted=print &position=&_r=0

Joseph Frey—Innocence Project. (n.d.). Retrieved from https://www.innocenceproject. org/cases/joseph-frey/

Junkin, T. (2004). *Bloodsworth: The true story of the first death row inmate exonerated by DNA.* Chapel Hill, NC: Algonquin Books of Chapel Hill.

Kalven, H., & Zeisel, H. (1966). *The American jury.* Boston, MA: Little Brown.

Kanin, E. J. (1994). *Archives of Sexual Behavior, 23,* 1, 81–92.

Kassin, S. M. (2007). Internalized false confessions. In M. P. Toglia, J. D. Read, D. F. Ross, & R. D. L. Lindsay (Eds.), *The handbook of eye-witness psychology (Vol. 1).* New York, NY: Taylor & Francis.

Kassin, S. M. (2015). The social psychology of false confessions. *Social Issues and Policy Review, 9*(1), 25–51.

Kassin, S. M., Bogart, D., & Kerner, J. (2012). Confessions that corrupt: Evidence from the DNA exoneration case files. *Psychological Science, 23,* 41–45.

Kassin, S. M., Drizin, S. A., Grisso, T. Gudjonsson, G. H., Leo, R. A., & Redlich, A. D. (2010). Police-induced confessions: Risk factors and recommendations. *Law and Human Behavior, 34,* 3–38.

Katz, L. S., Huffman, C., Cojucar, G. (2017). In her own words: Semi-structured interviews of women veterans who experienced military sexual assault. *Journal of Contemporary Psychotherapy, 47*(3), 181–189.

Kennedy, J. P. (2004). Writing the wrongs. The role of defense counsel in wrongful conviction—A commentary. *Canadian Journal of Criminology and Criminal Justice, 46,* 197–208.

Kim, K., Littlefield, C., & Etehad, M. (2017, June 17). Bill Cosby: A 50-year chronicle of accusations and accomplishments. *The Los Angeles Times.* Retrieved from http:// www.latimes.com/entertainment/la-et-bill-cosby-timeline-htmlstory.html

King, R. (2016). *Reclaiming innocence: Brooklyn's fight to reverse wrongful convictions.* Retrieved from http://thecrimereport.org/2016/05/19/ reclaiming-innocence-brooklyns-fight-to-reverse-wrongful-convictions/

King, G. (2012). *Devil in the grove: Thurgood Marshall, the Groveland Boys, and the dawn of a New America.* New York, NY: Harper Perennial.

Kinshasha, K. M. (2006). *Black resistance to the Ku Klux Klan in the wake of the Civil War.* Jefferson, NC: McFarland.

Kix, P. (2016, January 18). Recognition: How a travesty led to criminal-justice innovation in Texas. *The New Yorker.* Retrieved from http://www.newyorker.com/magazine/2016/01/18/recognition-annals-ofjustice-paul-kix

Klein, R. (2008). An analysis of thirty-five years of rape reform: A frustrating search for fundamental fairness. *Akron Law Review, 41,* 981–1057.

Klibanoff, H. (1980a, October 26). Sanders case—Questions of procedure. *The Boston Globe,* p. 1.

Klibanoff, H. (1980b, October 27). Sanders case: A photo and a suggestion. *The Boston Globe,* p. 1.

Klibanoff, H. (1980c, October 28). Police suggestiveness and the Sanders line-up. *The Boston Globe,* p. 1.

Klibanoff, H. (1980d, October 29). The Willie Sanders Case: How physical evidence deteriorated in the Sanders Case. *The Boston Globe,* p. 1.

Kotlowitz, A. (1999, February 9). The unprotected. *The New Yorker.* Retrieved from https://www.newyorker.com/magazine/1999/02/08/the-unprotected

Kovel, J. (1970). *White racism: A psycho-history*. New York, NY: Pantheon.

Krajicek, D. J. (2015). A freakishly rare anomaly. Retrieved from http://thecrimereport. org/2015/02/09/2015-02-a-freakishly-rare-anomaly/

Lacayo, R. (2000, April 2). Blood at the Root. *Time*. Retrieved from http://content.time. com/time/magazine/article/0,9171,42301,00.html?iid=sr-link1

LaFree, G. D. (1983). The effect of sexual stratification by race on official reactions to rape. *American Sociological Review, 45*, 842–854.

Lamb, M. E., Hershkowitz, I., Orbach, Y., & Esplin, P. W., (2008). *Tell me what happened: Structured investigative interviews of child victims and witnesses*. West Sussex, UK: Wiley.

Lampien, J. M., Neuschatz, J. S., & Cling, A. D. (2012). *The psychology of eye-witness identification*. New York, NY: Psychology Press.

Lautenschlager, P. A. (2003, December 17). *State of Wisconsin—Department of Justice: Avery review*. Retrieved from http://www.stevenaverycase.org/wp-content/ uploads/2016/03/WI-DOJ-Report-on-Avery-1985-Case.pdf

Lawson, M. L. (1977). Omaha, a city in ferment: Summer of 1919. *Nebraska History, 58*(3), 395–417. Retrieved from http://www.muchgrace.com/HistoricPapers/ CityinFerment.pdf

Leavy, W. (1987, March). Innocent man's eight year prison ordeal. *Ebony*, pp. 86, 88, 90, 91.

LeBeau, J. L. (1985). Rape and racial patterns. *Journal of Offender Counseling Services Rehabilitation, 9*(1–2), 125–148.

LeBeau, J. L. (1987). Patterns of stranger and serial rape offending: Factors distinguishing apprehended and at large offenders. *The Journal of Law & Criminology, 78*, 309–326.

Lee, H. (1960). *To kill a mockingbird*. Philadelphia, PA: Lippincott.

Leo, R. A. (2005). Rethinking the study of miscarriages of justice. *Journal of Contemporary Criminal Justice, 21*(3), 201–223.

Leo, R. A. (2008). *Police interrogation and American justice*. Cambridge, MA: Harvard University Press.

Leo, R. A. (2009). False Confessions: Causes, Consequences, and Implications. *The Journal of the American Academy of Psychiatry and the Law, 37*(3), 332–343.

Leo, R. A., & Davis, D. (2010). From false confession to wrongful conviction: Seven psychological processes. *The Journal of Psychiatry and Law, 38*, 9–56.

Leo, R. A., & Gould, J. B. (2009). Studying wrongful convictions: Learning from social science. *Ohio State Journal of Criminal Law, 7*, 7–30.

Levy, A. (2015, April 13). The price of a life: What's the right way to compensate someone for decades of lost freedom? *The New Yorker*. Retrieved from http://www.newyorker. com/magazine/2015/04/13/the-price-of-a-life

Liptak, A. (2008, March 25). Consensus on counting the innocent. *The New York Times*, p. A14.

Liptak, A. (2016). Supreme Court Finds Racial Bias in Jury Selection for Death Penalty Case. The New York Times, 5/23/16. Retrieved from https://www.nytimes.com/ 2016/05/24/us/supreme-court-black-jurors-death-penalty-georgia.html

Lisak, D., Gardinier, L., Nicksa, S. C., & Cote, A. M. (2010). False allegations of sexual assault: An analysis of ten years of reported cases. *Violence Against Women, 16*(12), 1318–34. doi:0.1177/1077801210387747

Lofquist, W. S. (2008). Whodunnit? An examination of the production of wrongful convictions. In S. Westervelt & J. Humphrey (Eds.), *Wrongly convicted: Perspectives on failed justice* (pp. 174–198). Newark, NJ: Rutgers University Press.

Loftus, E. F. (2005). Planting misinformation in the human mind: A 30-year investigation of the malleability of memory. *Memory & Learning, 12*, 361–366.

Loftus, E., & Ketcham, K. (1991). *Witness for the defense: The accused, the eyewitness, and the expert who puts memory on trial.* New York, NY: St. Martin's Press.

London, K., Bruck, M., Ceci, S. J., & Shuman, D. W. (2005). Disclosure of child sexual abuse: What does the research tell us about the ways that children tell? *Psychology, Public Policy, and Law, 11*(1), 194–226.

Lonsway, K. A., & Archambault, J. (2012). The "justice gap" for sexual assault cases: Future directions for research and reform. *Violence Against Women, 18*, 145–168.

Lowrey-Kinberg, B., Senn, S. L., Gould, J. B., & Hail-Jares, K. (2017). Pathways to suspicion: Causes and consequences of innocent suspects' origin of implication. *California Western Law Review, 54*, 2–50.

Lyon, T. D., & Ahern, E. C. (2011). Disclosure of child sexual abuse: Implications for interviewing. In J. E. B. Myers (Ed.), *The APSAC handbook on child maltreatment* (3rd ed.). Thousand Oaks, CA: Sage.

MacFarlane, B. A. (2004). *Convicting the innocent: A triple failure of the justice system.* Retrieved from http://www.canadiancriminallaw.com/articles%20pdf/convicting_the_innocent.pdf

Mann, C. R., & Selva, L. H. (1979). The sexualization of racism: The Black as rapist and white justice. *Western Journal of Black Studies, 3*, 168–177.

Manson v. Brathwaite, 432 U.S. 98 (1977).

Mark Clark—National Registry of Exonerations. (n.d.). Retrieved from https://www.law.umich.edu/special/exoneration/Pages/casedetail.aspx?caseid=3107

Martin, C. H. (1987). The civil rights Congress and southern Black defendants. *Georgia Historical Quarterly, 71*(1), 25–52.

Maston, C., & Klaus, P. (2003). Criminal victimization in the United States, 2002. Statistical Tables, 42 tbl.29. Washington, DC: US Department of Justice.

Maxwell v. Bishop, 398 U. S. 262 (1970).

McDermott, M. J. (1979). *Rape victimization in 26 American cities.* Washington, DC: Urban Institute, National Institute of Justice.

McGagin, K. (2007, October 11). *Letter to Gerald F. Uelman.* Retrieved from http://www.ccfaj.org/documents/reports/incompentence/expert/CVCGCB%2010-11-07.pdf

McGuire, D. L. (2010). *At the dark end of the street: Black women, rape, and resistance.* New York, NY: Knopf.

McVeigh, K. (2014, March 22). George Stinney was executed at 14. Can his family now clear his name? *The Guardian.* Retrieved from http://www.theguardian.com/theobserver/2014/mar/22/george-stinney-execution-verdict-innocent

Medwed, D. S. (2013). *Prosecution complex: America's race to convict and its impact on the innocent.* New York, NY: NYU Press.

Meili, T. (2003). *I am the Central Park jogger: A story of hope and possibility.* New York, NY: Scribner.

Meissner, C. A., & Brigham, J. C. (2001). Thirty years of investigating own race bias in memory for faces: A meta-analysis. *Psychology, Public Policy, and Law, 7*(3), 3–35.

Menaker, T. A., Campbell, B. A., & Wells, W. (2017). The use of forensic evidence in sexual assault investigation: Perceptions of sex crimes investigators. *Violence Against Women, 23*, 399–425.

Messick, R. E. (1985, November 19). High bail set in child murders. *The Star Ledger.*

Michael Mercer—Innocence Project. (n.d.). Retrieved from https://www.innocenceproject. org/cases/michael-mercer/

Mills, S. (2014, June 25). $40M for five wrongly convicted of Dixmoor rape, murder. *The Chicago Tribune.* Retrieved from http://www.chicagotribune.com/news/local/ breaking/chi-isp-agrees-to-pay-40m-to-five-wrongly-convicted-of-dixmoor-rape-murder-20140624-story.html

Mills, S., & Lighty, T. (2016a, September 1). Sex offender charged in 1991 rape, murder that led to Dixmoor 5 case. *The Chicago Tribune.* Retrieved from http://www. chicagotribune.com/news/local/breaking/ct-dixmoor-five-arrest-met-20160831-story.html

Mills, S., & Lighty, T. (2016b, November 17). Prosecutor admitted in FBI report that Englewood Four teens coerced into false confessions. *The Chicago Tribune.* Retrieved from   http://www.chicagotribune.com/news/ct-prosecutor-framed-englewood-four-met-20161117-story.html

Miranda v. Arizona, 384 U. S. 336 (1966).

Mnookin, J. L. (2018). The uncertain future of forensic science. *Daedalus, the Journal of the American Academy of Arts and Sciences, 147*, 99–118.

Moore, L. (2012, August 20). Rep. Todd Akin: The statement and the reaction. *The New York Times.* Retrieved from http://www.nytimes.com/2012/08/21/us/politics/ rep-todd-akin-legitimate-rape-statement-and-reaction.html

Moran, R. (2007, August 2). The presence of malice [Op-Ed]. *The New York Times.* Retrieved from https://www.nytimes.com/2007/08/02/opinion/02moran.html

Muhammad, K. (2010). *The condemnation of Blackness: Race, and the making of urban America.* Cambridge, MA: Harvard University Press.

Murty, K. S., & Vyas, A. G. (2010). Post-conviction DNA exonerations. *Journal of US–China Public Administration, 7*(7), 82–87.

Myers, J. E. (2013). *Evidence of interpersonal violence: Child maltreatment, intimate partner violence, rape, stalking and elder abuse.* New York, NY: Wolters Kluwer.

Nachman, D., & Hardy, D. (Directors). (2009). Witch hunt: Some convictions are criminal. The G-Machine, Inc.

Nathan, D. (2005). I'm Sorry; A Long-Delayed Apology from One of the Accusers in the Notorious McMartin Pre-School Molestation Case. *The Los Angeles Times*, 10/30/ 05, MM10.

Nathan, D., & Snedeker, M. (1995). *Satan's silence.* New York, NY: Basic Books.

National Academy of Sciences. (2009). *Strengthening forensic science in the United States: A path forward.* Washington, DC: National Academy of Sciences.

National Commission on Law Observance and Enforcement. (1931, January 7). *Report on the enforcement of the prohibition laws of the United States.* Retrieved from https:// www.ncjrs.gov/pdffiles1/Digitization/44540NCJRS.pdf

National Institute of Standards and Technology. (n.d.). Retrieved from https://www.nist. gov/interdisciplinary-topics/national-commission-forensic-science

National Registry of Exonerations. (n.d.). *About us.* Retrieved from http://www.law. umich.edu/special/exoneration/Pages/about.aspx

Neuschatz, J. S., Jones, Nicholas, Wetmore, S. A., & McClung, J. (2012). Unreliable informant testimony. In B. Cutler (Ed.), *Conviction of the innocent: Lessons from psychological research*. Washington, DC: American Psychological Association.

Newsome, M. (2007). The victim: A wrongful conviction. *O, The Oprah Magazine*, October, 2007.

Another Negro burned: Henry Smith Dies at the stake(1893, February 2). *The New York Times* Retrieved from http://query.nytimes.com/mem/archive-free/pdf?res=9F01E 5DE103BEF33A25751C0A9649C94629ED7CF

For action on race riot peril (1919, October 5). *The New York Times*. Retrieved from http://query.nytimes.com/mem/archive-free/pdf?_r=1&res=9C04E7D61F30E033 A25756C0A9669D946896D6CF&oref=slogin.

Negroes accuse Maryland bench: Double standard is charged in report on rape convictions. (1967, September 18). The New York Times, p. 33.arged in report on rape convictions.

Man's 4th rape case ends in acquittal. (1980, October 5). The New York Times, p. 33.

Ohio doctor accused of 36 rapes; man jailed for 3 of them is freed. (1982, September 24). *New York Times*, p. A16, col 3. Retrieved from http://www.nytimes.com/1982/ 09/24/us/ohio-doctor-accused-of-36-rapes-man-jailed-for-2-of-them-is-freed. html?pagewanted=print

Police review chemist's work (2003, March 13) *The New York Times*, p 22. Retrieved from http://www.nytimes.com/2003/03/13/us/national-briefing-mid-atlantic-maryland-police-review-chemist-s-work.html

Neuschatz, J. S., Jones, N., Wetmore, S. A., & McClung, J. (2012). Unreliable Informant Testimony. In B. Cutler (Ed.), *Conviction of the Innocent: Lessons From Psychological Research*. Washington, DC: American Psychological Association.

Norris v. Alabama (1935) 294 U.S. 587.

Norris, R. J., Weintraub, J. N., Acker, J. R., Redlich, A. D., & Bonventre, C. L. (2019, September). The criminal costs of wrongful convictions: Can we reduce crime by protecting the innocent? *Criminology and Public Policy*, 1–22.

Ochoa, C. (2005). Christopher Ochoa: My life is a broken puzzle. In C. Vollen & D. Eggers (Eds.), *Surviving justice: America's wrongfully convicted and exonerated*. San Francisco, CA: McSweeney's Books.

Ogletree, C. J. (2006). Making race matter in death matters. In C. J. Ogletree & A. Sarat (Eds.), *From lynch mobs to the killing state: Race and the death penalty in America*. New York, NY: New York University Press.

Olney, M., & Bonn, S. (2014). An exploratory study of the legal and non-legal factors associated with exoneration for wrongful conviction: The power of DNA evidence. *Criminal Justice Policy Review, 26*(4),400–420. doi:10.1177/0887403414521461

Olsen, J. (1991). *Predator: Rape, madness, and injustice in Seattle*. New York, NY: Dell.

Packer, H. (1968). *The limits of the criminal sanction*. Stanford, CA: Stanford University Press.

Parker, K. F., Dewees, M. A., & Radelet, M. L. (2001). Racial bias and the conviction of the innocent. In S. D. Westervelt & J. A. Humphreys (Eds.), *Wrongly convicted: Perspectives on failed justice* (pp. 114–131). New Brunswick, NJ: Rutgers University Press.

Partington, D. H. (1965). The incidence of death penalty for rape in Virginia. *Washington and Lee Law Review, 22*(1), 43–75.

Patterson, T. (2007). Innocent man shares his 20-year struggle behind bars. *CNN*. Retrieved from http://www.cnn.com/2007/US/law/10/25/innocence.project/index.html

Patterson, W. L. (Ed.). (1951). *We charge genocide: The crime of government against the Negro people*. New York, NY: Civil Rights Congress.

Pfeifer, M. J. (2004). *Rough justice: Lynching and American society, 1874–1947*. Chicago, IL: University of Illinois Press.

Philen, R. M., Kilbourne, E. M., McKinley, T. W., & Parrish, R. G. (1989, December 9). Mass sociogenic illness by proxy: Parentally reported epidemic in an elementary school. *The Lancet, 2*(8676), 1372–1376.

Pilger, L. (2016, July 6). Jury awards $28.1 million in Beatrice 6 case. *Lincoln Journal Star*. Retrieved from http://journalstar.com/news/local/911/jury-awards-million-in-beatrice-case/article_ec6b4cf9-1591-5b98-8357-825676e8c5c1.html

Planty, M., Langton, L., Krebs, C., Berzofsky, M., & Smiley-McDonald, H. (2013, March). *Female victims of sexual violence, 1994–2010* (NCJ 240655). US Department of Justice, Office of Justice Programs, Bureau of Justice Statistics. Retrieved from http://www.bjs.gov/content/pub/pdf/fvsv9410.pdf

Possley, M., Ferkenhoff, E., & Mills, S. (2002, February 8). Police arrest 2 in Roscetti case: Officials say tip led them to pair, who confessed. *The Chicago Tribune*. Retrieved from http://articles.chicagotribune.com/2002-02-08/news/0202080321_1_police-arrest-duane-roach-larry-ollins

Possley, M., & Mills, S. (2001, May 2). New evidence stirs doubt over murder convictions. *The Chicago Tribune*. Retrieved from http://www.chicagotribune.com/news/watchdog/chi-010502roscetti-story.html

Powell, M. (2014, May 14). He lost 3 years and a child, but got no apology. *The New York Times*. Retrieved from https://www.nytimes.com/2014/05/15/nyregion/he-lost-3-years-and-a-child-but-got-no-apology.html

Powell v. Alabama (1932), 287 U.S. 45.

Public Broadcasting System.org. (n.d.). Retrieved from https://www.pbs.org/wgbh/pages/frontline/the-confessions/timeline-of-the-case/. The Confessions, 9/9/10, Ofra Bikel.

Pumphrey v. State (1908) Alabama, 132 47 So. 156.

Rabinowitz, D. (1990, May). From the mouths of babes to a jail cell. *Harper's Magazine*, 52–63.

Radelet, M. L., Bedau, H. A., & Putnam, C. E. (1992). *In spite of innocence: Erroneous convictions in capital cases*. Boston, MA: Northeastern University Press.

Ralph Armstrong—National Registry of Exonerations. (n.d.). Retrieved from https://www.law.umich.edu/special/exoneration/Pages/casedetail.aspx?caseid=2997

Ramsey, R. J. (2020). *Understanding Wrongful Conviction: How Innocent People are Convicted of Crimes They Did Not Commit*. Cognella, Academic Publishing: USA.

Randall Lynn Ayers—National Registry of Exonerations. (n.d.). Retrieved from https://www.law.umich.edu/special/exoneration/Pages/casedetail.aspx?caseid=3006

Ray Spencer—National Registry of Exonerations. (n.d.). Retrieved from https://www.law.umich.edu/special/exoneration/Pages/casedetail.aspx?caseid=3657

Reddington, F. P. (2009). A brief history of rape law and rape law reform in the United States. In F. P. Reddington & B. W. Kreisel (Eds.), *Sexual assault: The victims, the perpetrators, and the criminal justice system*. Durham, NC: Carolina Academic Press.

Reddington, F. P., & Kreisel, B. W. (Eds.). (2005). *Sexual assault: The victims, the perpetrators, and the criminal justice system*. Durham, NC: Carolina Academic Press.

Ressler, R. K., & Shachtman, T. (1992). *Whoever Fights Monsters: My Twenty Years Tracking Serial Killers for the FBI*. New York, NY: St. Martin's Press.

Reuters. (2017, March 21). *Virginia governor pardons "Norfolk Four" sailors in 1997 rape-murder*. Retrieved from https://www.reuters.com/article/us-virginia-norfolkfour/virginia-governor-pardons-norfolk-four-sailors-in-1997-rape-murder-idUSKBN16S2UN

Ricardo Rachell—Innocence Project. (n.d.). Retrieved from https://www.innocenceproject.org/cases/ricardo-rachell/

Ricciardi, L., & Demos, M. (Producers). (2015). *Making a murderer* [Television series]. Manitowoc County, WI: Netflix.

Rickey Johnson—National Registry of Exonerations. (n.d.). Retrieved from https://www.law.umich.edu/special/exoneration/Pages/casedetail.aspx?caseid=3334

Rise, E. W. (1992). Race, rape, and radicalism: The case of the Martinsville Seven, 1949–1951. *Journal of Southern History, 58*(3), 461–490.

Risinger, D. M. (2007). Innocents convicted: An empirically justified factual wrongful conviction rate. *Journal of Criminal Law and Criminology, 97*(3), 761–806.

Robert, M. (2013, August 5). Robert Dewey, wrongly convicted of murder, to receive $1.2 million compensation? *Westword*. Retrieved from http://www.westword.com/news/robert-dewey-wrongly-convicted-of-murder-to-receive-12-million-compensation-5894637

Robert Kelly—National Registry of Exonerations. (n.d.). Retrieved from https://www.law.umich.edu/special/exoneration/Pages/casedetail.aspx?caseid=3346

Robert McClendon—National Registry of Exonerations. (n.d.). Retrieved from https://www.innocenceproject.org/cases/robert-mcclendon/

Robertson, C. (September 17, 2010). 30 years later, freedom in a case with tragedy for all involved. *The New York Times*, p. 12.

Rodney Roberts—Innocence Project. (n.d.). Retrieved from https://www.innocenceproject.org/cases/rodney-roberts/

Rodney Roberts—National Registry of Exonerations. (n.d.). Retrieved from https://www.law.umich.edu/special/exoneration/Pages/casedetail.aspx?caseid=4402

Rosen, I., & Schonder, G. (Producers). (2012). Chicago: The false confession capital. *Sixty Minutes*. CBS News. Retrieved from http://www.cbsnews.com/news/chicago-the-false-confession-capital/

Rosenmerkel, S., Durose, M., & Farole, D. (2009). *Felony sentences in state courts, 2006*. Washington, DC: US Department of Justice, Bureau of Justice Statistics.

Rosenthal, R. (1995). *State of New Jersey v. Margaret Kelly Michaels*: An overview. *Psychology, Public Policy, and Law, 1*(2), 246–271.

Rossmo, D. K. (2006). Criminal investigative failures: Avoiding the pitfalls (Part II). *FBI Law Enforcement Bulletin, 75*(9), 1–8.

Rossmo, D. K. (2009). Errors in probability: Chance and randomness in forensics and profiling. In D. K. Rossmo (Ed.), *Criminal investigative failures*. Boca Raton, FL. CRC Press.

Royster, J. J. (1997). *Southern horrors and other writings: The anti-lynching campaign of Ida B. Wells, 1892–1900*. Boston, MA: Bedford/St. Martin's.

Russell, D. E. H. (1984). *Sexual exploitation: Rape, child sexual abuse, and workplace harassment.* Beverly Hills, CA: Sage.

Russell, K. K. (2001). Toward developing a theoretical paradigm and typology for petit-apartheid. In D. Milovanovic & K. K. Russell (Eds.), *Petit apartheid in the US criminal justice system.* Durham, NC: Carolina Academic Press.

Ryan, N. E. (2002). Affirmation in response to motion to vacate judgment of conviction, Indictment No. 4762/89. Retrieved from www. ManhattanDA.org

Sagarin, E. (1977). Forcible rape and the rights of the accused. In D. Chappell, R. Geis, & G. Geis (Eds.), *Forcible rape: The crime, the victim, and the offender* (p. 146). New York, NY: Columbia University Press.

Sanchez, R., & Foster, P. (2015, June 18). "You rape our women and are taking over our country," Charleston church gunman told Black victims. *The Telegraph.* Retrieved from http://www.telegraph.co.uk/news/worldnews/northamerica/usa/11684957/You-rape-our-women-and-are-taking-over-our-country-Charleston-church-gunman-told-black-victims.html

Sands, A. (1981, January). Rape and racism in Boston: An open letter to white feminists. *Off Our Backs,* pp, 16–17.

Santtila, P., Junkkila, J., & Sandnabba, N. K. (2005). Behavioural linking of stranger rapes. *Journal of Investigative Psychology and Offender Profiling, 2,* 87–103.

Saywitz, K. J., Lyon, T. D., & Goodman, G. S. (2011). Interviewing children. In J. E. B. Myers (Ed.), *The APSAC handbook on child maltreatment* (3rd ed.). Thousand Oaks, CA: Sage.

Scheck, B., Neufeld, P., & Dwyer, J. (2001). *Actual innocence: When justice goes wrong and how to make it right.* New York, NY: Signet.

Schiff, K. G. (2005). *Lighting the way: Nine woman who changed modern America.* New York, NY: Miramax.

Schreiber, N., Bellah, L. D., Martinez, Y., McLaurin, K. A., Strok, R., Garven, S., & Wood, J. M. (2006). Suggestive interviewing in the McMartin Preschool and Kelly Michaels daycare abuse cases: A case study. *Social Influence, 1*(1), 16–47.

Schwartzapfel, B. (2012, January/February). No country for innocent men. *Mother Jones.* Retrieved from http://www.motherjones.com/politics/2011/12/tim-cole-rick-perry

Scully, J. A. M. (2008). Rotten apple or rotten barrel: The role of civil rights lawyers in ending the culture of police violence. *National Black Law Journal, 21,* 137–172.

Shaw, J. (2011). Exoneration and the road to compensation: The Tim Cole Act and comprehensive compensation for persons wrongfully imprisoned. *Texas Wesleyan Law Review, 17,* 593–617.

Shaw, J., Campbell, R., & Cain, D. (2016). The view from inside the system: How police explain their response to sexual assault. *American Journal of Community Psychology, 58,* 446–462.

Skagerberg, E. M. (2007). Co-witness feedback in line-ups. *Applied Cognitive Psychology, 21*(4), 489–497. doi:10.1002/acp.1285

Slater, C., Woodhams, J., & Hamilton-Giachritsis, C. (2015). Testing the assumptions of crime linkage with stranger sex offenses: A more ecologically-valid study. *Journal of Criminal Psychology, 30,* 261–273.

Slone, A. E., Brigham, J. C., & Meissner, C. A. (2000). Social and cognitive factors affecting the own-race bias in Whites. *Basic & Applied Social Psychology, 22,* 71–84.

Smalarz, L., Scherr, K. C., & Kassin, S. M. (2016). Miranda at 50: A psychological analysis. *Current Directions in Psychological Science, 25*(6), 455–460.

Smallbone, S. W., & Wortley, R. K. (2001). Child sexual abuse. Offender characteristics and modus operandi. *Trends and Issues in Criminal Justice, 193*, 1–6.

Smith, A. M., & Cutler, B. L. (2013). Conclusion: Identification test reforms. In B. L. Cutler (Ed.), *Reform of eyewitness identification procedures*. Washington, DC: American Psychological Association.

Smith, E., & Hattery, A. J. (2011). Race, wrongful conviction & exoneration. *Journal of African American Studies, 15*, 74–94. doi:10.1007/s12111-010-9130-5

Smith, M., & Padzer, L. (1980). *Michelle remembers*. New York, NY: Congdon & Lattes.

Snook, B., & Cullen, R. M. (2009). Bounded rationality and criminal investigations: Has tunnel vision been wrongfully convicted? In D. Kim Rossmo (Ed.), *Criminal investigative failures*. Boca Raton, FL: CRC Press.

Sommerville, D. M. (2004). *Rape and race in the nineteenth-century south*. Chapel Hill, NC: University of North Carolina Press.

South Carolinians abolishing the death penalty. (n.d.). Retrieved from https://sc-abolish. org/stories/witness-id-kirk-bloodsworth/

Spohn, C., & Horney, J. (1992). *Rape law reform: A grassroots revolution and its impact*. Berlin, Germany: Springer.

Spohn, C., & Horney, J. (1996). The impact of rape law reform on the processing of simple and aggravated rape cases. *Journal of Criminal Law and Criminology, 86*(3), 861–884.

Stack, L. (2017, July 18). Dennis Hastert, Ex-House speaker who admitted sex abuse, leaves prison. *The New York Times*. Retrieved from https://www.nytimes.com/2017/07/18/us/dennis-hastert-released.html

Stainthorpe, J. L. (1998). Litigating police torture Chicago. In S. Salzman (Ed.), *Civil rights litigation and attorney fee's handbook* (Vol. 13, pp. 1–35). New York, NY: Clark Boardman,

State v. Cromedy, 727 A.2d 457, 459 (N. J. 1999).

State v. Henderson, 208 N. J. 208 (2011).

State v. Lawson, 352 Or. 724, 291 P.3d 673 (2012).

State v. Michaels, Supreme Court of New Jersey, 136 N. J. 299; 642 A.2d 1372. (1994).

State v. Walker, 80 N. J. 187 (1979).

Steblay, N. M., & Loftus, E. F. (2008). Eye witness memory and the legal system. In E. Shafir (Ed.), *The behavioral foundations of policy* (pp. 145–162). New York, NY: Russell Sage.

Stevenson, B. (2014). *Just Mercy: A Story of Justice and Redemption*. New York, NY: Spiegel and Grau.

Sterling, G. (1986, November 6). Exonerated: Blood test 12 years late clears a "lifer." *The Star-Ledger*, pp. 1, 20.

Stern, R., & Sundberg, A. (Directors). (2006). *The trials of Darryl Hunt*. [Motion picture]. United States: Home Box Office.

Sullivan, T. (1992). *Unequal verdicts: The Central Park jogger trials*. New York, NY: American Lawyer Books/Simon & Schuster.

Synder, L. C., McQuillan, P. J., Murphy, W. L., & Joselson, R. (2007). *Report on the conviction of Jeffrey Deskovic*. White Plains, New York. Westchester County District

Attorney's Office. Retrieved from www.westchesterda.net/jeffrey%20 deskovic%20 com%20 rpt.pdf

Taslitz, A. E. (2006). Wrongly accused: Is race a factor in convicting the innocent. *Ohio State Journal of Criminal Law, 4*, 121–133.

Terry, K. J. (2008). Stained Glass: The nature and scope of child sexual abuse in the Catholic Church. *Criminal Justice and Behavior, 35*(5), 549–569.

Theoharis, J. (2013). *The rebellious life of Mrs. Rosa Parks.* Boston, MA: Beacon Press.

Thompson, C. (2016, January 5). *Penny Beerntsen, the rape victim in* Making A Murderer, *speaks out.* The Marshall Project. Retrieved from https://www.themarshallproject.org/2016/01/05/penny-beernsten-the-rape-victim-in-making-a-murderer-speaks-out#.pbzut2rQC

Thompson-Cannino, J., Cotton, R., & Torneo, E. (2009). *Picking cotton: Our memoir of injustice and redemption.* New York, NY: St. Martin's Griffin.

Timothy Cole—Innocence Project. (n.d.). Retrieved from https://www.innocenceproject.org/cases/timothy-cole/

Torpy, B., & Rankin, B. (2007). DNA clears man in 1985 rape. *The Atlanta Journal Constitution.* Retrieved from http://truthinjustice.org/willie-williams.html

Tulsa Race Riot Commission. (2001, February 28). Tulsa *race riot:* A *report by* the Oklahoma Commission to *study* the Tulsa *race riot* of 1921. Retrieved from http://www.okhistory.org/research/forms/freport.pdf

Tulsa Tribune. (1921, May 31). *Nab Negro for attacking girl in an elevator.* Retrieved from http://www.tulsaworld.com/archives/nab-negro-for-attacking-girl-in-an-elevator/article_758e0217-1077-5282-bdb9-4eef81f8e12d.html

US Department of Justice, Office of Justice Programs, National Institute of Justice. (1999). Eyewitness evidence: A guide for law enforcement. Retrieved from http://www.nij.gov/pubs-sum/178240.htm

Vincent Thames—National Registry of Exonerations. (n.d.). Retrieved from https://www.law.umich.edu/special/exoneration/Pages/casedetail.aspx?caseid=3844

Vitello, P. (2012, October 15). George Whitmore Jr., who falsely confessed to 3 murders in 1964, dies at 68. *The New York Times.* Retrieved from http://www.nytimes.com/2012/10/16/nyregion/george-whitmore-jr-68-dies-falsely-confessed-to-3-murders-in-1964.html

Wall, P. M. (1964). *Eye-witness identification in criminal cases.* Springfield, IL: Thomas.

Wang, A. B. (2017, January 10). NYPD captain apologizes after saying "true stranger rapes" are more troubling than others. *The Washington Post.* Retrieved from https://www.washingtonpost.com/news/post-nation/wp/2017/01/08/nypd-captain-draws-outrage-after-saying-true-stranger-rapes-are-more-troubling-than-others/?utm_term=.17ac4050a410

Warden, R. (2004). *The snitch system: How snitch testimony sent Randy Steidl and Other innocent Americans to death row.* Chicago, IL: Center on Wrongful Convictions, Bluhm Legal Clinic.

Warren, A. G. (2013). *Handbook on questioning children* (3rd ed.). Washington, DC: American Bar Association.

Washington, M. (2006, May 5). Federal jury awards Earl Washington Jr. $2.25 million. *The Virginian-Pilot.* Retrieved from http://pilotonline.com/news/federal-jury-awards-earl-washington-jr-million/article_08dd164f-0493-5d48-995f-8baf07e5a2a8.html

Weinberg, S. (2003, August 3). Trials and errors; features. *Sunday Age*. Retrieved from http://www.theage.com.au/articles/2003/08/03/1059849267718.html

Weinstein, H. (2006, June 21). Freed man gives lesson on false confessions. *The Los Angeles Times*. Retrieved from http://articles.latimes.com/2006/jun/21/local/me-confess21/2

Welborn, V. (2008). Leesville man freed after wrongful conviction. *Shreveport Times*. Retrieved from http://truthinjustice.org/rickey-johnson.html

Wells, G. A., & Quigley-McBride, A. (2016). Applying eye-witness identification research to the legal system: A glance at where we have been and where we could go. *Journal of Applied Research in Memory and Cognition, 5*, 290–294.

Wells, G. L. (1978). Applied eyewitness-testimony research: System variables and estimator variables. *Journal of Personality and Social Psychology, 36*(12), 1546–1557.

Wells, G. L. (2006). Eye-witness identification: Systemic reforms. *Wisconsin Law Review, 2006*, 615–643.

Wells, G. L., & Hasel, L. E. (2007). Facial composite production by eyewitnesses. *Current Directions in Psychological Science, 16*, 6–10.

Wells, G. L., Small, M., Penrod, S., Malpass, R. S., Fulero, S. M., & Brimacombe, C. A. E. (1998). Eyewitness identification procedures: Recommendations for lineups and photospreads. *Law and Human Behavior, 22*(6), 603–647. http://dx.doi.org/10.1023/A:1025750605807

Wells, T., & Leo, R. A. (2008). *The wrong guys: Murder, false confessions, and the Norfolk four*. New York, NY: New Press.

Wildeman, J., Costelloe, M., & Scheur, R. (2011). Experiencing wrongful and unlawful conviction. *Journal of Offender Rehabilitation, 50*, 411–432.

Wilkinson, J. (2016, August 15). Hillary Clinton's website removed promise to "believe" all sexual assault survivors after return of allegations that Bill Clinton raped Juanita Broaddrick and Hillary threatened her to keep quiet. *The Daily Mail*. Retrieved from http://www.dailymail.co.uk/news/article-3741760/Hillary-Clinton-s-website-removed-promise-believe-sexual-assault-survivors-emergence-Bill-Clinton-Juanita-Broaddrick-historic-rape-allegations.html.

Williamson, E. J., Stricker, J. M., Irazola, S. P., & Niedzwiecki, E. (2016). Wrongful convictions: Understanding the experiences of the original crime victims. *Violence & Victims, 31*(1), 155–166.

Willie Davidson—Innocence Project. (n.d.). Retrieved from https://www.innocenceproject.org/cases/willie-davidson/

Willie Jackson—Innocence Project. (n.d.). Retrieved from https://www.innocenceproject.org/cases/willie-jackson/

The Willie Sanders Defense Committee. (1980). *From Scottsboro 1930 to Boston 1980: The frame-up Continues*. Roxbury, MA: Author.

Wilson, W. J. (1978). *The declining significance of race*. Chicago, IL: University of Chicago Press.

Wilson, W. J. (1987). *The truly disadvantaged: The inner city, the underclass, and public policy*. Chicago, IL: University of Chicago Press.

Wolfgang, M. E., & Reidel, M. (1973). Race, judicial discretion, and the death penalty. *Annals of the American Academy, 407*, 119–133.

Wood v. Alaska 957 F. 2d 1544 (9th Cir. 1992).

WRAL.com. (2008a, May 5). *Man indicted in 1987 Goldsboro rape case*. Retrieved from http://www.wral.com/news/local/story/2835370/

WRAL.com. (2008b, May 9). *Rape victim apologizes to wrongfully convicted man*. Retrieved from http://www.wral.com/news/local/story/2862438/

WRAL.com. (2010, April 28). *Man sentenced to life in prison in 1987 Goldsboro rape case*. Retrieved from http://www.wral.com/man-sentenced-to-life-in-prison-in-1987-goldsboro-rape-case/7499351/

Wriggins, J. (1983). Rape, racism, and the law. *Harvard Women's Law Journal, 6*, 103–141. Retrieved from http://papers.ssrn.com/sol3/papers.cfm?abstract_id=2038544

X, M. (1964). *The ballot or the bullet* [Speech]. Malcolm X, 1925-1965, audio collection. North Hollywood, CA: Pacifica Radio Archives.

Yardley, J. (2000, October 17). Texas inmate's confession slips through the cracks. *The New York Times*. Retrieved from http://www.nytimes.com/2000/10/17/us/texas-inmate-s-confession-slips-through-the-cracks.html?_r=0

Zambito, T. (2014, April 6). *Newark man set free after serving 17 years for a rape he says he did not commit*. NJ.com. Retrieved from http://www.nj.com/news/index.ssf/2014/04/newark_man_freed_after_17_year

Zeigarnik, B. (1927). Das Behalten erledigter und unerledigter Handlungen [Remembering finished and unfinished tasks]. Psychologische Forschung, *9*, 1–85.

Zeigarnik, B. (1938). On finished and unfinished tasks. In W. D. Ellis (Ed.), *A source book of Gestalt psychology* (pp. 300–314). Gouldsboro, ME: Gestalt Journal Press.

For the benefit of digital users, indexed terms that span two pages (e.g., 52–53) may, on occasion, appear on only one of those pages.

Tables and figures are indicated by *t* and *f* following the page number

For the benefit of digital users, indexed terms that span two pages (e.g., 52–53) may, on occasion, appear on only one of those pages.